CRANE ORIGAMI

Wishing World Peace and Health for Its People

Why Cranes?

Perhaps you have seen colorful paper cranes stringed into tiered bunches on ceremonial occasions or in hospital rooms. Being called "*Senbazuru*" or thousand cranes, they are made with prayers for someone's happiness, recovery from illness or injury. Also the crane patterns have been a must for Japanese wedding gowns and *obi* sashes. Obviously the crane has been an auspicious symbol for the Japanese. Why not dragons or rabbits but cranes?

Cranes are migrant birds which travel from one place in the world to another depending on the climate. The Japanese crane has pure white feathers characteristically tinted with red at the crest, black at wing tips. They must have fascinated people when they paid visits showing their beautiful streamlined silhouettes with widespread wings. It's easy to imagine that people would look at such elegant cranes as messengers of good luck who never fail to appear at a certain time of the year. Over time, the crane fitted into the country's scenery and made appearances in proverbs and legends, taking root in everyday life as a highly esteemed creature.

Cranes, however, are not as common as sparrows or pigeons which show up constantly around your house. In the hope of observing cranes more often, people thought of creating one by drawing, painting, carving, weaving and folding the figure, and later during the Edo Period when origami became an amusing hobby, crane origami spread widely across the country.

Why one thousand?

An old saying goes "Cranes live up to a thousand years, turtles ten thousand years," which urged people to create as many pieces as they could wishing friends' good luck while working on these elaborate folds. Originally, *senbazuru* were created out of a rectangular sheet of paper, by making one or several slits to separate each and to link each at wings, tails or beaks as illustrated on pages 6 to 25. Today *senbazuru* generally means a bunch of separate cranes each made from a square sheet of origami.

This book will introduce those traditional or "hidden" crane models with detailed instructions. Each model seems rather difficult at first, but with a little patience you will be glad you made one yourself!

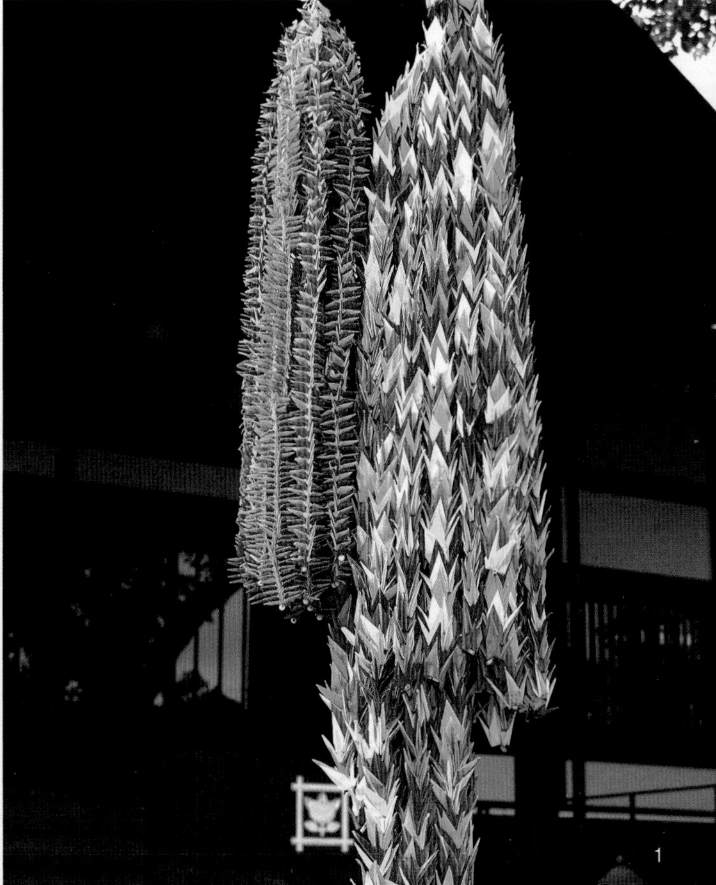

BASIC CRANE FOLDING

This common version is a must to practice before you go on to the traditional methods. As crane origami involves most of the basic folds such as valley fold, mountain fold, and inside reverse fold, get used to these folds and the procedure using store-bought square origami paper "Crane Base" introduced here will serve as a base for many other models including popular animals and flowers.

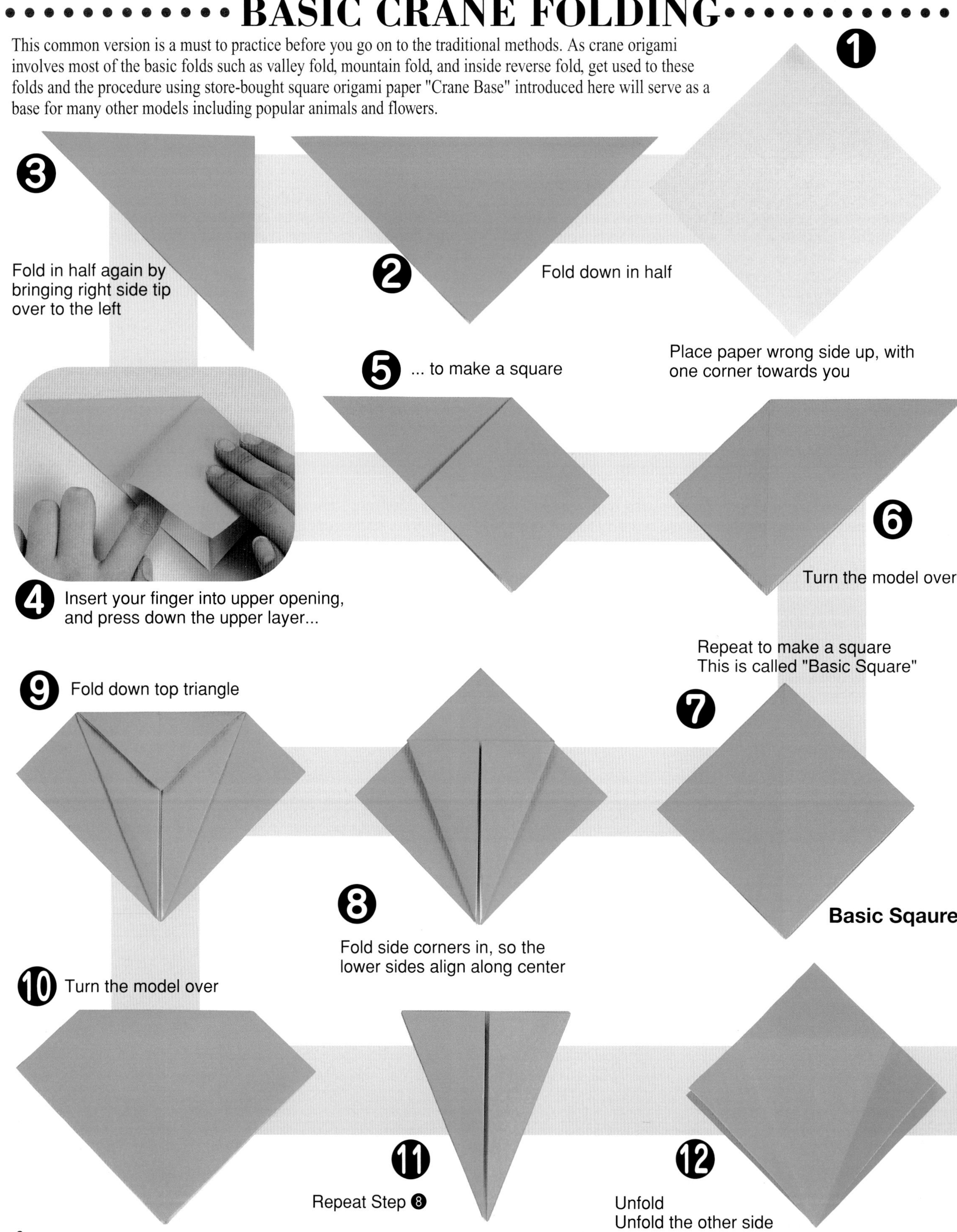

1
Place paper wrong side up, with one corner towards you
2
Fold down in half
3
Fold in half again by bringing right side tip over to the left
4
Insert your finger into upper opening, and press down the upper layer...
5
... to make a square
6
Turn the model over
7
Repeat to make a square This is called "Basic Square"
Basic Sqaure
8
Fold side corners in, so the lower sides align along center
9
Fold down top triangle
10
Turn the model over
11
Repeat Step 8
12
Unfold
Unfold the other side

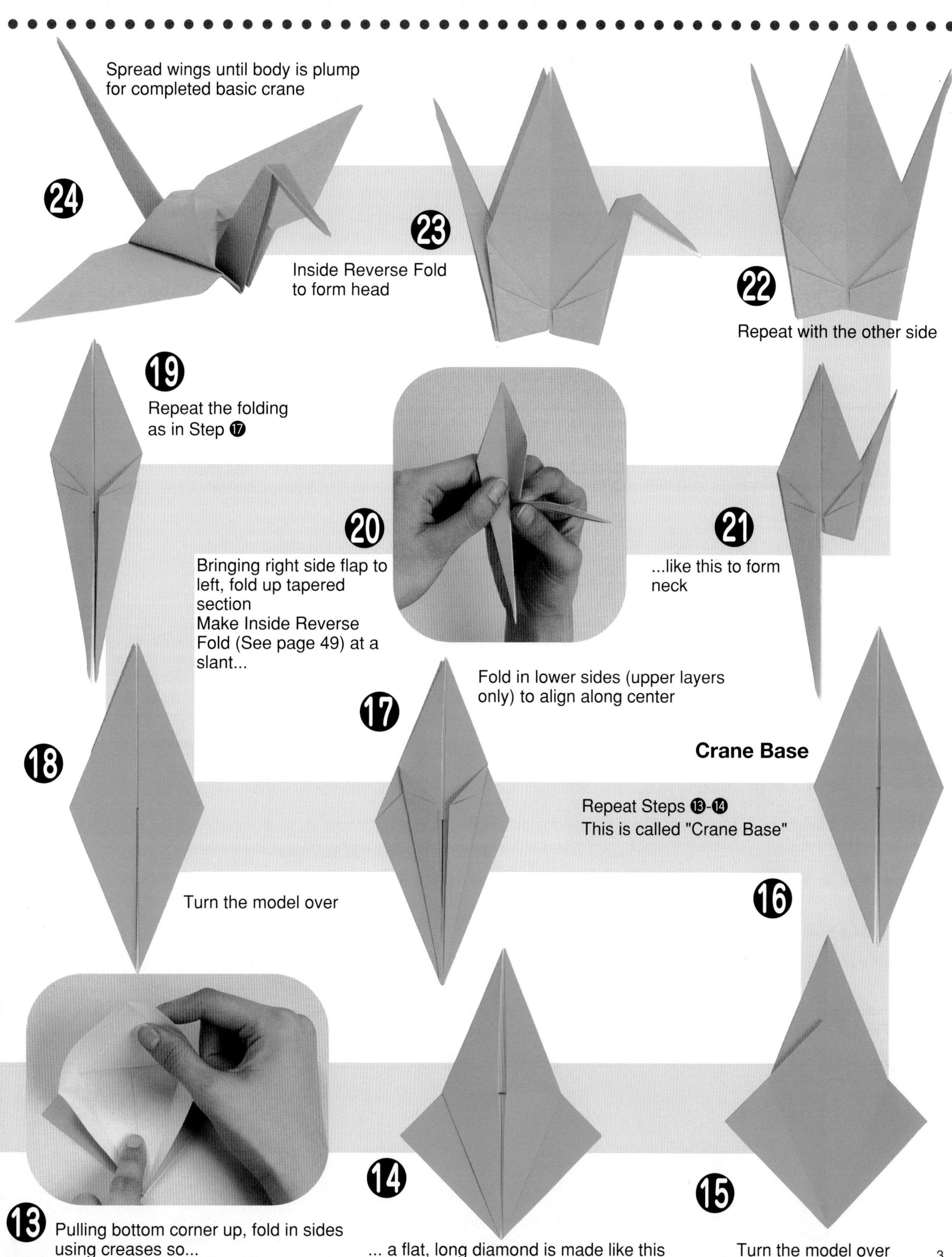
24
Spread wings until body is plump for completed basic crane
23
Inside Reverse Fold to form head
22
Repeat with the other side
19
Repeat the folding as in Step 17
20
Bringing right side flap to left, fold up tapered section
Make Inside Reverse Fold (See page 49) at a slant...
21
...like this to form neck
17
Fold in lower sides (upper layers only) to align along center
18
Turn the model over
Crane Base
Repeat Steps 13-14
This is called "Crane Base"
16
13
Pulling bottom corner up, fold in sides using creases so...
14
... a flat, long diamond is made like this
15
Turn the model over

Secret Thousand Crane Folding
THOUSAND CRANES OF KUWANA

Front cover of original "*Senbazuru Orikata*"
(Kuwana City Museum Collection)

"Origami" is not a new word in many English dictionaries, but the word has a checkered past. Originally origami did not mean the paper craft. It used to mean a formal letter or list folded precisely in half. In the Edo Period (17-19 C), such folded pieces of paper were used as certificates to be attached to works of art, including *samurai* swords. Eventually origami came to represent such certificates. Even now you might hear a phrase "origami-*tsuki*," meaning "with origami." It means the quality is certified.

Origami as a pastime paper craft would be called "*orikata*" or "*orimono*" until just eighty years ago. Numerous origami designs have been developed by now, but it all started from ancient rituals, ceremonies or gift-giving customs of Japan. Shinto rituals called for white or natural paper folded neatly into special shapes called *Gohei* and *Shide*, which are still seen in shrines or at traditional festivals. This started in the seventh century when paper-making methods were introduced to the country. Then in later times, people would fold paper to wrap or envelop gifts in addition to the use of *furoshiki*, a wrapping cloth. (The Japanese never

"Senbazuru of Kuwana" as permanent exhibit at the museum (part)

A scene of crane kite flying from the book

Linked Crane Folding

When folding a Basic Crane (page 2), the first thing to do is making two diagonal creases that cross each other. However, when folding a crane to link, only one crease is made diagonally. This is to make the elaborate-looking work easier. The initial diagonal crease connects head and tail. This line will work as a guide when telling head or tail from wings. Also, the resulting crane will not show unwanted creases on their wings.

Place right side up

2 Fold up in half

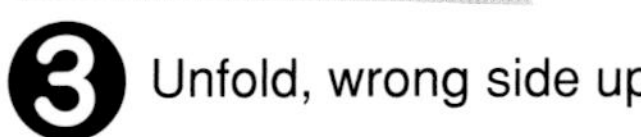
3 Unfold, wrong side up

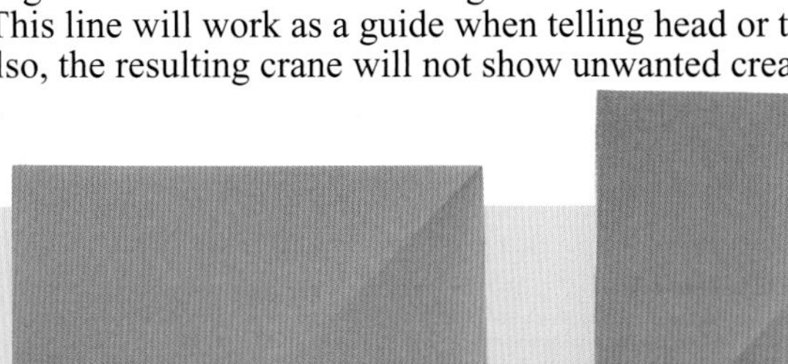
4 Fold in half

5 Unfold, and fold in half the other way

"HIDEN SENBAZURU ORIKATA"

present gifts or money without wrapping them. They would show respect and thanks to the recipients in how they wrap them. This is why the gifts from the Japanese have layers of wrapping paper, sometimes making you feel they are unnecessarily decorative!)

About two hundred years ago, a surprising method was discovered by a chief priest in Kuwana, Mie Prefecture, mid-south of Japan. Roko Angido of Choanji Temple created two to ninety-eight linked cranes out of a single sheet of paper by making carefully planned slits. It was published as "*Hiden Senbazuru Orikata*" by Yoshinoya Tamehachi, a publisher in Kyoto. This oldest origami book includes not only the instructions but *kyoka*, or a short poem, for each model. *Kyoka* is a type of informal poem containing everyday fun, humorous cynicism and depictions of the lifestyle of that era.

The classic text is preserved in Kuwana City Museum and is exhibited along with all forty-nine of the actual linked crane models from the book. The City of Kuwana approved it as an intangible cultural resource and uses origami crane as its logo.

"Senbazuru of Kuwana" as permanent exhibit at the museum

Special thanks to: Kuwana City Museum

Illustrations for "*Mitsu-ga-ichi*," or triple cranes, and "*Kazaguruma*," or pinwheel

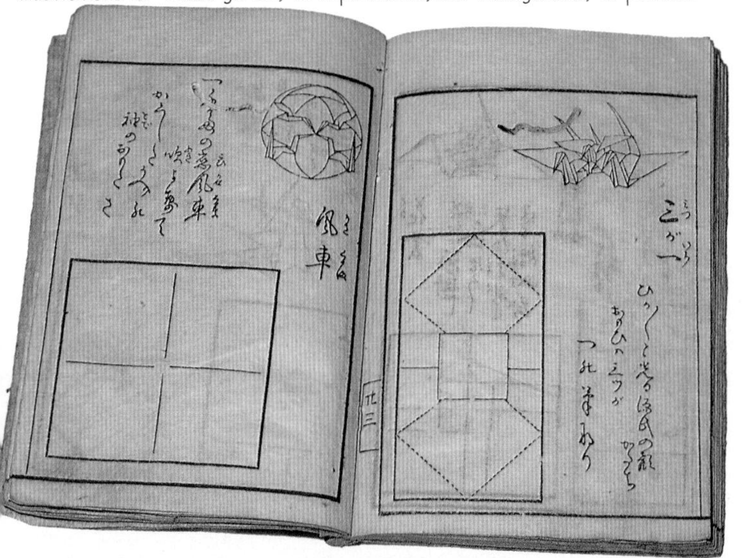

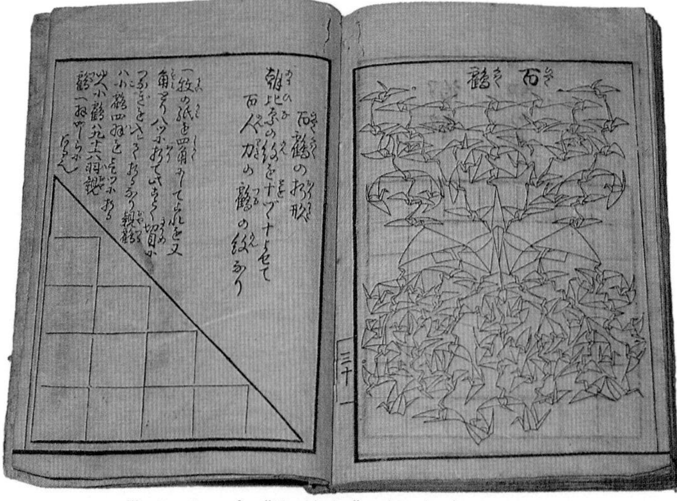

Illustrations for "*Hyakkaku*," or hundred cranes

7 Using the creases, fold into a square so the center point becomes the top

6 Unfold, right side up

Beginning Square

8 The resulting square is called "Beginning Square"

The rest is made in the same manner as BASIC CRANE
See Steps 8-24 on pages 2-3

Completed crane with smooth wings

TRADITIONAL LINKED CRANES MADE FROM ONE SHEET

Here is a selection of eleven typical linked cranes found in the literature "*HIDEN SENBAZURU ORIKATA*" cited on previous pages. Except for *Imoseyama* shown on this page, each project has plural cranes linked only with ⅛-inch width which makes the work challenging. Use thin *washi* paper to avoid breakage while folding or twisting. Since sizes of the paper are not indicated as in the literature, feel free to work with a size you are comfortable with.

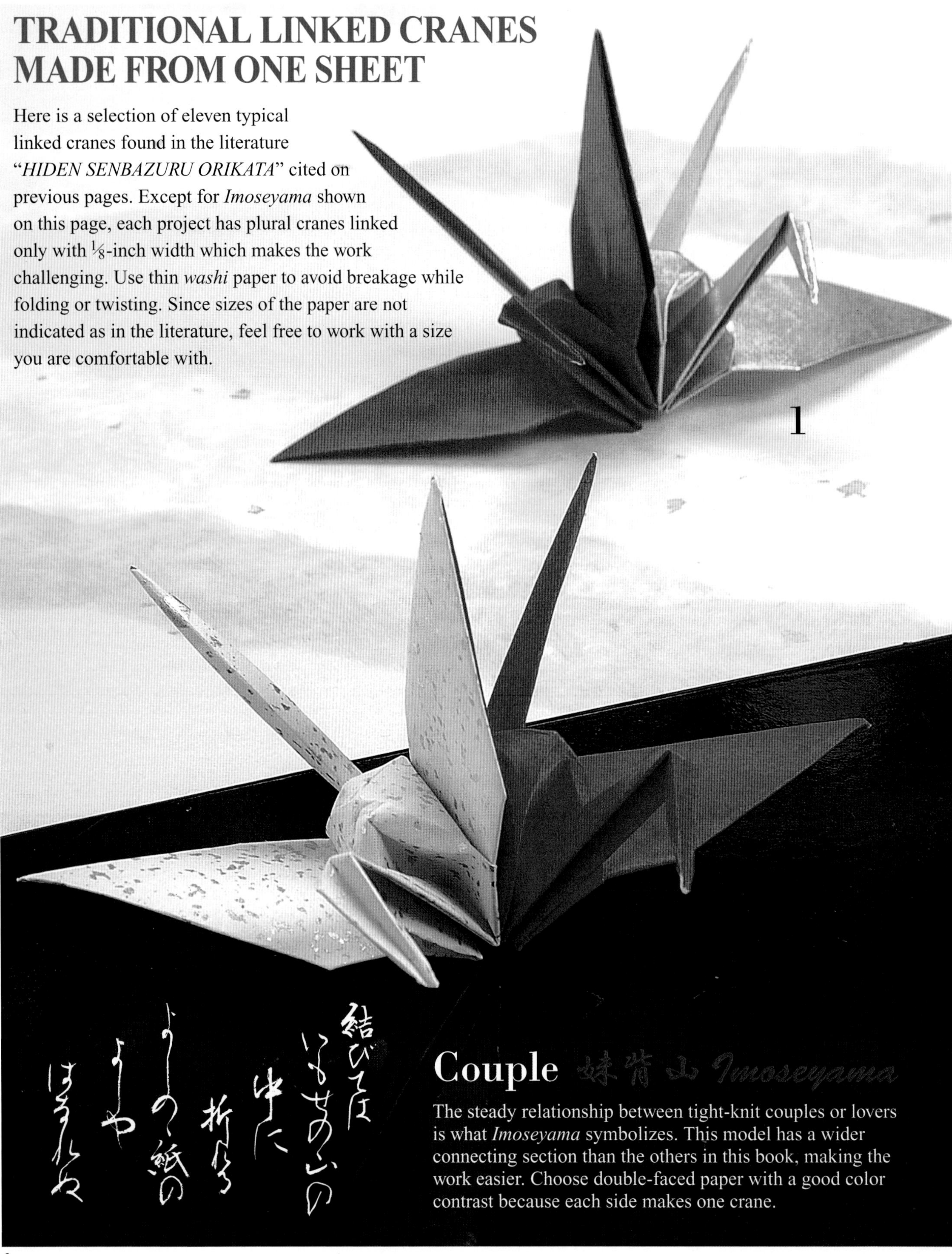

1

Couple 妹背山 *Imoseyama*

The steady relationship between tight-knit couples or lovers is what *Imoseyama* symbolizes. This model has a wider connecting section than the others in this book, making the work easier. Choose double-faced paper with a good color contrast because each side makes one crane.

USE A RECTANGLAR SHEET OF PAPER (2:1 RATIO).

According to the layout below, make creases and fold in half (right sides out). Make creases for Beginning Square (See pages 4-5) on the layers.

Fold the layers into Beginning Square. There should be no center crease on both sides.

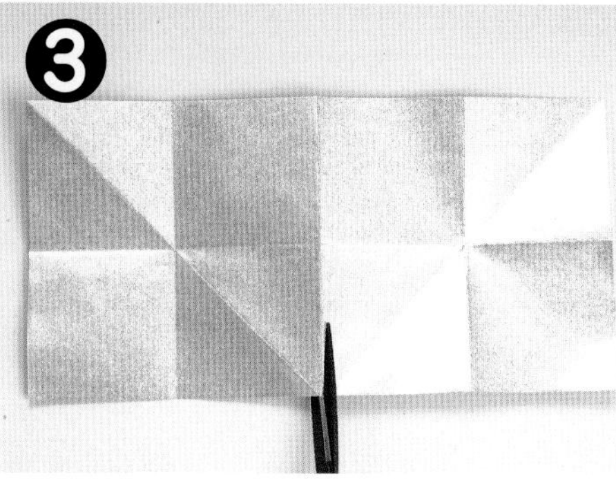

Unfold, and cut a slit in the middle, to reach the center point.

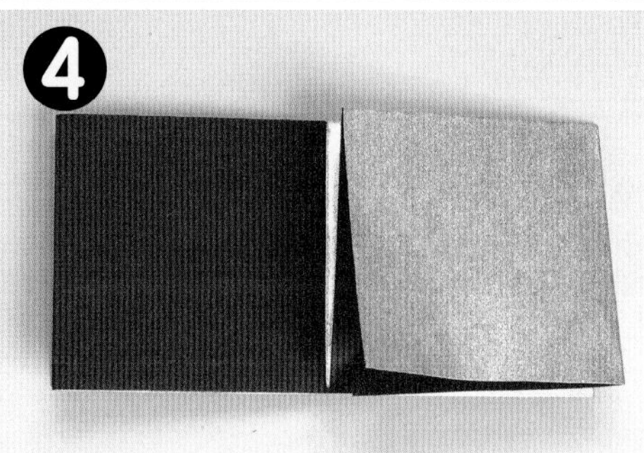

Fold each half into Beginning Square according to creases.

Bring left and right flaps of one side to align at center (See Steps ❸-❹, page 96.) Turn over and repeat. Fold down top triangle. Repeat with the other square.

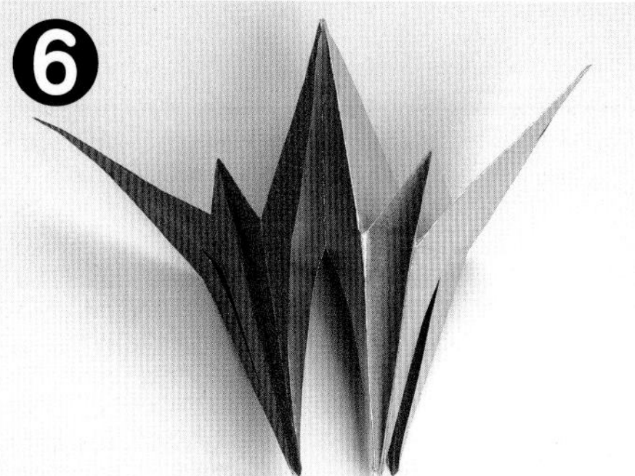

Unfold and form a long diamond. Repeat with all remaining diamonds to form Crane Base. For Crane Base, see Steps ⓭-⓰, page 3.

△ This corner to be made into head

--- Valley fold: See Steps ❷-❸, page 4 (Do not crease crossing diagonals, to avoid unwanted centerlines on finished wings)

>— Cut here

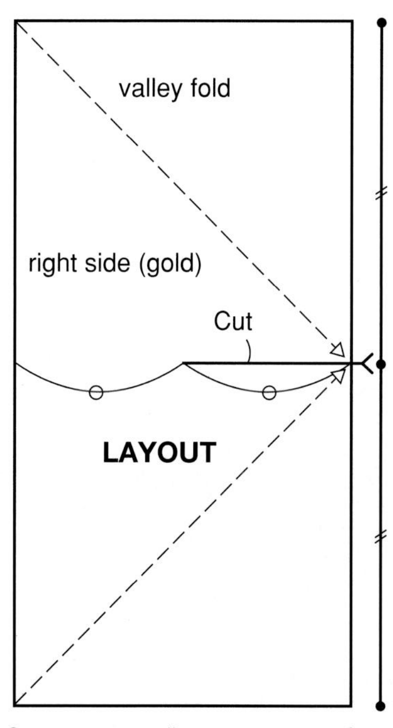

Bring left and right flaps to align at center to form narrow neck and tail (See Steps ⓱-⓳, page 3). Repeat with the other Crane Base.

Note: When making linked cranes, you will have to carry along the linked section(s) during the procedure without folding them into the design. The models often require folding in the air, instead of on a tabletop.

Bring the narrow flap over, and fold up, creasing at an angle. Form beak with Inside Reverse Fold to finish (See Steps ⓴-㉔, page 3). Gently pull out the wings and fluff the bodies.

Drawing from the original book: The beaks are folded so the two face each other.

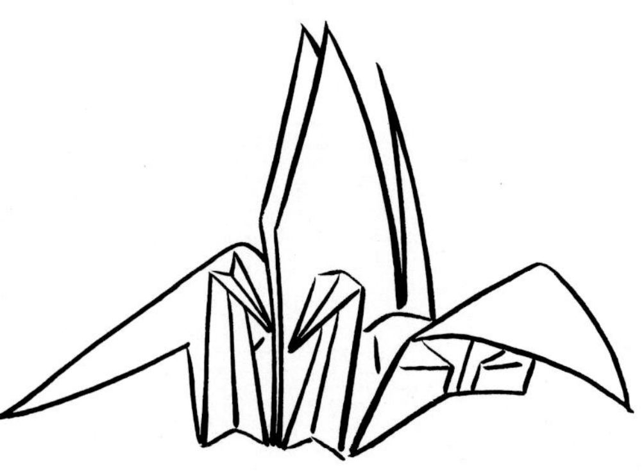

Feeding 拾餌 *Ehiroi*

The loving, beak-to-beak position shows the mother bird feeding the baby crane, all made from a single sheet of paper. Fold the beaks adjusting angles.

2

USE A RECTANGULAR SHEET OF *WASHI* PAPER (4:3 RATIO).

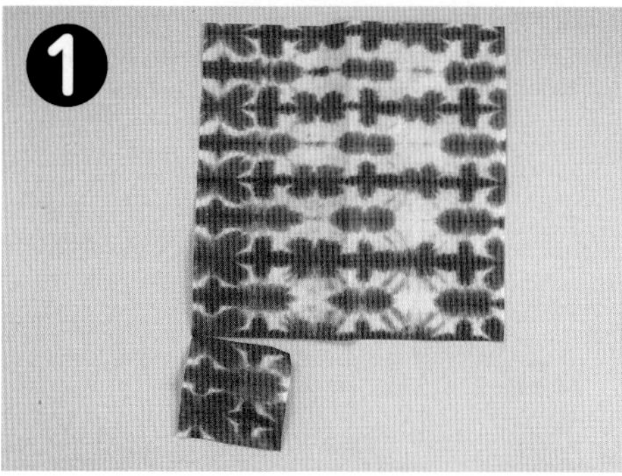

❶ According to the layout below, trim and make creases. Make further creases for Beginning Squares (See pages 4-5), and cut slit.

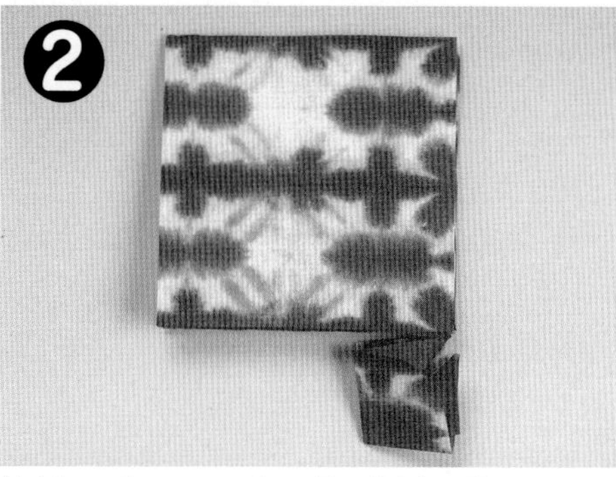

❷ Fold each square into Beginning Square using creases.

❸ Bring left and right flaps of one side to align at center (See Steps ❸-❹, page 96.) Turn over and repeat. Fold down top triangle. Repeat with the other square.

❹ First with smaller crane, pull open the triangles, and press down into a diamond. Repeat with the back side (See Steps ⓭-⓰, page 3).

❺ Then fold large crane into a diamond.

❻ First with smaller crane, make tapered neck and tail by folding sides in. Bring the flap over, and fold up in half (See Steps ⓱-㉑, page 3).

❼ Then repeat with large crane.

❽ Make heads by Inside Reverse Fold (See Steps ㉒-㉔, page 3) to finish. Pull wings apart and fluff bodies.

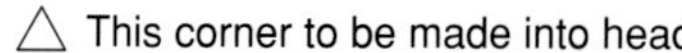

△ This corner to be made into head

--- Valley fold: See Steps ❷-❸, page 4 (Be sure to crease one diagonal per each square and do not crease crossing diagonals, to avoid unwanted centerlines on finished wings)

≻— Cut here(Leave ⅛" as uncut connection)

LAYOUT

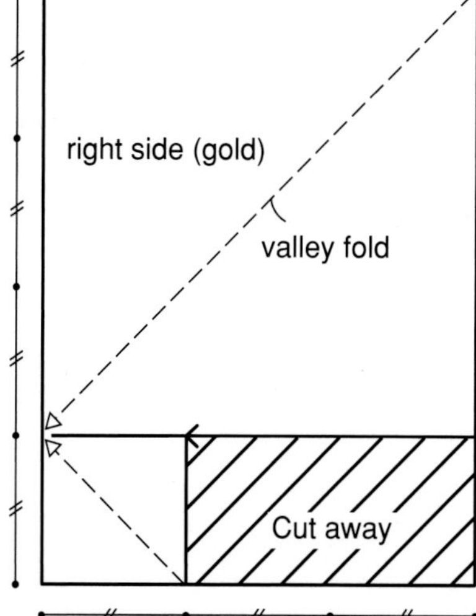

Drawing from the original book:
By altering angles of each section, a different expression will appear.

3
一筆の恋風車
ゆきゝ寄せて
かくした文の
袖のおもたさ

Pinwheel 風車 *Kazaguruma*

Four cranes connected at beaks and wings resemble a pinwheel that is just about to spin, hence the name. Curl the wings slightly so that they touch each other only at their tips.

USE A SQUARE SHEET OF *WASHI* PAPER.

According to the layout below, make creases. Make further creases for 4 Beginning Squares (See pages 4-5), and then cut slits.

Fold each square into Beginning Square, using creases.

Bring left and right flaps of one side to align at center (See Steps ❸-❹, page 96.) Turn over and repeat. Fold down top triangle. Repeat with remaining squares.

All the squares are folded in the same manner.

Unfold and fold into a diamond (See Steps ⓭-⓰, page 3), carefully so as not to break the connection.

All four diamonds are completed. The wings are folded down because of the linkage.

Carefully bring sides in to make tapered neck and tail (See Steps ⓱-⓳, page 3).

Repeat with all remainders.

Fold them up by Inside Reverse Fold, and make heads in the same manner (See Steps ⓴-㉔, page 3). Shape wings and fluff bodies.

Drawing from the original book:
Tails can be stood upright like this.

LAYOUT

△ This corner to be made into head

--- Valley fold: See Steps ❷-❸, page 4 (Be sure to crease one diagonal per each square and do not crease crossing diagonals, to avoid unwanted centerlines on finished wings)

≻— Cut here(Leave ⅛" as uncut connection)

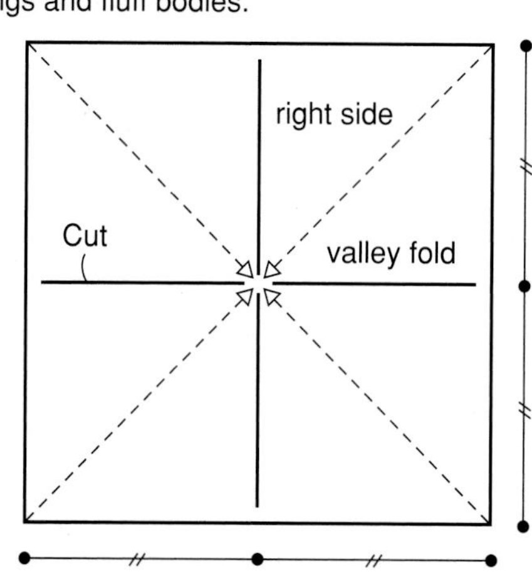

Eight Cranes in Circle 八橋 *Yatsuhashi*

Yatsuhashi literally means eight bridges, but in fact it was small stepping platforms placed in a zigzag pattern over marshy land. Later it became a design theme often with iris flowers. The cranes here form a circle as if "hand in hand."

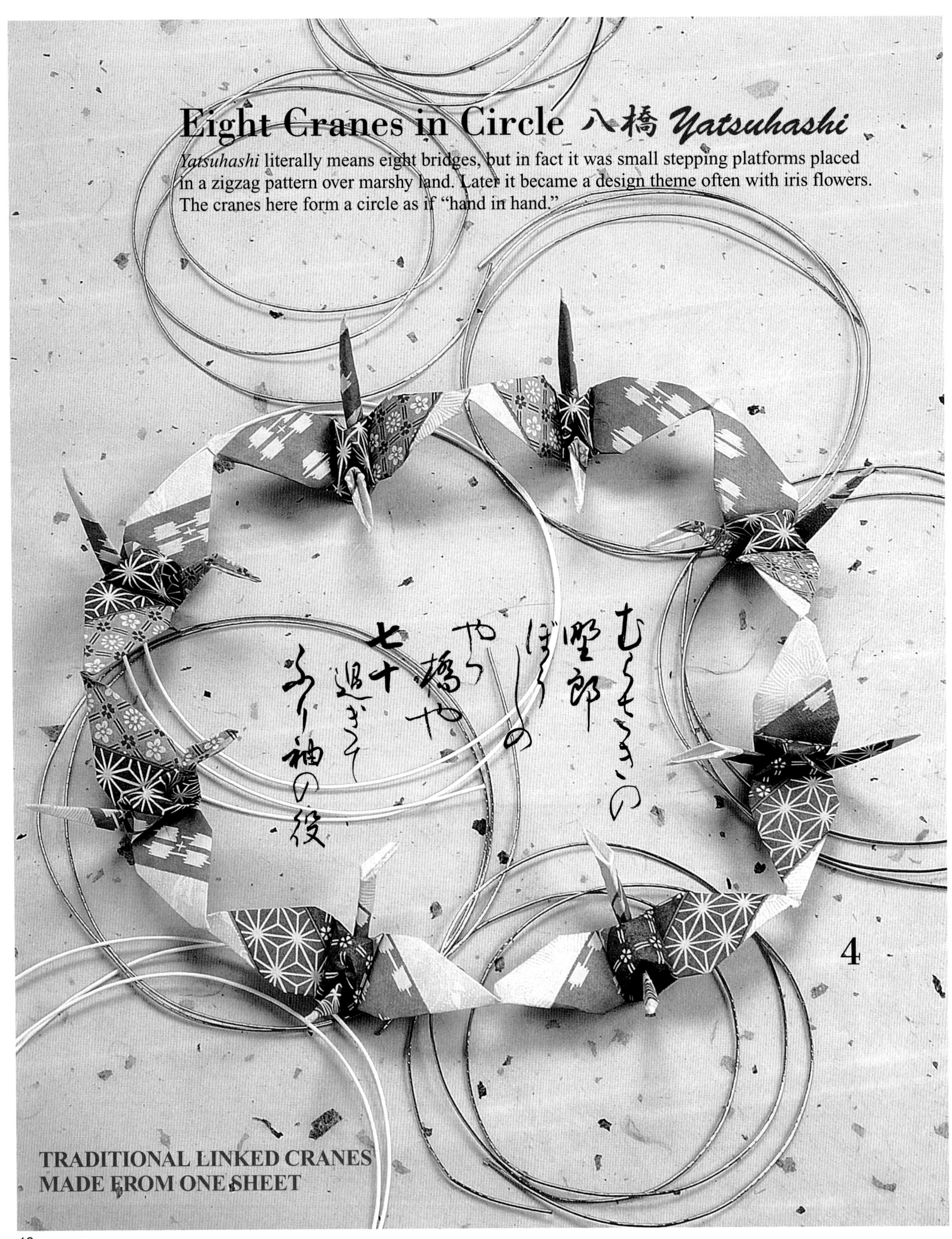

4

TRADITIONAL LINKED CRANES
MADE FROM ONE SHEET

USE A SQUARE SHEET OF *WASHI* PAPER.

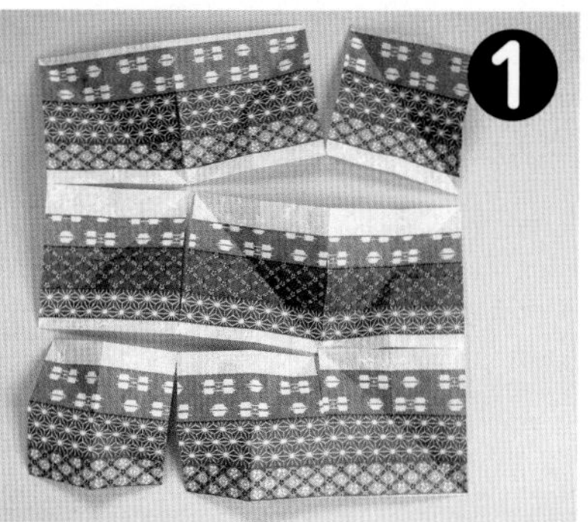

❶
According to the layout below, make creases. Make further creases for 9 Beginning Squares (See pages 4-5), and then cut slits.

❷
Fold each square into Beginning Square using creases.

❸
Bring left and right flaps of one side to align at center (See Steps ❸-❹, page 96.) Turn over and repeat. Fold down top triangle. Repeat with remaining squares.

Unfold and fold into a diamond (See Steps ⓭-⓰, page 3) carefully so as not to break the connection. Leave the end squares undone.

Unfold end squares (★) and layer them precisely corner to corner. Refold the layers and then into a diamond.

Make tapered necks and tails by bringing sides in (See Steps ⓱-⓳, page 3).

Fold up necks and tails by Inside Reverse Fold (See Steps ⓴-㉔, page 3) to finish up.

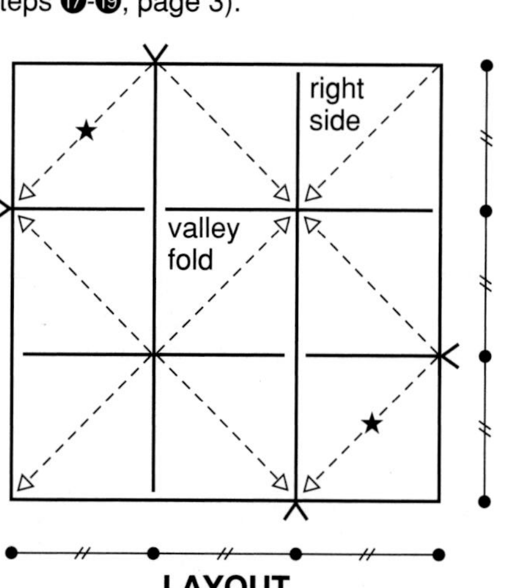

△ This corner to be made into head

--- Valley fold: See Steps ❷-❸, page 4 (Be sure to crease one diagonal per each square and do not crease crossing diagonals, to avoid unwanted centerlines on finished wings)

≻— Cut here (Leave ⅛" as uncut connection)

★ Squares with this symbol are to be layered and folded as if it were a single sheet

Drawing from the original book

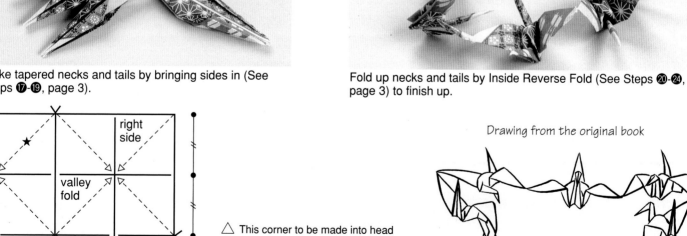

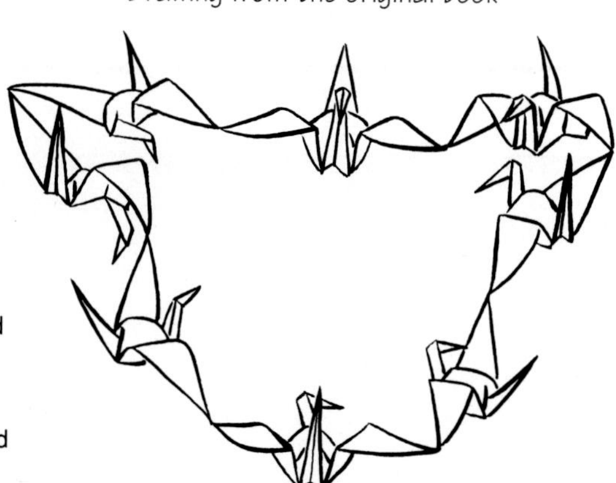

Wind Chime 鳴子 *Naruko*

Made of bamboo sticks, Japanese wind chimes were hung over farmland to drive away animals that eat the crops. Here, a parent crane is looking after child birds, resembling such a chime.

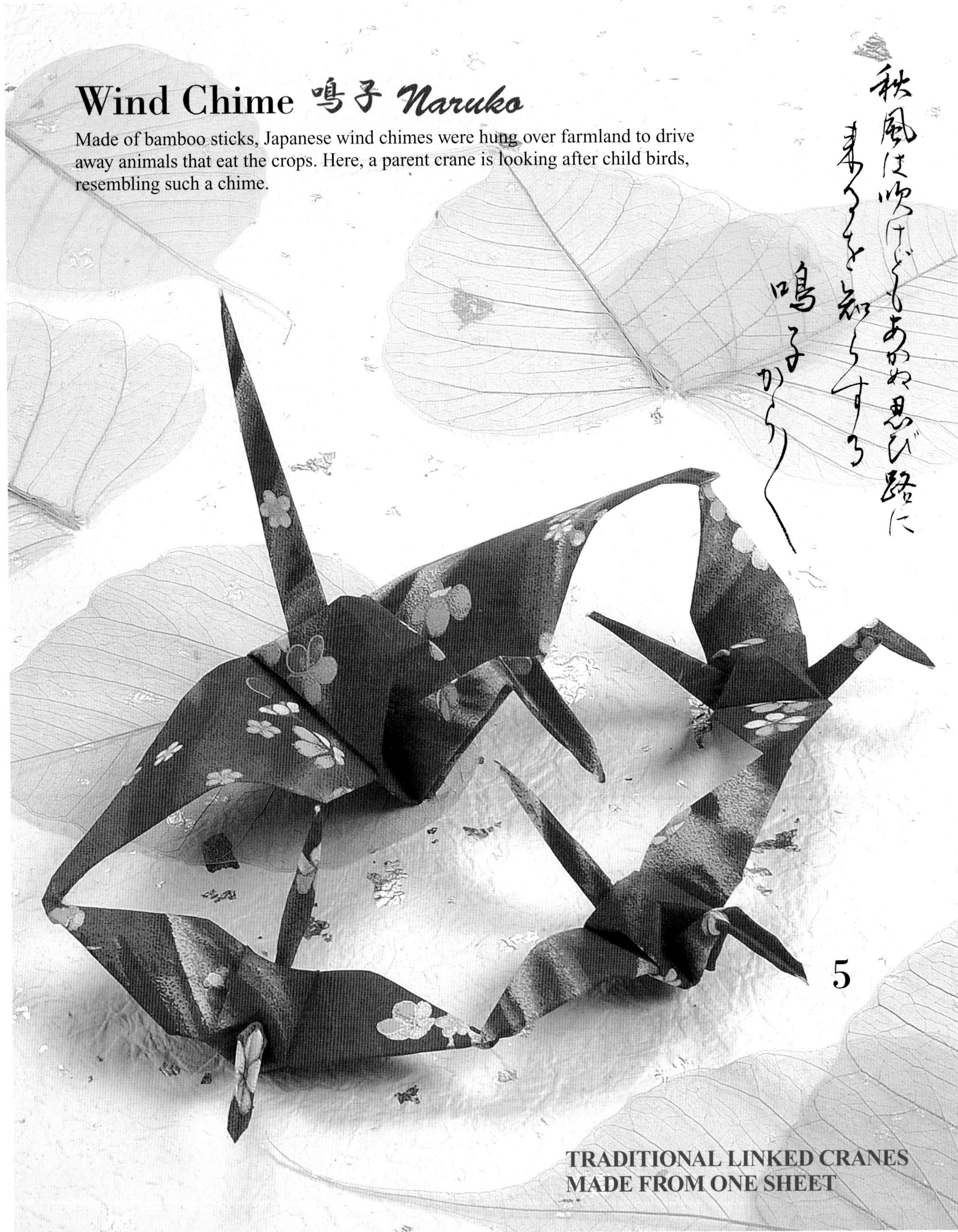

5

TRADITIONAL LINKED CRANES MADE FROM ONE SHEET

USE A SQUARE SHEET OF *WASHI* PAPER.

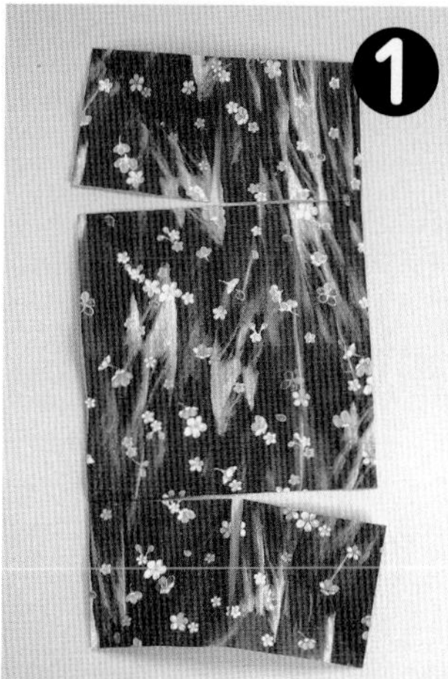

According to the layout below, make creases. Make further creases for 5 Beginning Squares (See pages 4-5), and then cut slits.

Fold each square into Beginning Square using creases.

Bring left and right flaps of one side to align at center (See Steps ❸-❹, page 96.) Turn over and repeat. Fold down top triangle. Repeat with remaining squares.

Unfold flaps and fold into a diamond (See Steps ⓭-⓰, page 3) carefully so as not to break the connection. Lastly, unfold end pieces (★), layer precisely, and fold into a diamond.

❺ One large crane and three small ones are folded into Crane Bases.

❻ Make tapered necks and tails by bringing sides in (See Steps ⓱-⓳, page 3).

❼ Fold up necks and tails by Inside Reverse Fold (See Steps ⓴-㉔, page 3) to finish up.

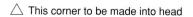

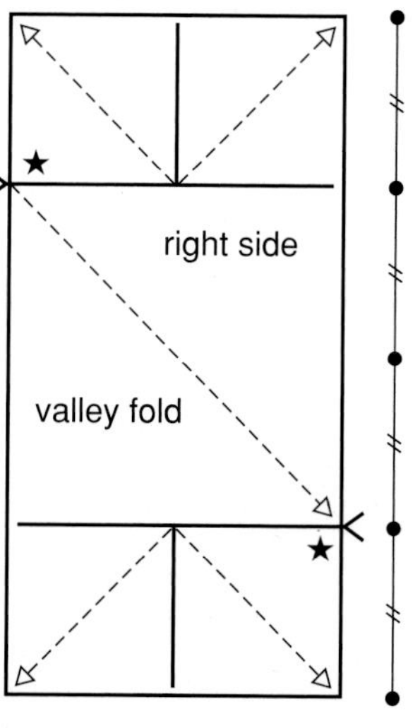

△ This corner to be made into head

--- Valley fold: See Steps ❷-❸, page 4 (Be sure to crease one diagonal per each square and do not crease crossing diagonals, to avoid unwanted centerlines on finished wings)

≻— Cut here (Leave ⅛" as uncut connection)

★ Squares with this symbol are to be layered and folded as if it were a single sheet

Drawing from the original book

Legendary Bird 九万里 *Kumanri*

Tiny ones sitting on the wingtips of the large bird emphasize the length of the wings. *Kumanri* is a legendary, gigantic bird whose wingspan measures seven thousand miles which enables it to fly up to *kuman-ri* (nine-*ri*, or something like 576,000 miles) with a single beat of wings.

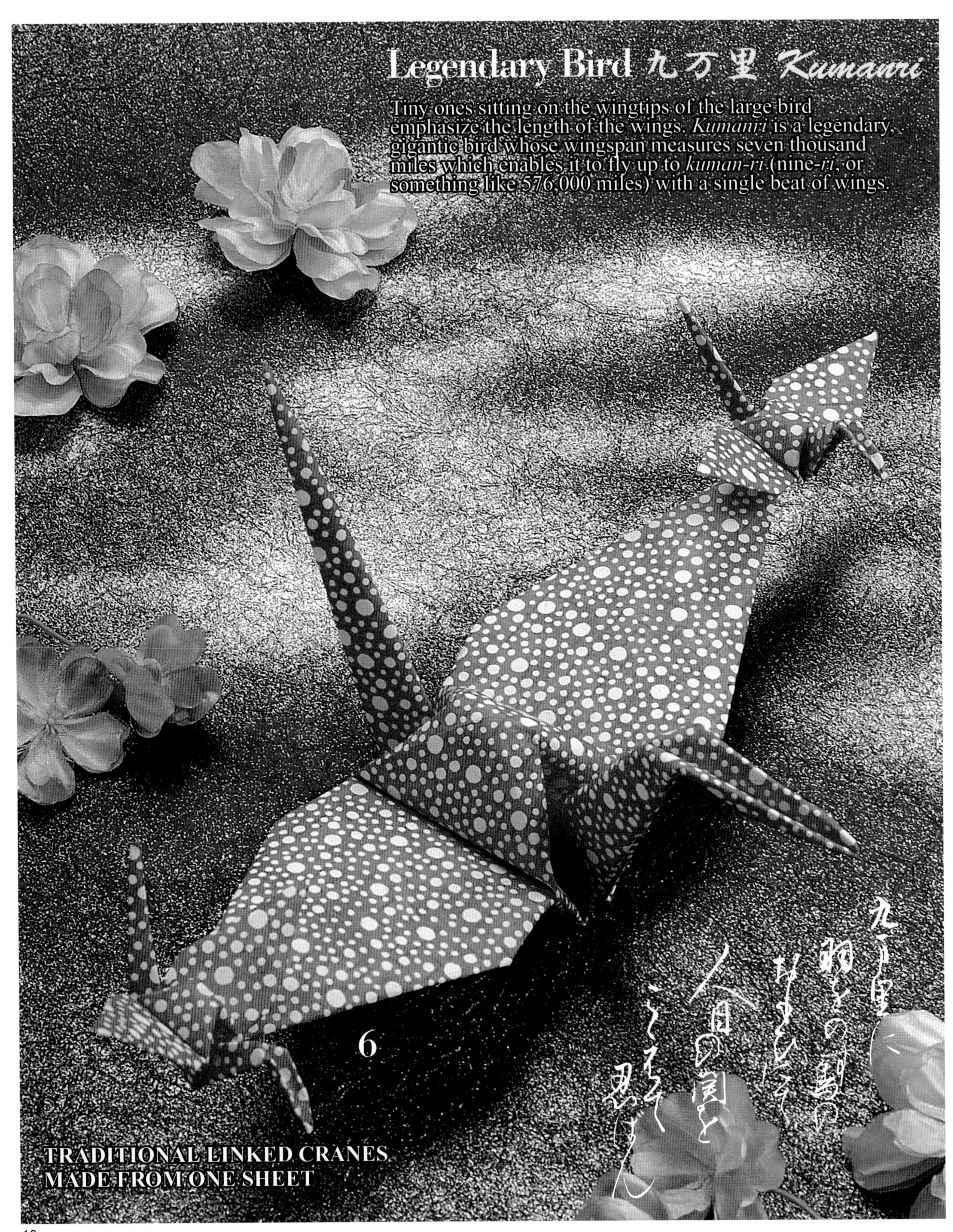

6

TRADITIONAL LINKED CRANES MADE FROM ONE SHEET

USE A RECTANGULAR SHEET OF *WASHI* PAPER (4:6 RATIO).

According to the layout below, trim and make creases on small squares. Make further creases for Beginning Squares (See pages 4-5), and then cut slits.

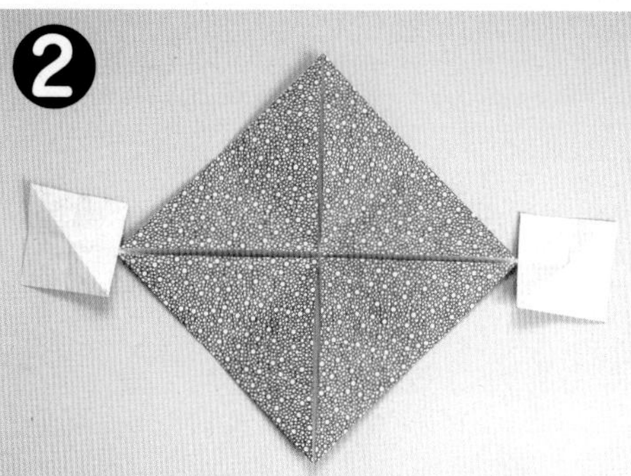

Turn over, and bring all four corners of large square to the center point, using creases. Make creases for Beginning Square.

Fold each square into Beginning Square (See page 5).

Bring left and right flaps of one side to align at center (See Steps ❸-❹, page 96). Turn over and repeat. Repeat with the other square.

Unfold and fold into a diamond (See Steps ⓭-⓰, page 3 for Crane Base) carefully so as not to break the connections.

Make tapered necks and tails by bringing sides in to align at center (See Steps ⓱-⓳, page 3).

Fold up necks and tails by Inside Reverse Fold (See Steps ⓴-㉔, page 3) to finish up.

LAYOUT

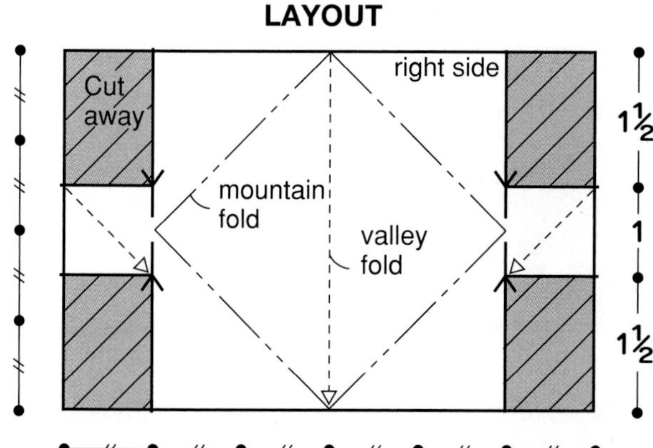

Divide short side into quarters. Cut away 1½ : 1 ratio rectangle from each corner.

△ This corner to be made into head

---Valley fold: See Steps ❷-❸, page 4

-·-·-Mountain fold

≻— Cut here (Leave ⅛" as uncut connection)

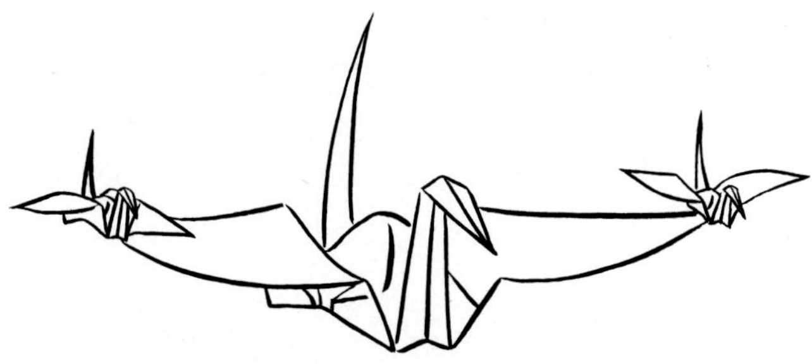

Drawing from the original book

忍び路の恋を見つけて
むら雲の中から
バアと月の顔出す
7

Above the Clouds 村雲 *Murakumo*

Tiny little crane on top of the soaring tail creates an aura of the distant moon over *murakumo*, or gathering clouds.

USE A RECTANGULAR SHEET OF *WASHI* PAPER (4:3 RATIO).

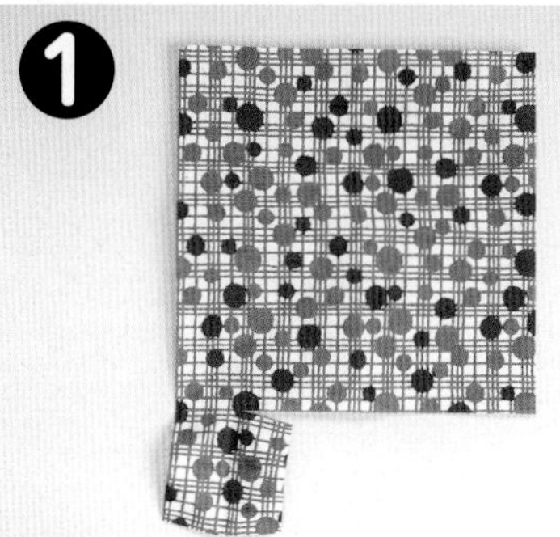

❶ According to the layout below, trim and make creases. On large square, make further creases for Beginning Square (See pages 4-5), and then cut slits.

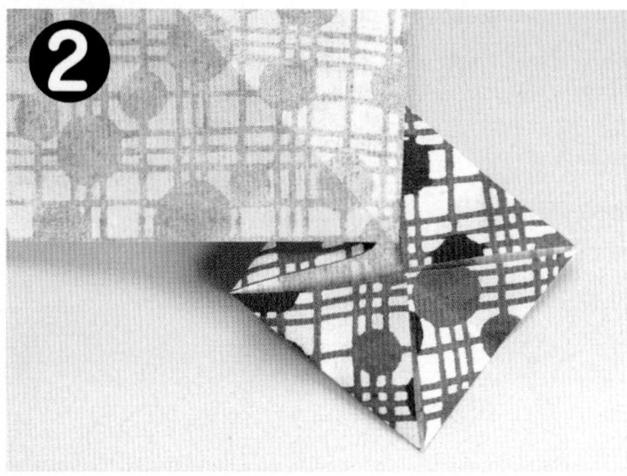

❷ Turn over, and bring all four corners of small square to the center point, using creases. Make creases for Beginning Square.

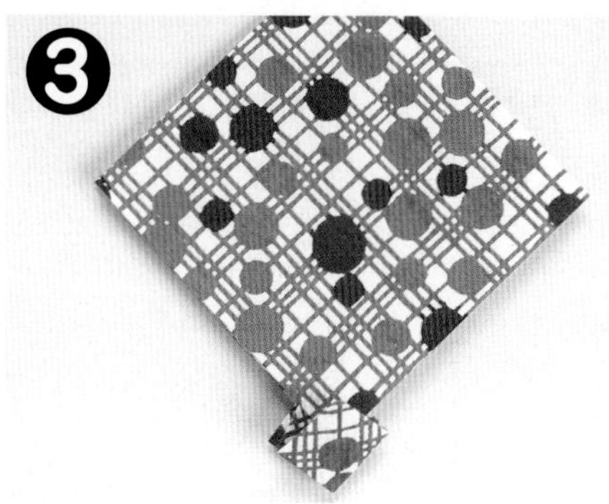

❸ Fold each square into Beginning Square, using creases.

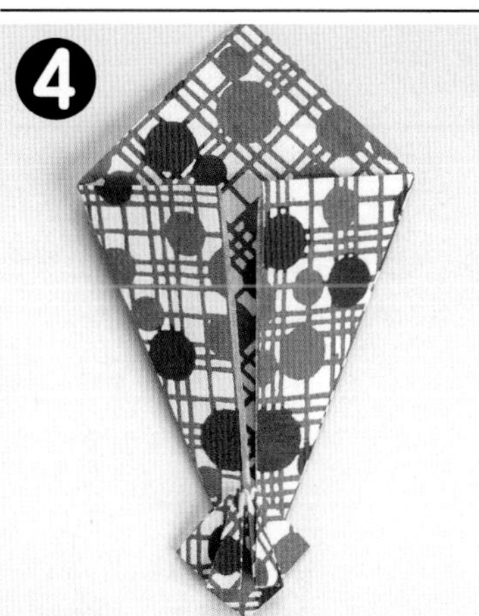

❹ Bring left and right flaps of one side to align at center (See Steps ❸-❹, page 96). Turn over and repeat. Repeat with the other square.

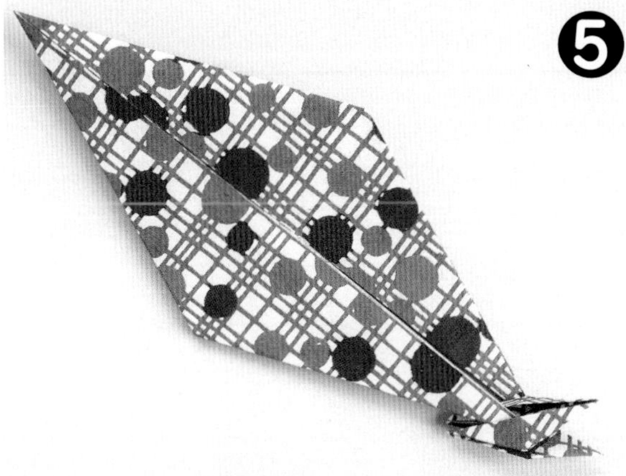

❺ Unfold and fold into a diamond (See Steps ⓭-⓰, page 3, for Crane Base) carefully so as not to break the connection.

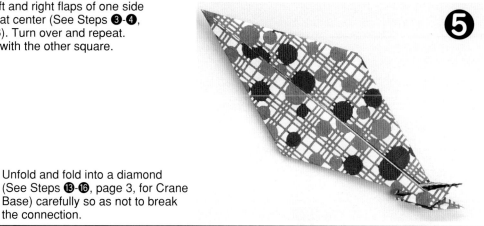

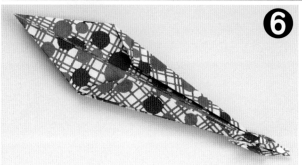

❻ Make tapered necks and tails by bringing sides in to align at center (See Steps ⓱-⓳, page 3).

❼ Fold up necks and tails of each, by Inside Reverse Fold (See Steps ⓴-㉔, page 3). Pull apart wings and fluff bodies to finish up.

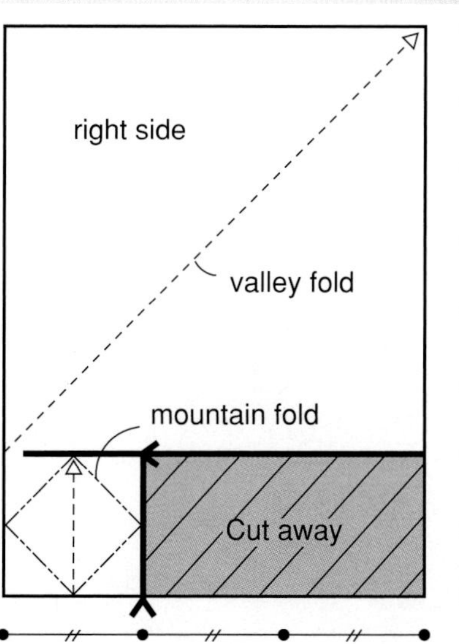

LAYOUT

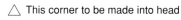

△ This corner to be made into head

--- Valley fold: See Steps ❷-❸, page 4

-·-·- Mountain fold

>— Cut here (Leave ⅛" as uncut connection)

Drawing from the original book: By altering angles of each section, a different expression will appear.

TRADITIONAL LINKED CRANES MADE FROM ONE SHEET

8
Parent and Child 瓜の蔓 *Uri-no-Tsuru*

A parent crane embracing two chicks under its wings. "*Uri-no-tsuru*" means vines of gourd, suggesting "*Uri-no-tsuru ni nasubi wa naranu,*" meaning "Vines of gourd won't bear eggplant." In other words, the apple doesn't fall far from the tree. How ironical they sang about the wonders of DNA!

Type A:
Chicks are linked at their wings. Cut a longer slit into the back of the wings when pulling them out to the front to make the twisting easy.

Type B (original):
One chick is hung upside down in this method. Turn it 90 degrees. Twist the other chick and pull out to front by folding the tip of its tail.

Both types are folded in the same manner.

USE A RECTANGULAR SHEET OF *WASHI* PAPER (3:2 RATIO).

According to the layout below, make creases. Make further creases for Beginning Squares (See pages 4-5), and then cut slits.

Fold each square into Beginning Square, using creases.

Bring left and right flaps of one side to align at center (See Steps ❸-❹, page 96). Turn over and repeat. Fold down top triangle. Repeat with the other square.

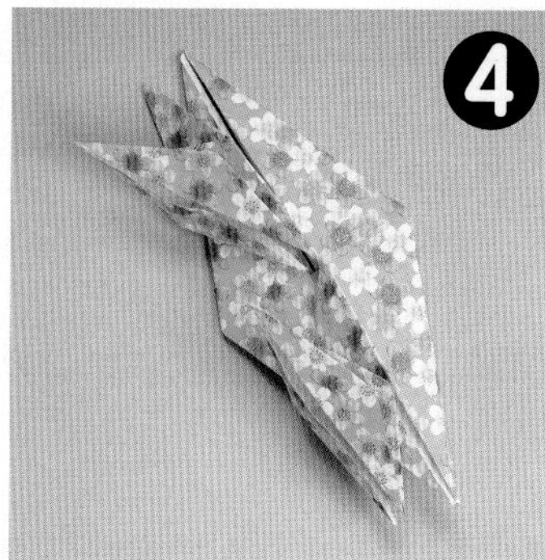

Unfold and fold into a diamond (See Steps ⓭-⓰, page 3, for Crane Base) carefully so as not to break the connections.

For type A, cut an additional slit from the connection to the fold. Work on both cranes.

Showing the connections that remain.

First with smaller crane, make tapered necks and tails by folding sides in. Bring over the flaps, and fold up (See Steps ⓱-⓳, page 3).

Repeat with the large crane. Fold up neck and tail by Inside Reverse Fold (See Steps ⓴-㉔, page 3).

Then make heads and tails of smaller cranes.

To sit smaller cranes next to the mother bird, twist at each connection.

Drawing from the original book

LAYOUT (Type A)

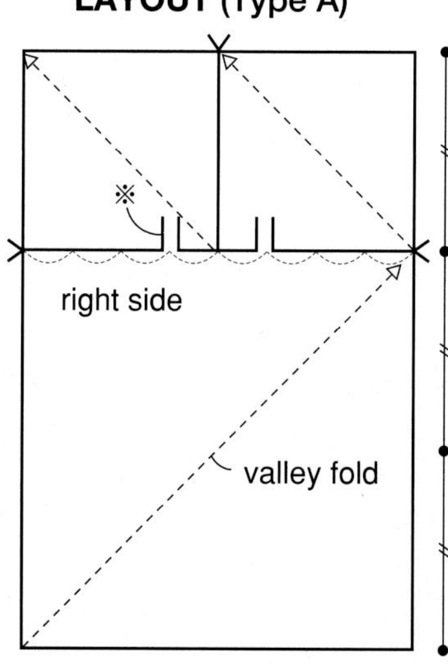

△ This corner to be made into head

--- Valley fold: See Steps ❷-❸, page 4 (Be sure to crease one diagonal per each square and do not crease crossing diagonals, to avoid unwanted centerlines on finished wings)

>— Cut here (Leave ⅛" as uncut connection)

※This part is to be cut in Steps ❺. It enables you to twist and pull out the model easily.

Carefully turn the tail of front chick which is held in the neck of large crane. The upside-down chick should be twisted around, and the wingtip bended at the connection.

LAYOUT (Type B)

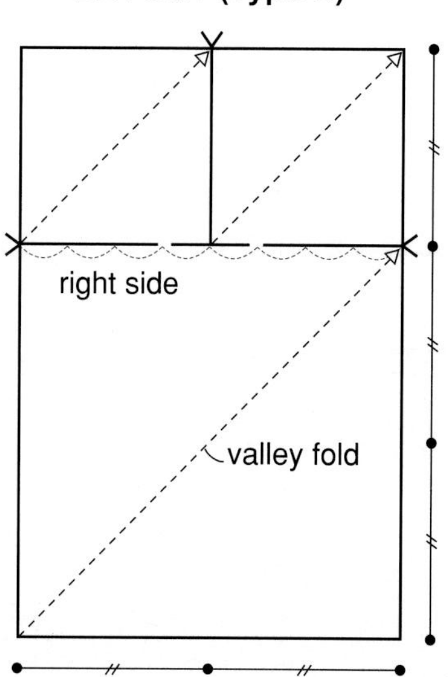

9

Kissing Cranes 相生 *Aioi*

Aioi stands for loving couple, and the word is often used at weddings and anniversaries as a word of celebration. This is not an easy one because half of the crane body is made of three layers of paper while the other half is made of one sheet.

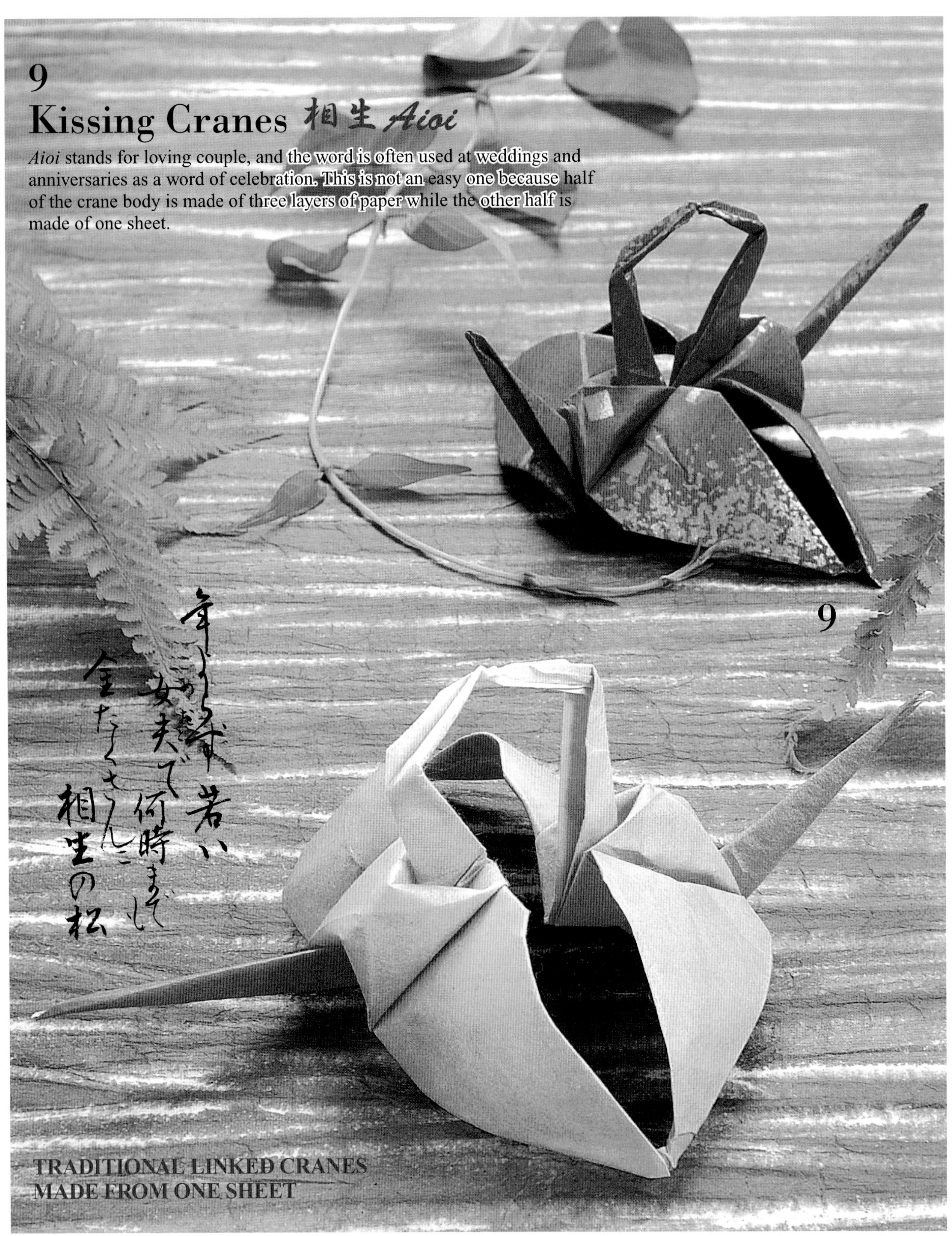

9

TRADITIONAL LINKED CRANES
MADE FROM ONE SHEET

USE A SQUARE SHEET OF THIN *WASHI* PAPER.

According to the layout below, make creases. Make further creases for 4 Beginning Squares (See pages 4-5), and then cut slits.

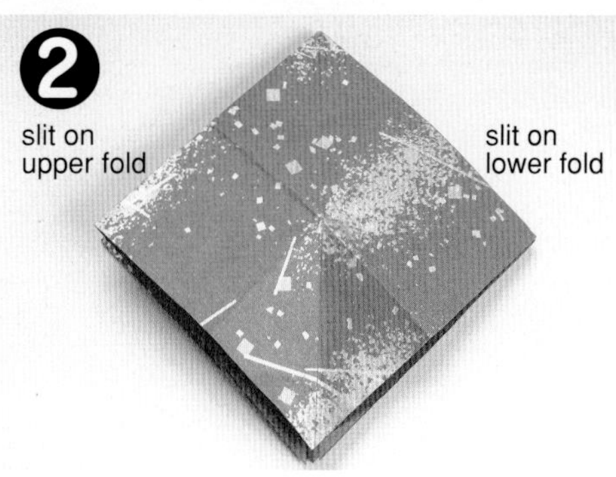

Fold the whole sheet into Beginning Square, using creases.

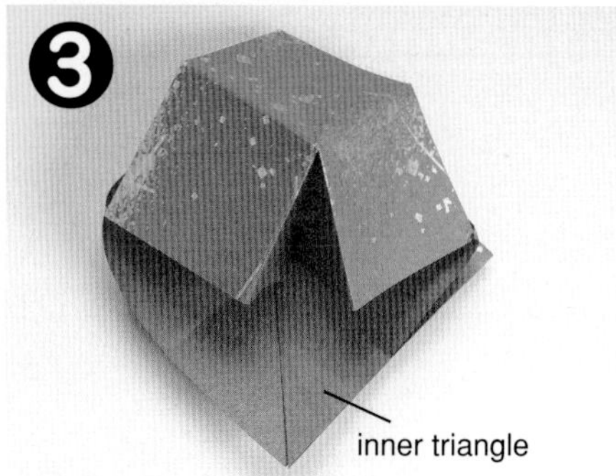

Start folding upper square into Basic Square again, this time together with one of inner triangles. Do not fold top square at this stage. Holding near edges together, turn over.

Repeat on remaining half, and then push in top squares to complete Beginning Squares.

Bring left and right flaps to align at center (See Steps ❸-❹, page 96), so thin flaps and thick flaps face each other. Unfold.

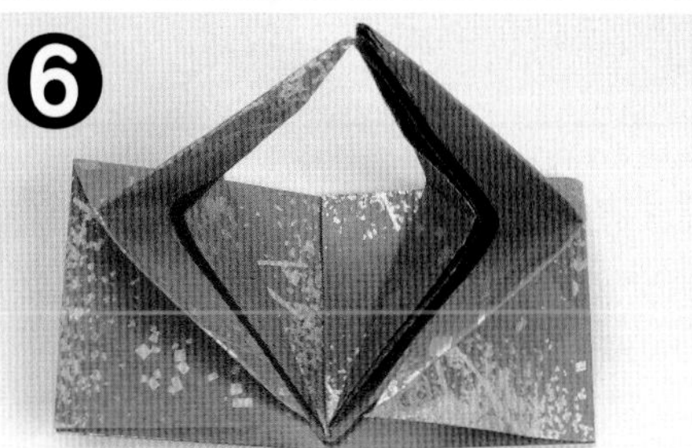

Pull open the triangles, and press down into a diamond (See Crane Base, Steps ⓭-⓰, page 3). Repeat with the other side carefully so as not to break connections.

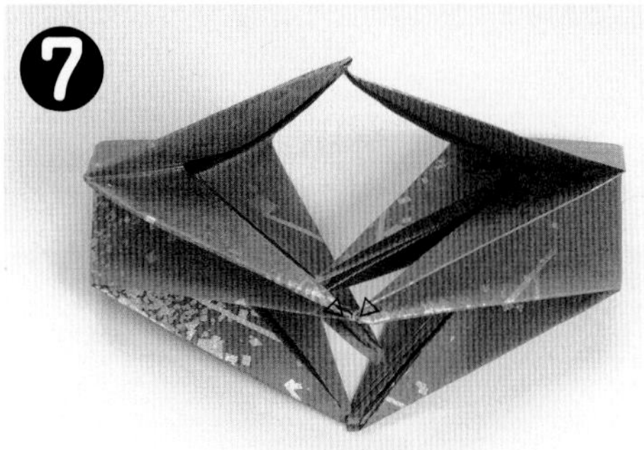

Repeat with the other side to form Crane Base. Check that they link up with each other at three points.

Make tapered neck and tail by folding sides in. Fold neck portions alternately to avoid breakage. Check that there are three connections.

Fold up neck and tail by Inside Reverse Fold. Since three points are joined, pull wings apart to fold heads (Steps ⓴-㉔, page 3).

LAYOUT

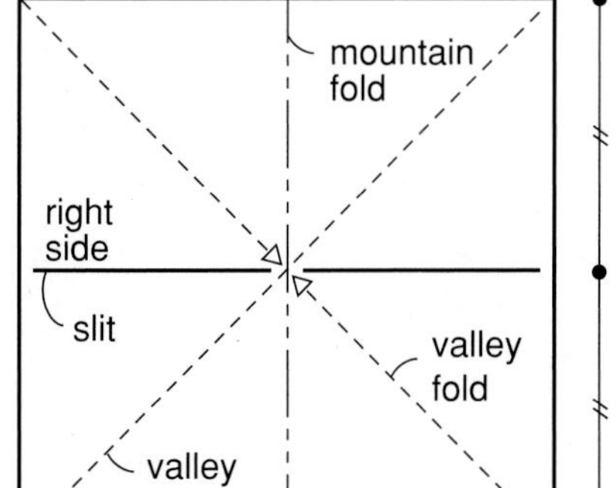

Note: It is advisable to place small markings for heads so that you can pick the right portions.

△ This corner to be made into head

--- Valley fold: See Steps ❷-❸, page 4 (Be sure to crease one diagonal per each square and do not crease crossing diagonals to avoid unwanted centerlines on finished wings)

-·-·- Mountain fold

≻— Cut here (Leave ⅛" as uncut connection)

Drawing from the original book

Hanging Vessel 釣ふね *Tsurifune*

An image of a boat-shaped flower vessel is created, with small birds resembling the chain or string, and the large one as a crescent vessel.

10

TRADITIONAL LINKED CRANES MADE FROM ONE SHEET

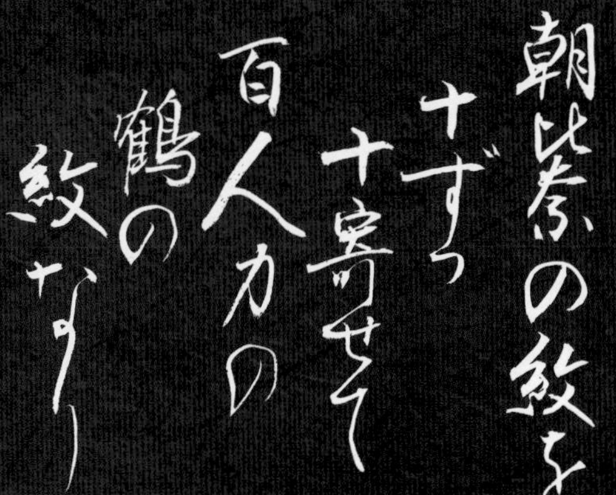

Hundred Cranes 百鶴 *Hyakkaku*

An awesome flock of linked cranes. A single sheet of paper is divided into a hundred squares, and the central crane uses four squares, leaving ninety-seven linked cranes in all.

11

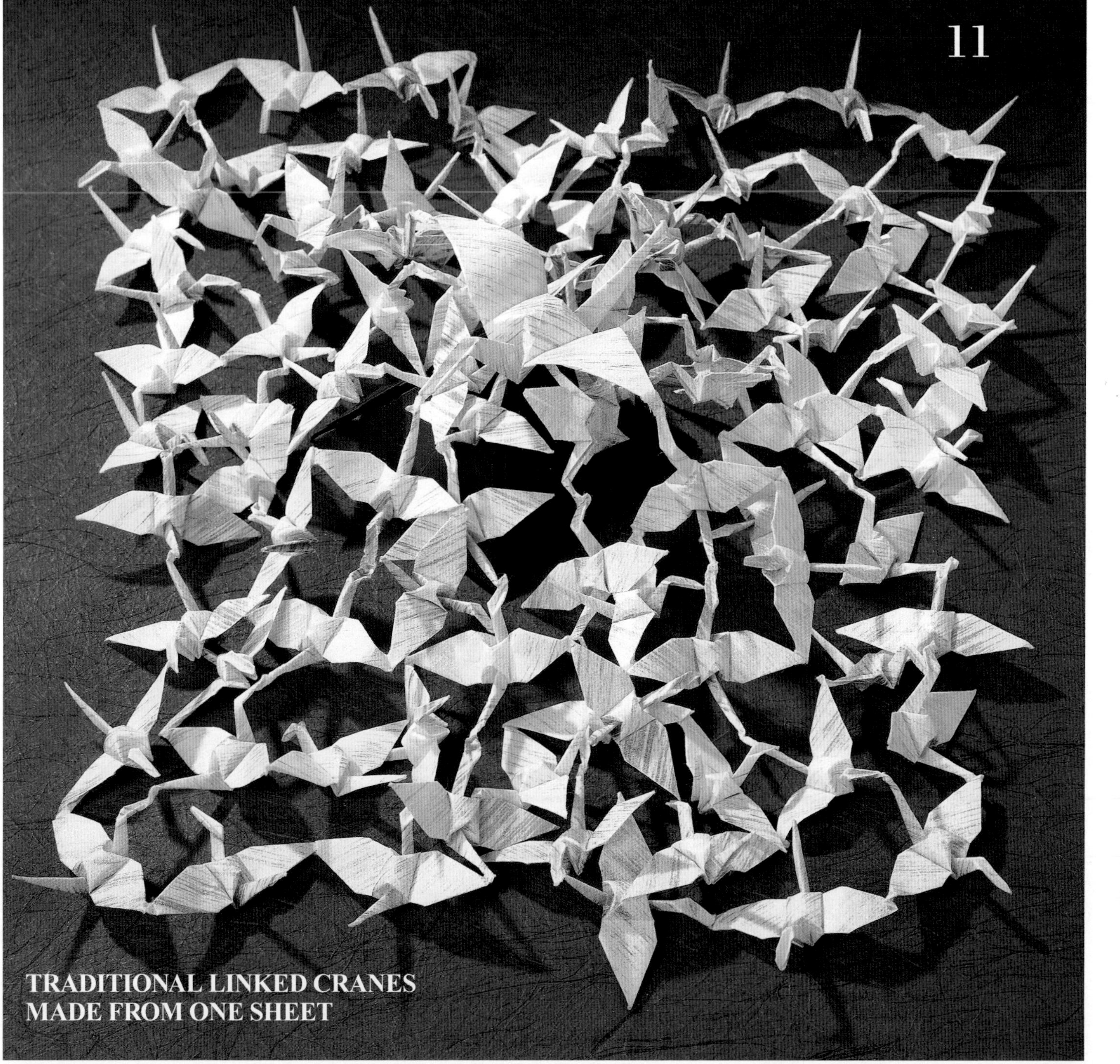

TRADITIONAL LINKED CRANES MADE FROM ONE SHEET

Everyday Uses and Special Occasions

Chopstick Rests

Why don't you prepare chopstick/silverware rests for your next dinner party? Your guests might want to take your one-of-a-kind ornaments home. Select a stiff paper, and it's easier than you think.

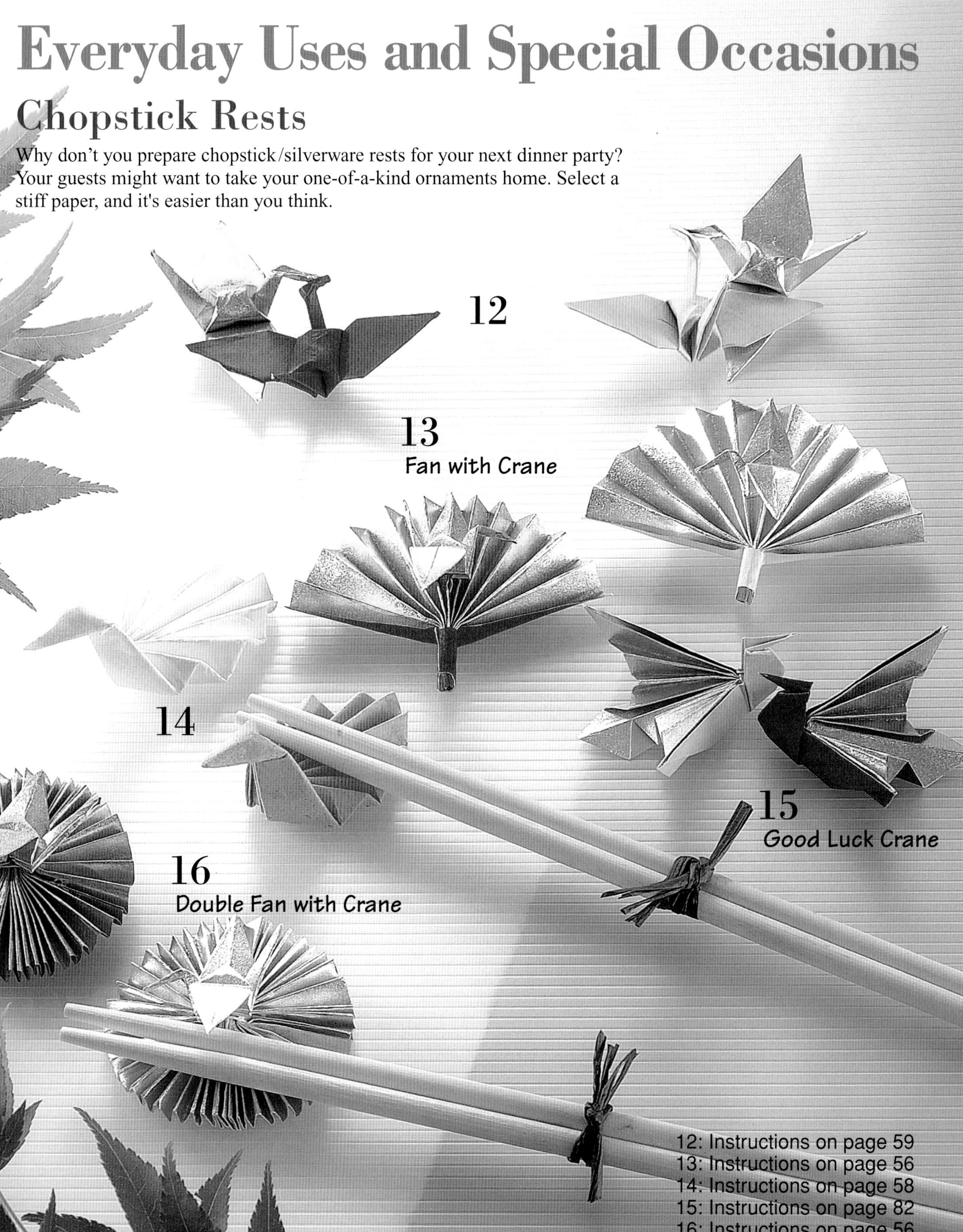

12: Instructions on page 59
13: Instructions on page 56
14: Instructions on page 58
15: Instructions on page 82
16: Instructions on page 56

Chopstick Covers

On New Year's Day, the Japanese used to fold *washi* paper into crisp chopstick covers and feel a festive mood of the first meal of the year.

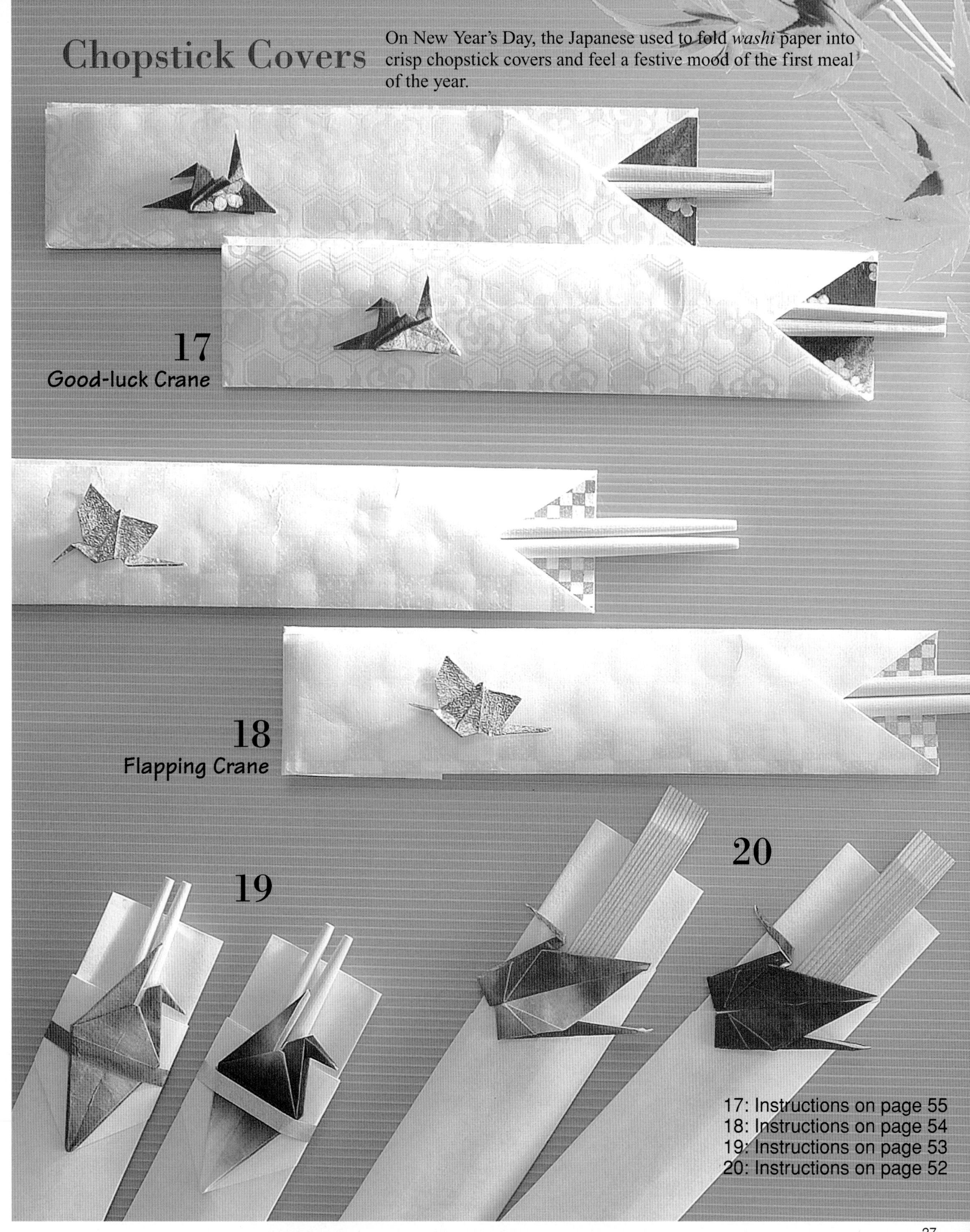

17
Good-luck Crane

18
Flapping Crane

19

20

17: Instructions on page 55
18: Instructions on page 54
19: Instructions on page 53
20: Instructions on page 52

Plate Doilies

This is a decorative version of *kaishi*, a small *washi* paper napkin used at tea ceremonies. A slit is made to the edge of the sheet to create various shapes of crane. Enjoy making a different version for each guest.

Instructions on page 60

21

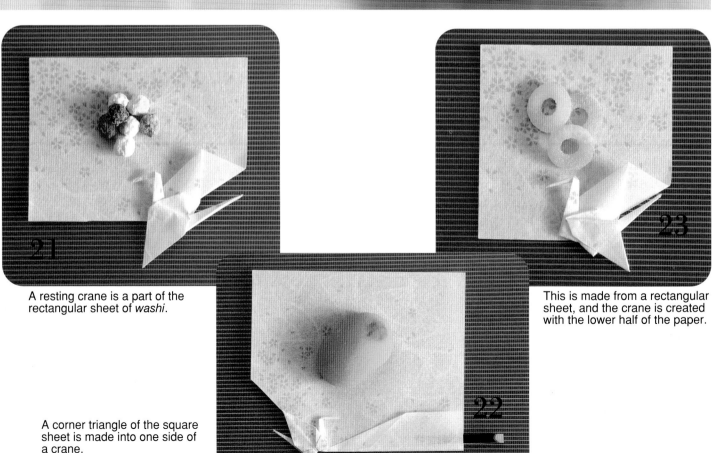

A resting crane is a part of the rectangular sheet of *washi*.

23

This is made from a rectangular sheet, and the crane is created with the lower half of the paper.

22

A corner triangle of the square sheet is made into one side of a crane.

A plain sheet of paper can turn into such, heart-warming plate liners. Serve tempura or any fried food.

Instructions on page 61

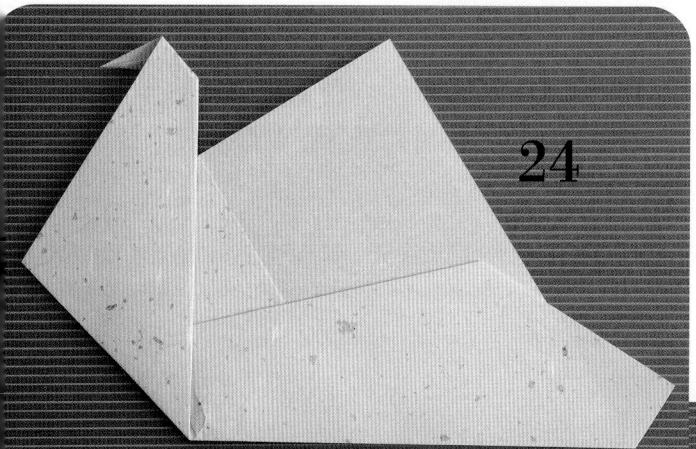

Only four folds, and voila! An artistic shape emerges so easily.

A practical design on which to lay more food.

Perfect for a small serving.

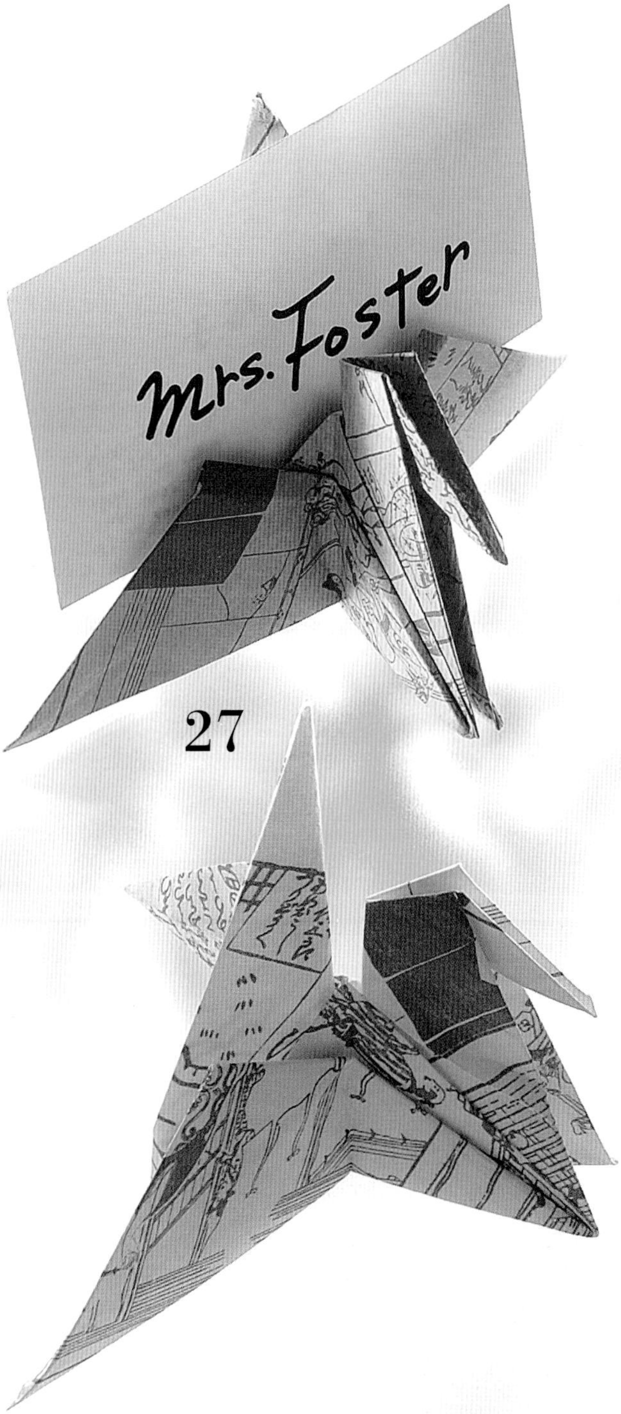

28

27

Card Holders

Crisp folded cranes will enhance your table. Two holding styles are shown here: front-facing and side-facing. Use front facing type to hold thicker cards.

Instructions on page 62

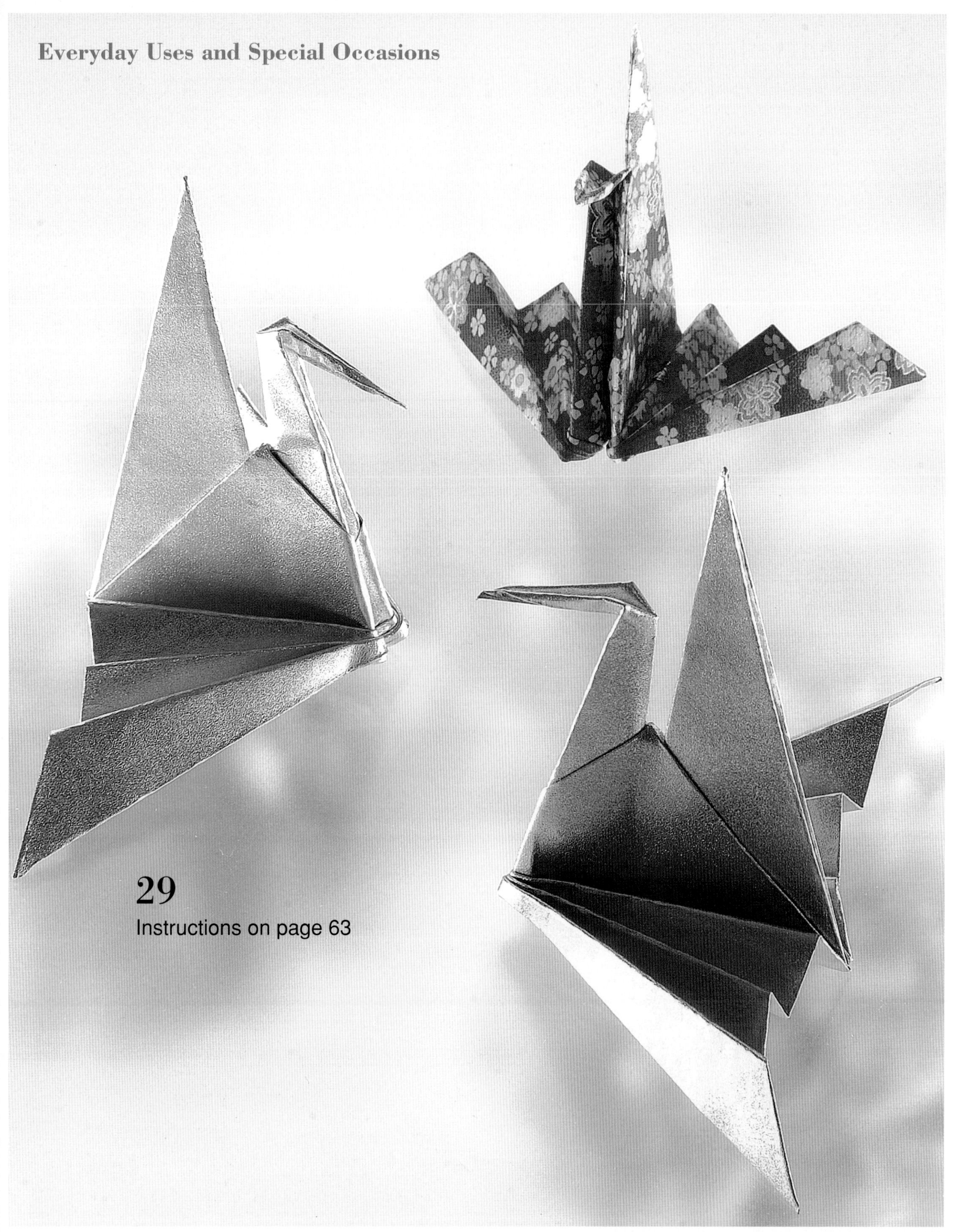

29

Instructions on page 63

Gift Envelopes

These were originally made for monetary gifts, but adjust the size, and the possibilities are endless. Photos, CDs, your origami projects, etc.

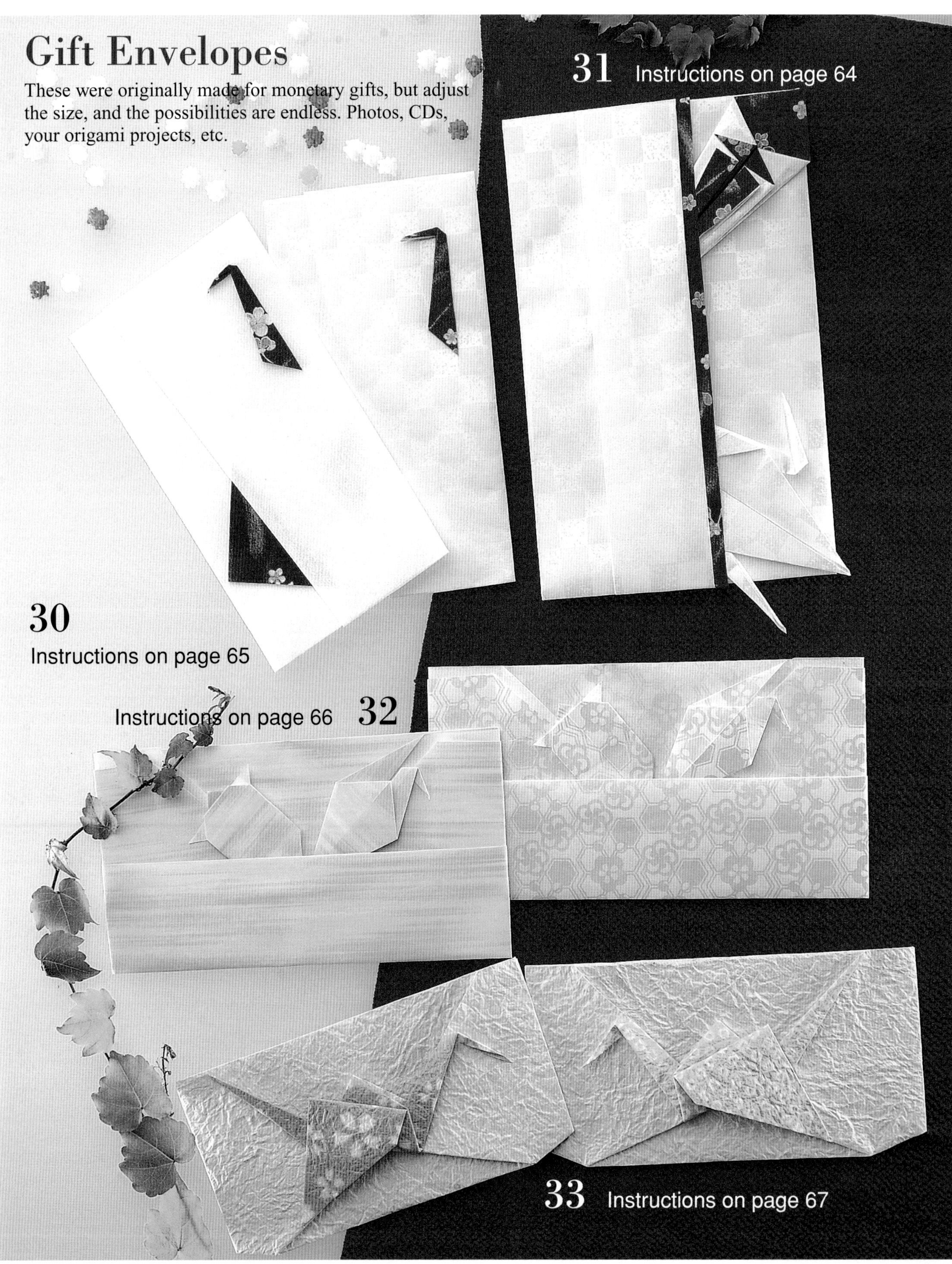

31 Instructions on page 64

30 Instructions on page 65

32 Instructions on page 66

33 Instructions on page 67

Flying Crane Quartets

Small cranes fly, pulling a sheet together in the air. By using a thick type of *washi* paper, you can create a charming container or a small gift.

Instructions on page 80

Original Plan by Gengo Ichihashi

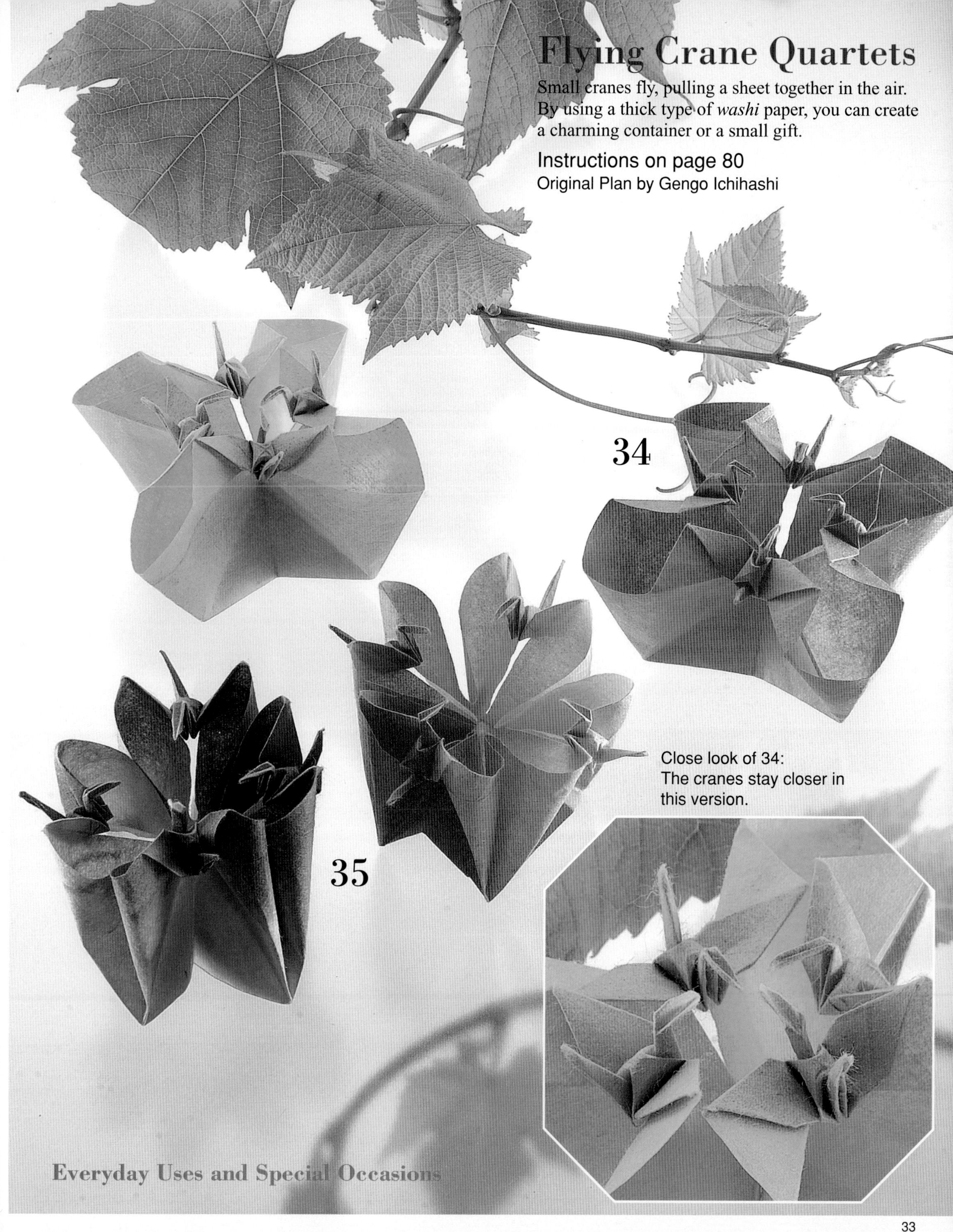

34

35

Close look of 34:
The cranes stay closer in this version.

Gift Card Envelopes

Small-size folded envelopes will convey your feelings when you add a folded crane that is extended from the envelope. Patterned paper will make a color contrast with the white of the reverse side. Perfect for electronic gift cards.

Instructions on page 68

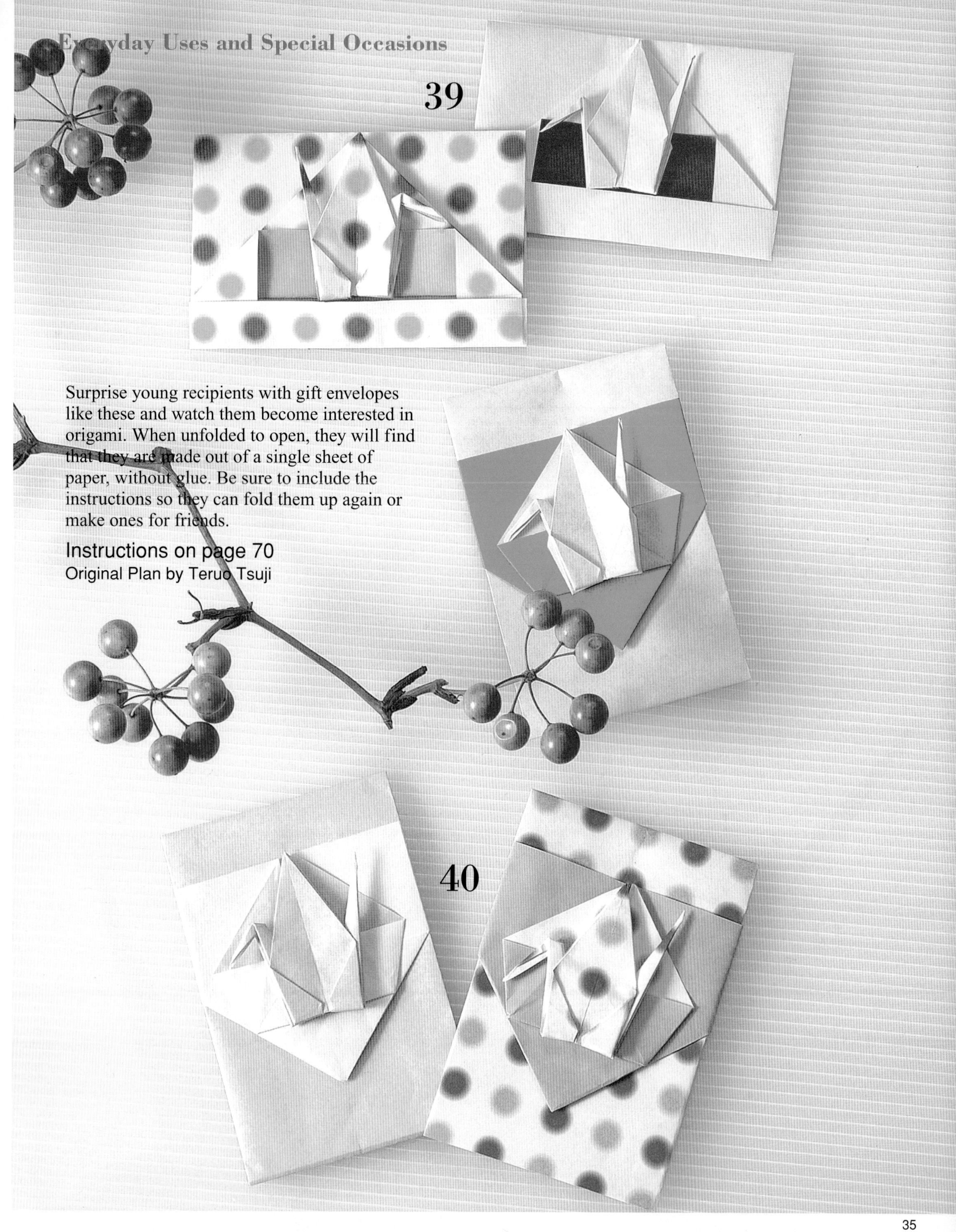

39

Surprise young recipients with gift envelopes like these and watch them become interested in origami. When unfolded to open, they will find that they are made out of a single sheet of paper, without glue. Be sure to include the instructions so they can fold them up again or make ones for friends.

Instructions on page 70

Original Plan by Teruo Tsuji

40

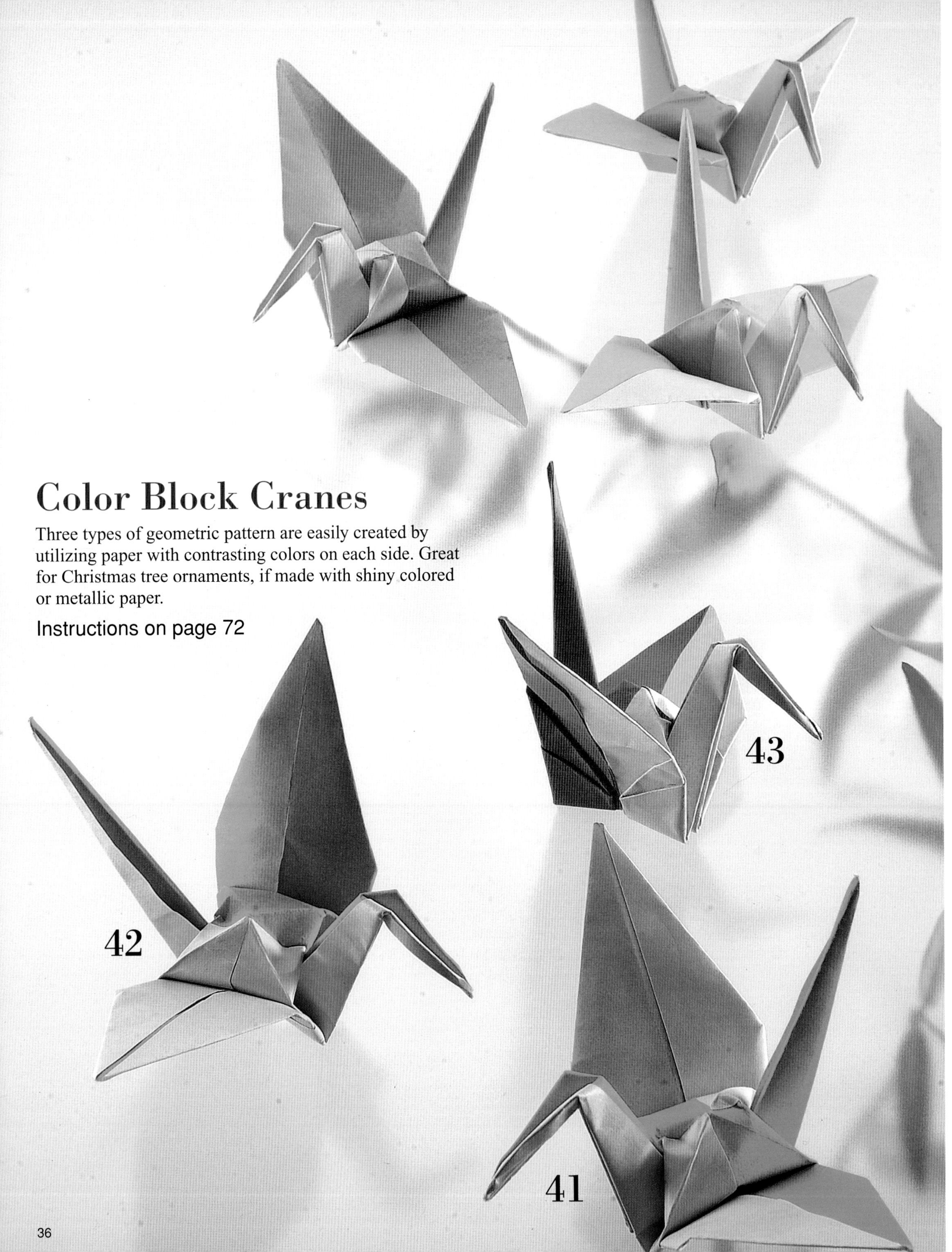

Color Block Cranes

Three types of geometric pattern are easily created by utilizing paper with contrasting colors on each side. Great for Christmas tree ornaments, if made with shiny colored or metallic paper.

Instructions on page 72

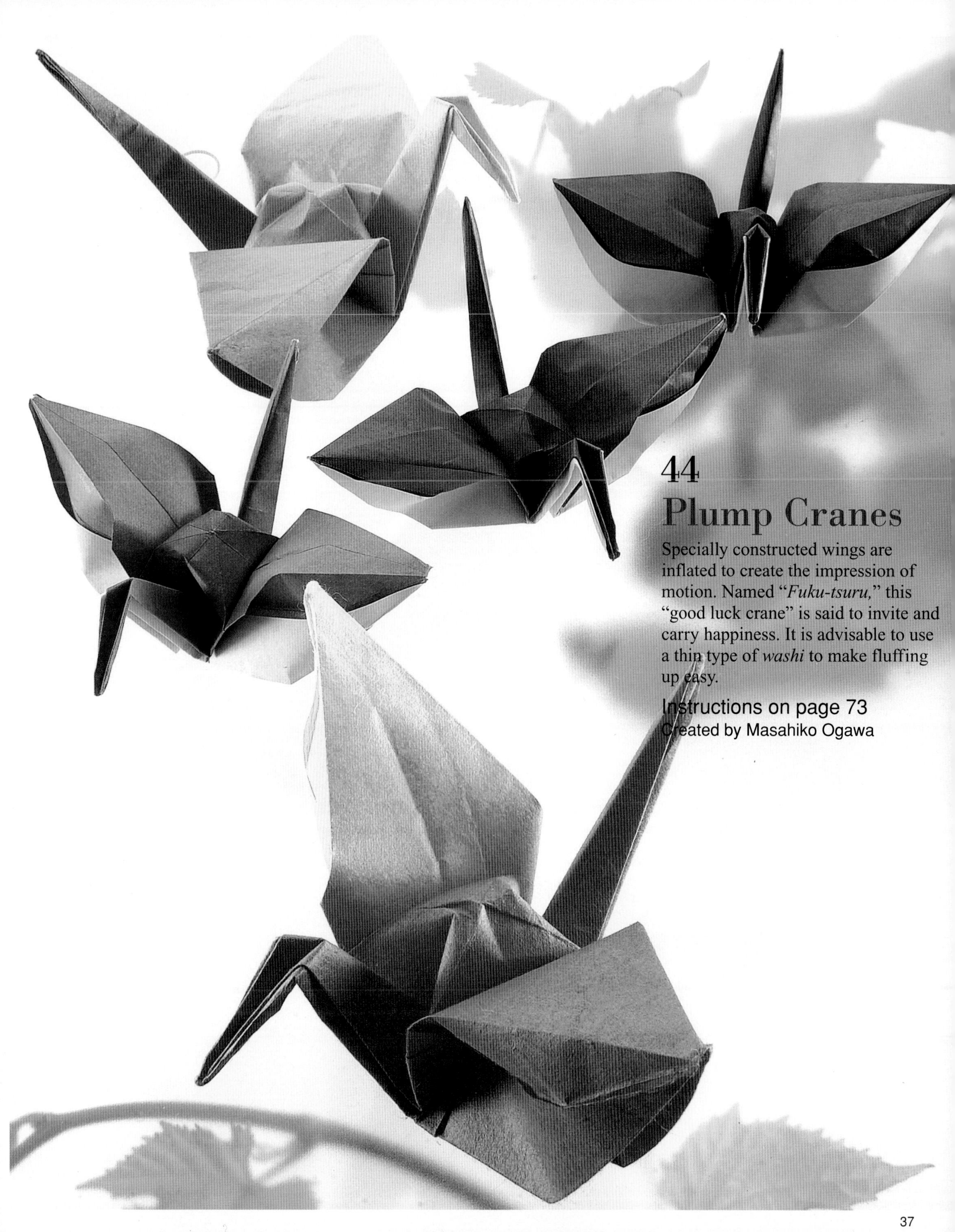

44
Plump Cranes

Specially constructed wings are inflated to create the impression of motion. Named "*Fuku-tsuru,*" this "good luck crane" is said to invite and carry happiness. It is advisable to use a thin type of *washi* to make fluffing up easy.

Instructions on page 73

Created by Masahiko Ogawa

45
Crane Containers

An unusual type of bird shaped container. Adjust the size of paper depending on the content, and use thicker paper for more stability.

Instructions on page 74

Crane Boxes

Traditionally popular origami boxes called "*orisue*" are adorned with tiny cranes created by altering the flap design. Make a dozen in several sizes and use as sorting boxes.

Instructions on page 76

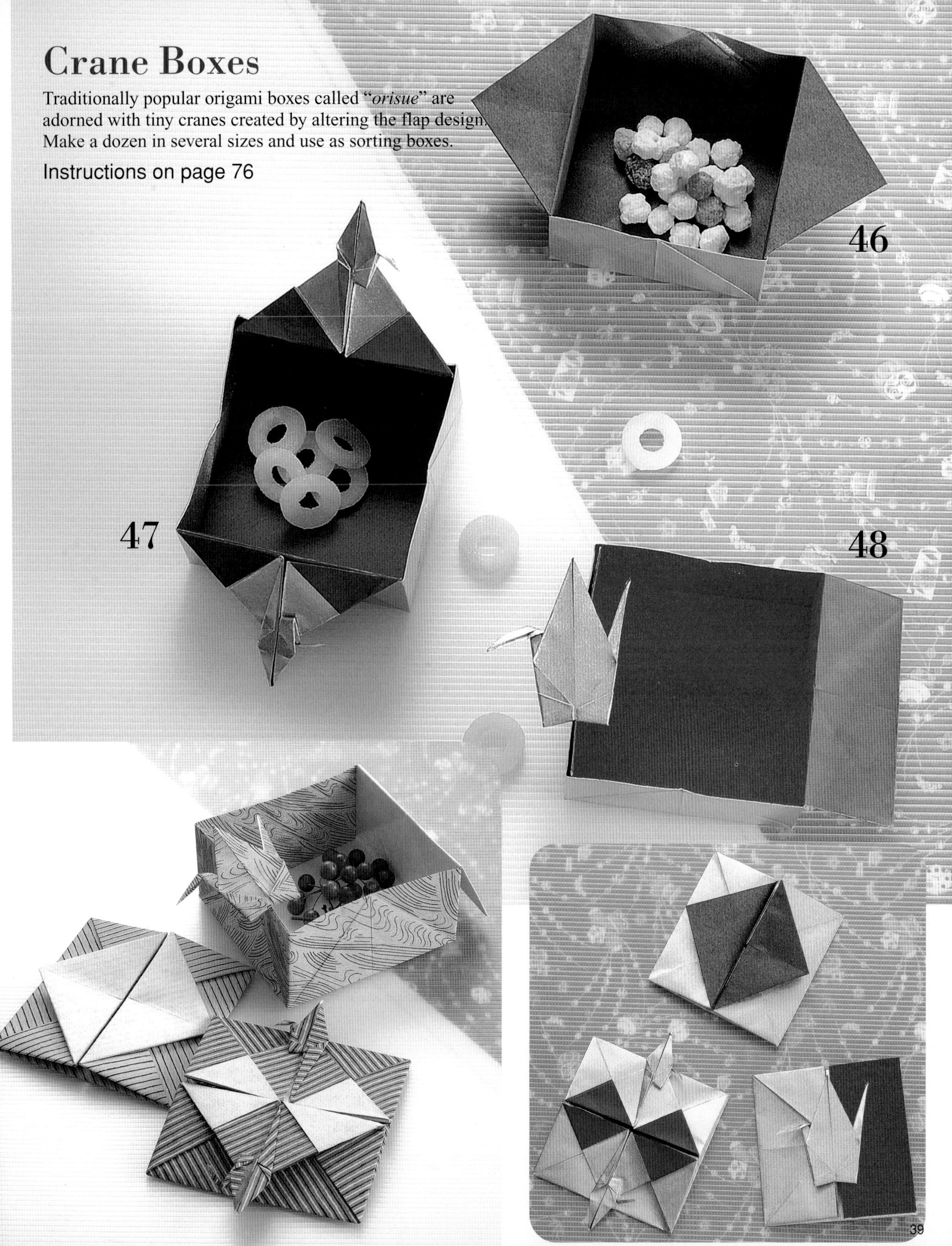

49
Sitting Cranes

Beautiful outline from the pointed head towards the wings folded as in rest. The body section serves as a container for tabletops and desks. A stiff type of paper is recommended.

Instructions on page 78

Created by Kazukuni Endo

50
Good Luck Cranes

These simple yet impressive cranes proudly show their wings in this pleated folds. This model is a new version of "*kujaku-zuru*" created by the late Toshio Chino, an origami artist.

Instructions on page 82

51
Happy Cranes

Regardless of the size, these chubby cranes will enhance any happy occasion with their petal-like, three-dimensional wings. This model is a new version of "*Iwai-zuru*" created by the late Mitsuo Okuda, an origami artist.

Instructions on page 84

New Year Wreaths

52

A paper-craft New Year wreath arranged with Christmassy colors. Crisply folded cranes are used as a good luck symbol adorning a *washi* paper base together with the traditional happy trio of pine, bamboo and plum blossom.

Instructions on page 86

53

A flapping crane centers the straw wreath which is accentuated with fresh pine and plum twigs.

Instructions on page 88

54

This one has a larger crane and red berries for more impact.

Instructions on page 88

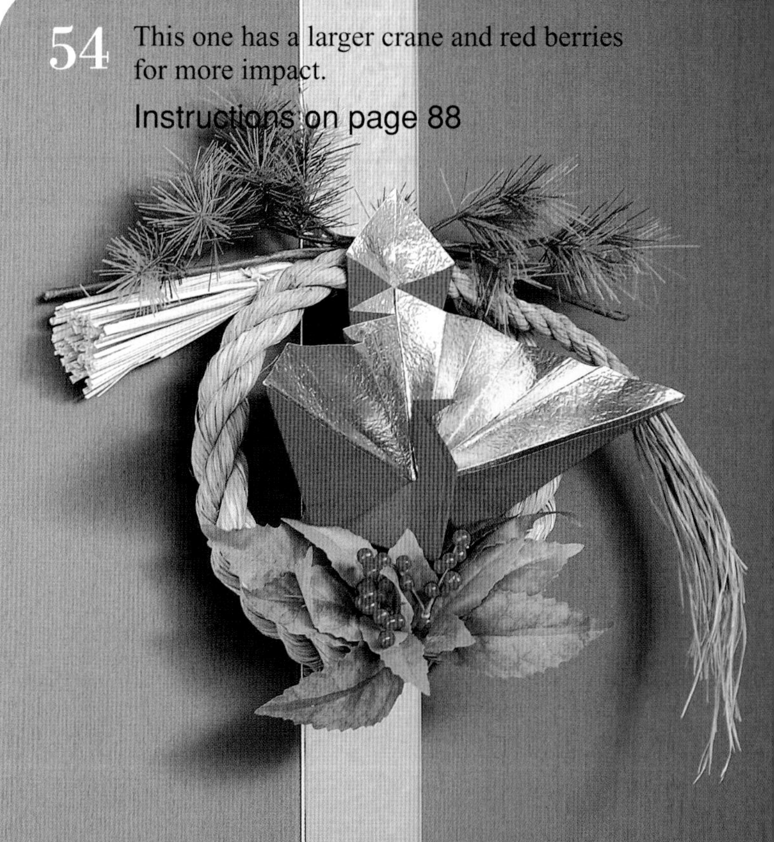

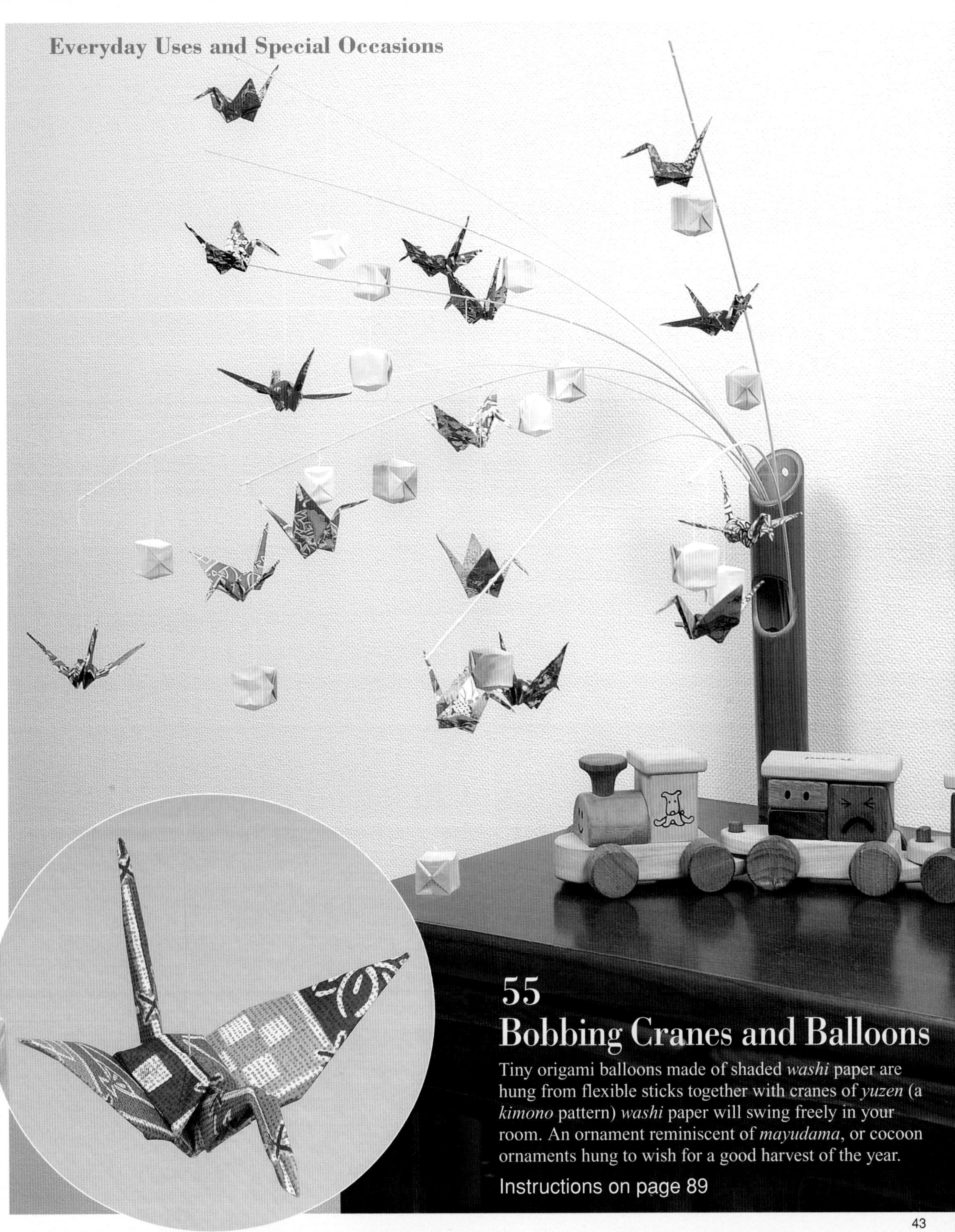

55
Bobbing Cranes and Balloons

Tiny origami balloons made of shaded *washi* paper are hung from flexible sticks together with cranes of *yuzen* (a *kimono* pattern) *washi* paper will swing freely in your room. An ornament reminiscent of *mayudama*, or cocoon ornaments hung to wish for a good harvest of the year.

Instructions on page 89

56
Wall Hanging

Beautiful translucent *washi* paper layered over gradated blue *washi* will suggest a breezy day. Arrange flapping cranes freely.

Instructions on page 92

57
Clustered Flowers

Each of the florets is made of a folded crane, the inflated body being the center of flower. Try with shaded paper for an unexpected effect.

Instructions on page 91

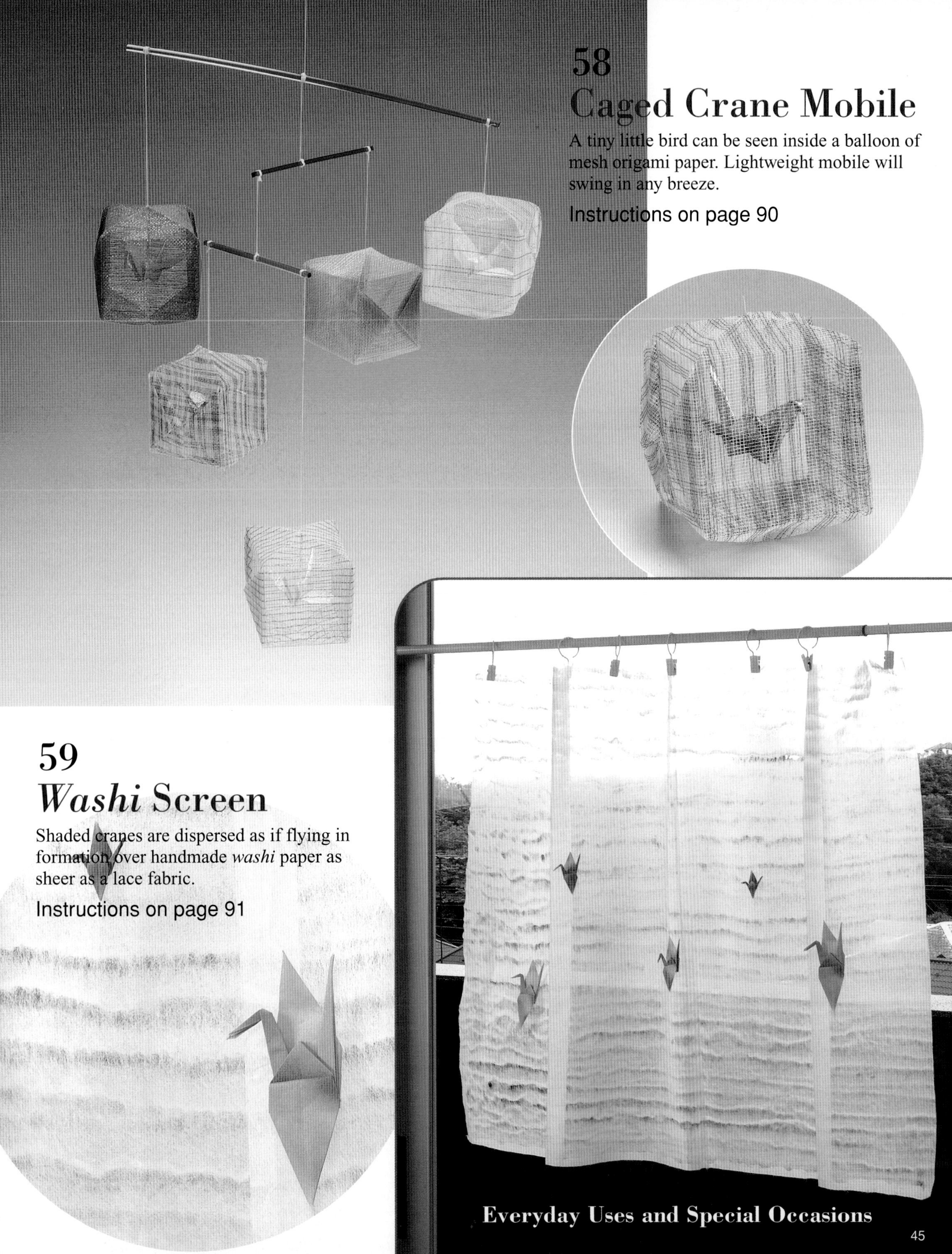

58 Caged Crane Mobile

A tiny little bird can be seen inside a balloon of mesh origami paper. Lightweight mobile will swing in any breeze.

Instructions on page 90

59 *Washi* Screen

Shaded cranes are dispersed as if flying in formation over handmade *washi* paper as sheer as a lace fabric.

Instructions on page 91

60
Light Diffuser

Through *washi* paper, the brightness of the light is softened to make you relax.

Instructions on page 92

61
Nightlight

Let your nightlight guide you with its gentle glow and elegant crane.

Instructions on page 93

Lamp Shades

62

Sturdy *washi* paper hand-pressed with fabric is made into a simple column shade, embellished with cranes of shaded *washi*.

Instructions on page 93

63

Unbleached *washi* paper has windows of wax paper, to display elegant cranes made from cut-out sections.

Instructions on page 94

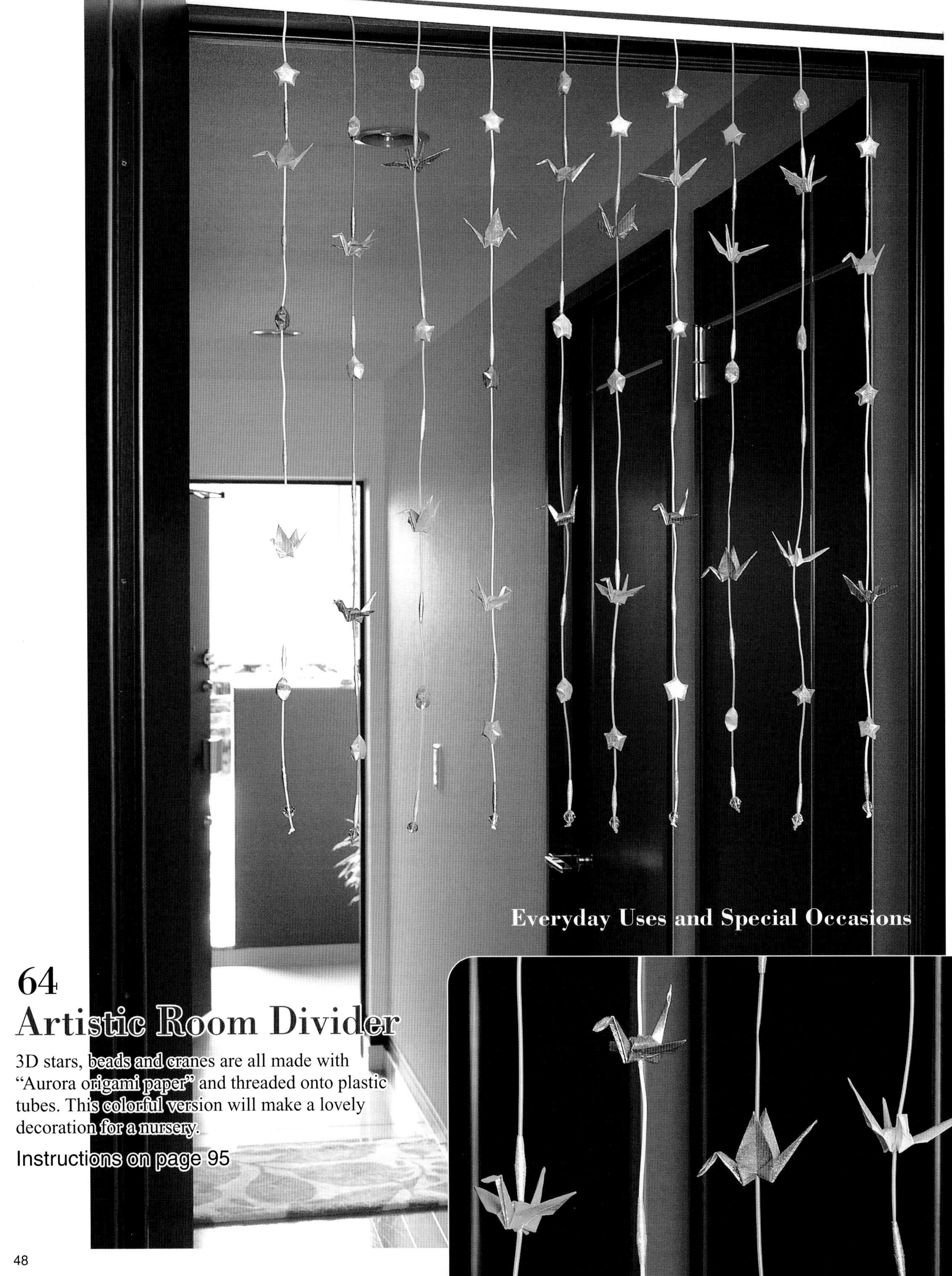

64
Artistic Room Divider

3D stars, beads and cranes are all made with "Aurora origami paper" and threaded onto plastic tubes. This colorful version will make a lovely decoration for a nursery.

Instructions on page 95

ORIGAMI SYMBOLS

Fold carefully checking dotted lines and arrows

Right side

Wrong side

Mountain fold

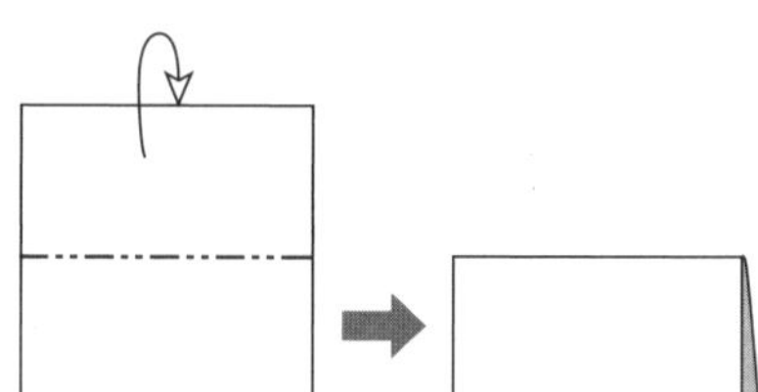

Valley fold

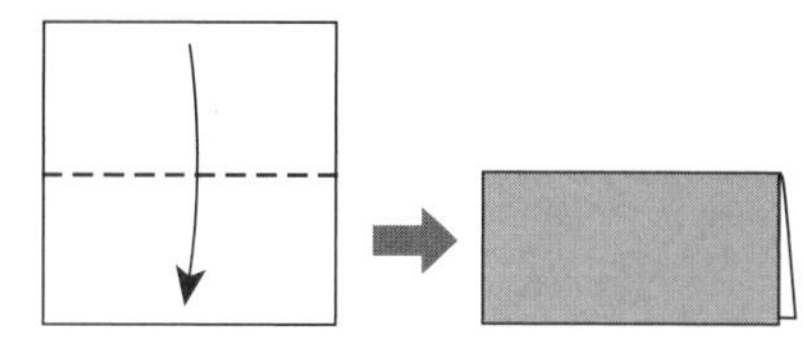

Turn over

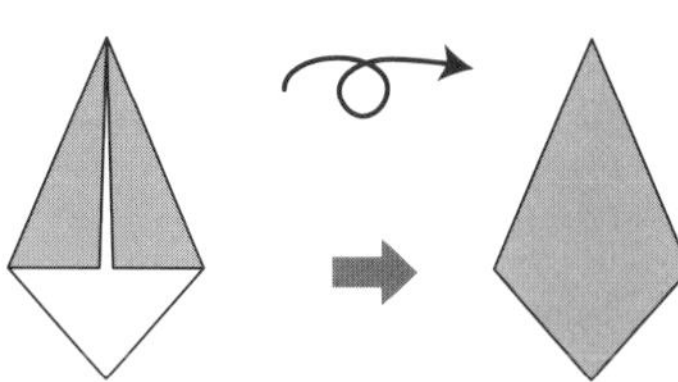

Crease (Fold and unfold)

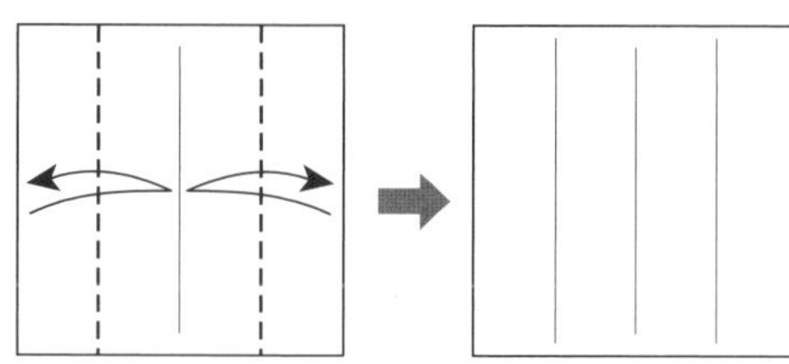

Fold over and over (Roll)

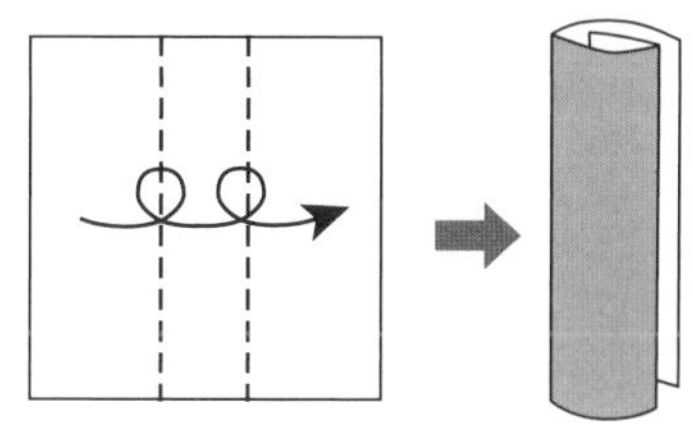

Rotate

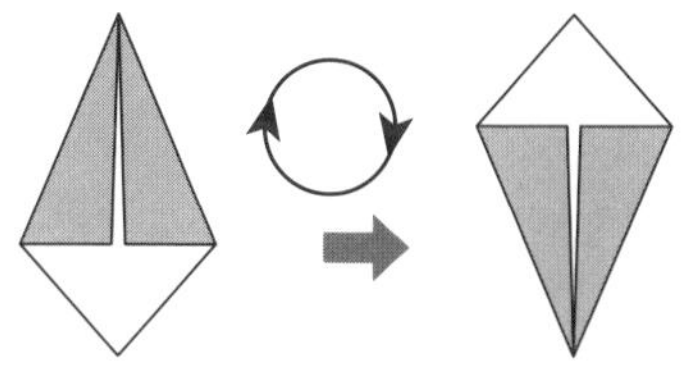

Step-fold (Pleat fold)

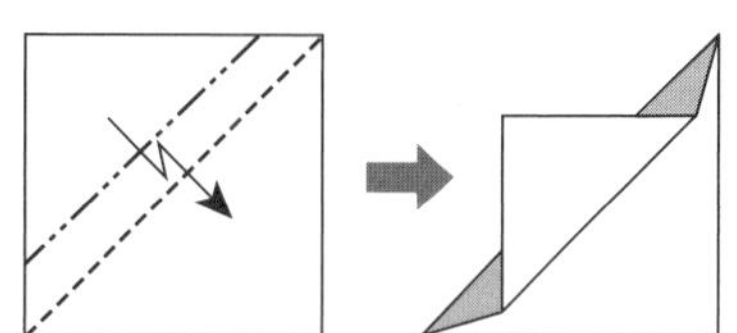

Reverse fold

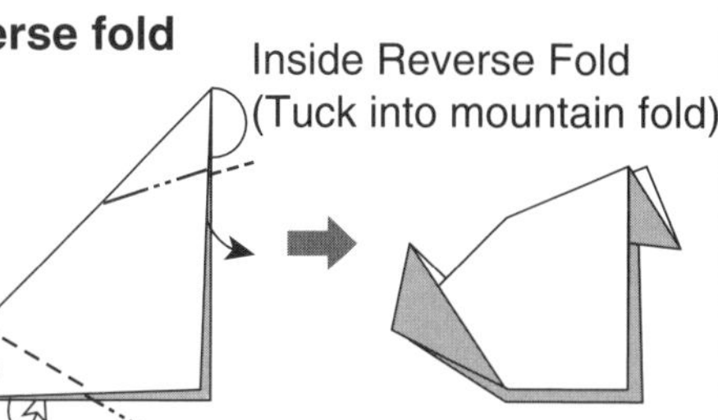

Enlarged / Reduced view

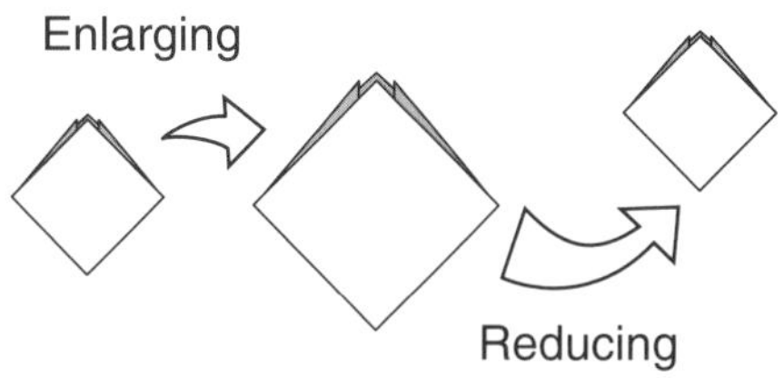

Pull out

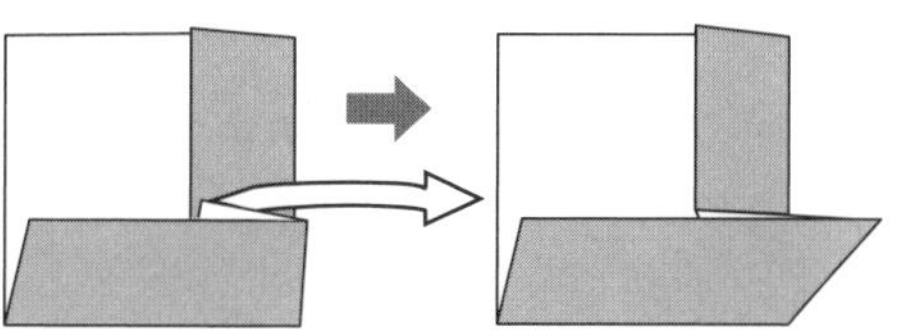

Insert

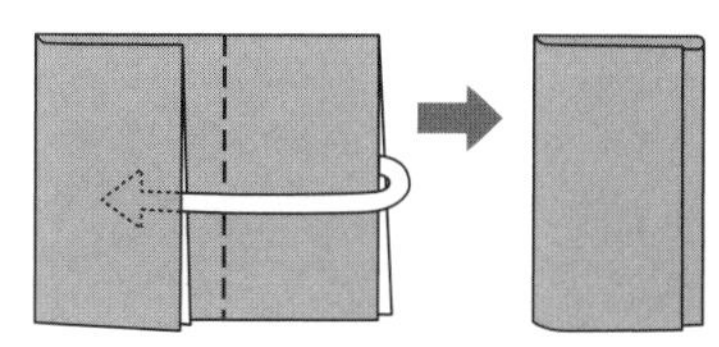

Push inside

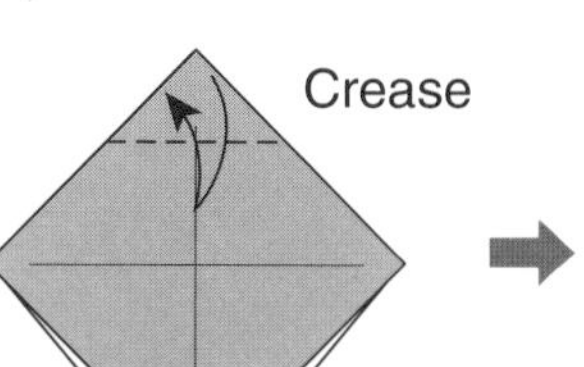

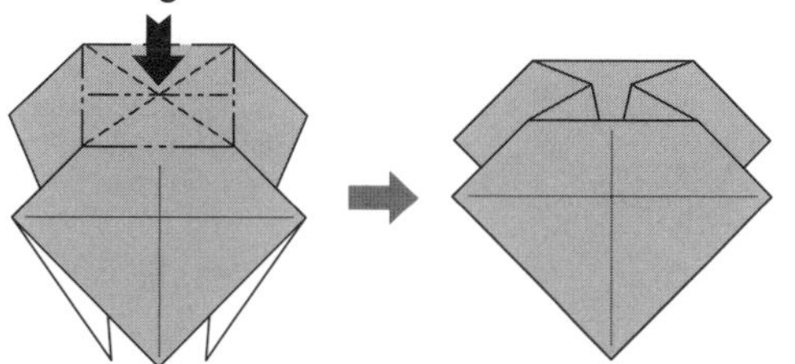

Open and flatten

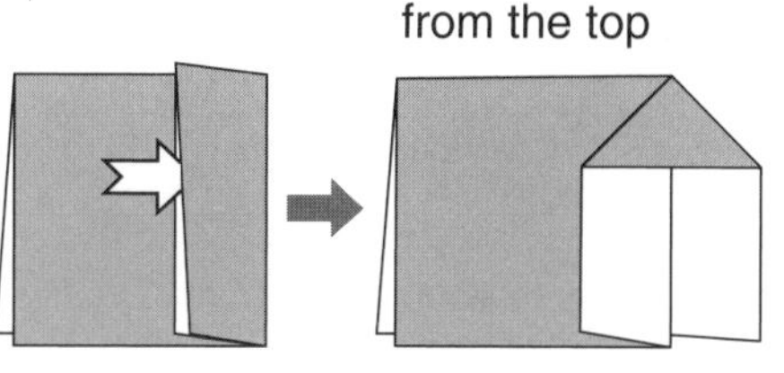

USE A FAIRLY LARGE *WASHI* PAPER. DRAW CUTTING LINES ACCORDING TO THE LAYOUT.

Folding Orders

Cut slits as indicated in Layout. Crease as indicated, and fold each square into Beginning Square (See pages 4-5), first with the large one, then from the connected small one towards the ends, one by one until two rows of six squares are made.

Unfold the sixth squares, layer them corner to corner, and fold again into Beginning Square. Continue working with remaining squares.

Fold each Beginning Square into Crane Base (See Step ⑯, page 3) carefully with the connections. Secure the sixth small crane base with a paper clip.

Continue folding each into a crane carefully.

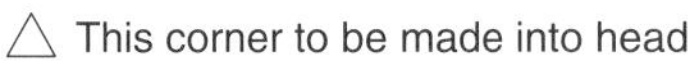

--- Valley fold: See Steps ❷-❸, page 4 (Be sure to crease one diagonal per each square and do not crease crossing diagonals, to avoid unwanted centerlines on finished wings)

>— Cut here (Leave ⅛" as uncut connection)

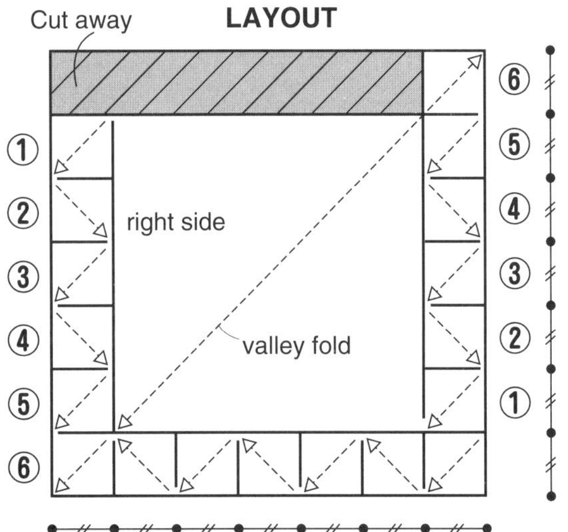

Layer ⑥ and ⑥ and fold as if it were a single sheet.

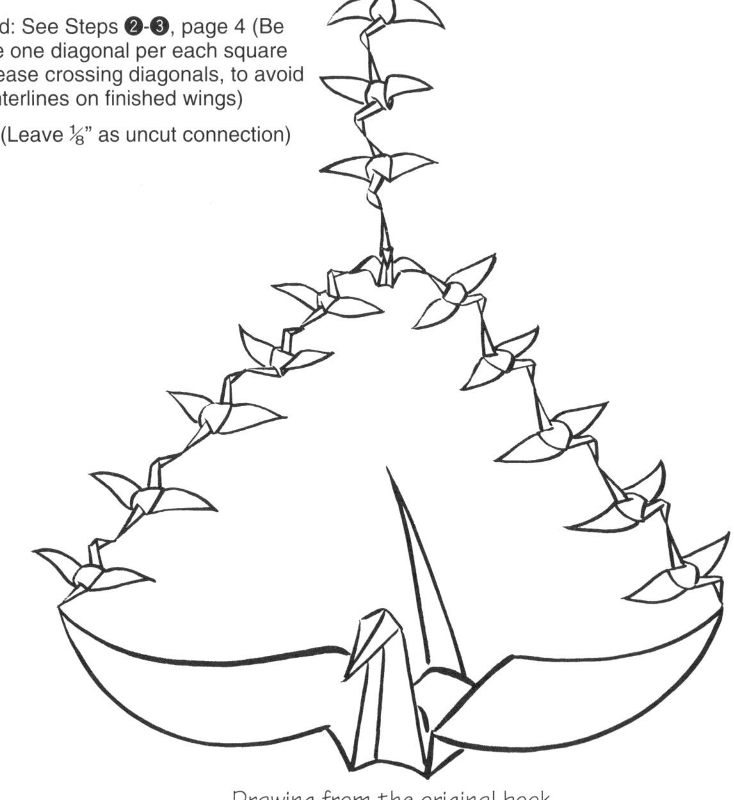

Drawing from the original book

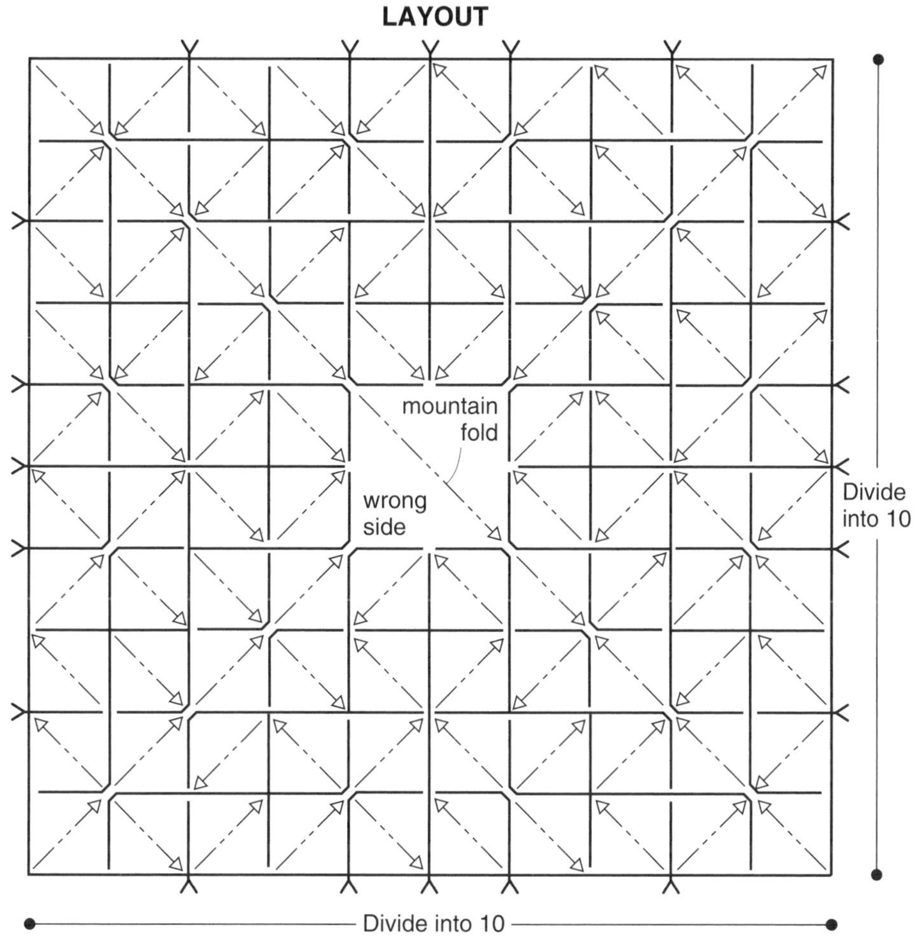

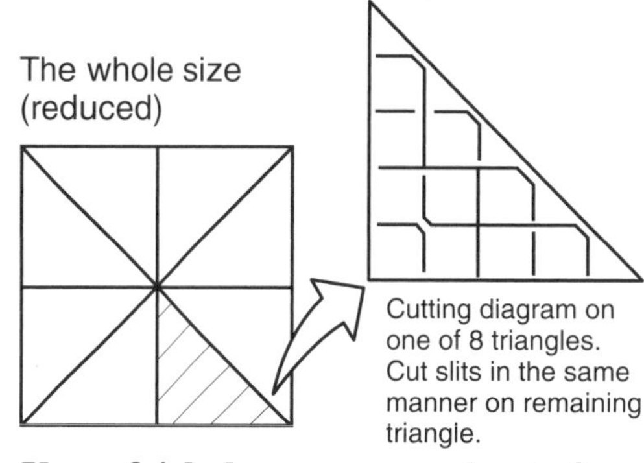

Cutting diagram on one of 8 triangles. Cut slits in the same manner on remaining triangle.

Use a fairly large square sheet of *washi* paper. To avoid confusing, mark crane head positions (△) on the wrong side before cutting.

See pages 4-5 for linked crane folding.

△ This corner to be made into head

–··– Mountain fold: Do not crease crossing diagonals, to avoid unwanted centerlines on finished wings)

>— Cut here (Leave ⅛" as uncut connection)

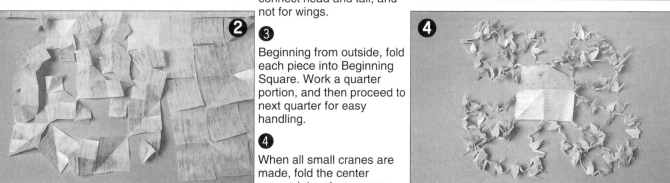

Folding Orders

Cut slits as indicated in Layout. Crease as indicated, and fold each square into Beginning Square (See pages 4-5).

Be sure to fold diagonally in the right direction for each square. The fold will connect head and tail, and not for wings.

❸

Beginning from outside, fold each piece into Beginning Square. Work a quarter portion, and then proceed to next quarter for easy handling.

When all small cranes are made, fold the center square into a large crane.

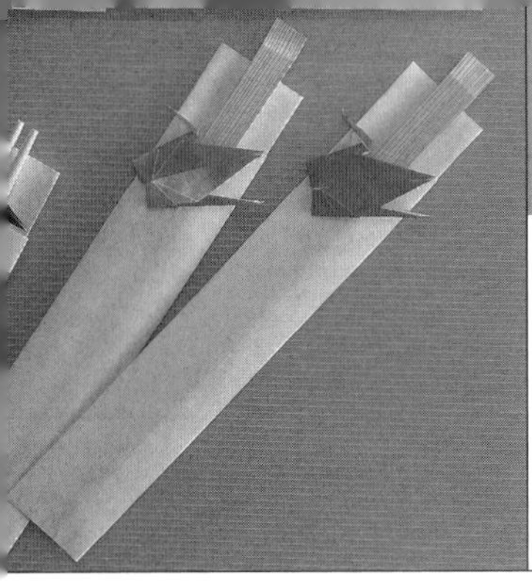

#20 Chopstick Cover Page 27

Materials

4"×18" *hosho* or white *washi* paper for cover
4"×4" colored *washi* paper for crane, cut into half triangles

See page 96 for crane folding.

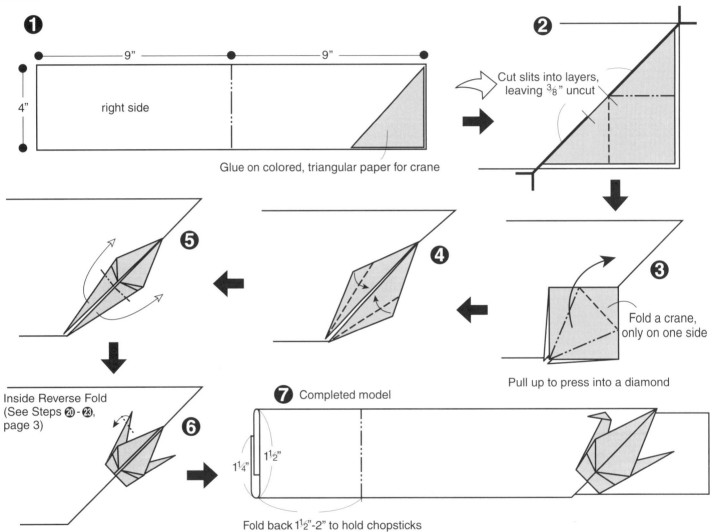

1

9" 9"

4"

right side

Glue on colored, triangular paper for crane

2

Cut slits into layers, leaving $\frac{3}{8}$" uncut

3

Fold a crane, only on one side

Pull up to press into a diamond

4

5

6

Inside Reverse Fold (See Steps ⑳-㉓, page 3)

7 Completed model

$1\frac{1}{4}$" $1\frac{1}{2}$"

Fold back $1\frac{1}{2}$"-2" to hold chopsticks

FOLDING COVERS #17 AND #18 on page 27

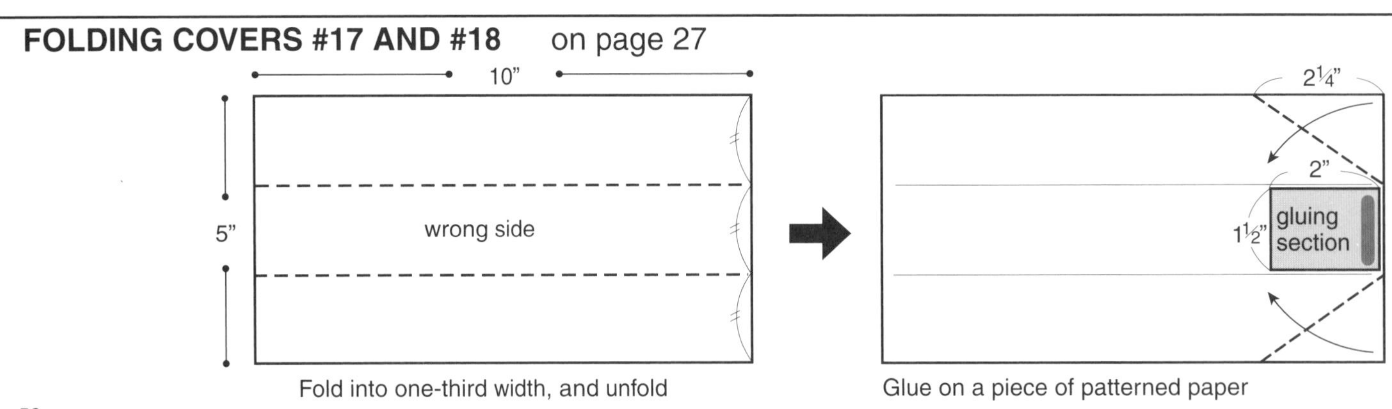

Fold into one-third width, and unfold

Glue on a piece of patterned paper

#19 Chopstick Cover

Page 27

Materials

4"×21" *hosho* or white *washi* paper for cover
4"×2" shaded *washi* paper for crane
¼"×4" shaded *washi* paper for band

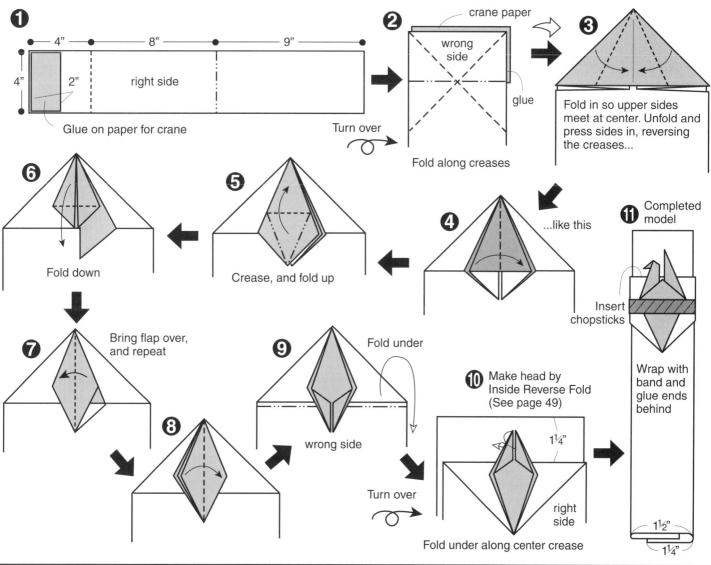

1

4" 8" 9"

4" 2" right side

Glue on paper for crane

2

crane paper

wrong side

glue

Turn over

Fold along creases

3

Fold in so upper sides meet at center. Unfold and press sides in, reversing the creases...

4

...like this

5

Crease, and fold up

6

Fold down

7

Bring flap over, and repeat

8

9

Fold under

wrong side

Turn over

10

Make head by Inside Reverse Fold
(See page 49)

1¼"

right side

Fold under along center crease

11

Completed model

Insert chopsticks

Wrap with band and glue ends behind

1½"

1¼"

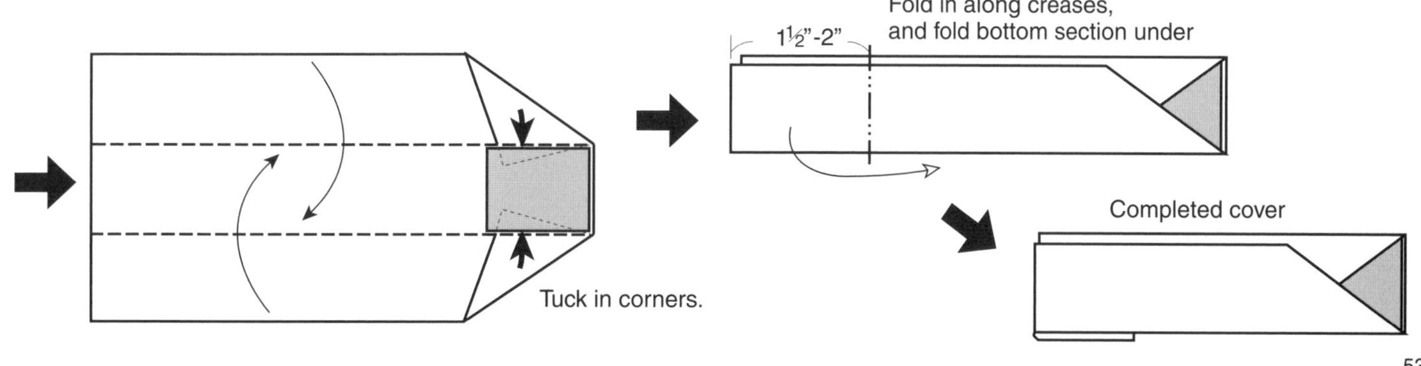

#18 Chopstick Cover Page 27

Materials

5"×10" block printed *washi* paper for cover
1½"×2" patterned *washi* paper
2" square gold *washi* paper for flapping crane

See page 52 for folding cover.

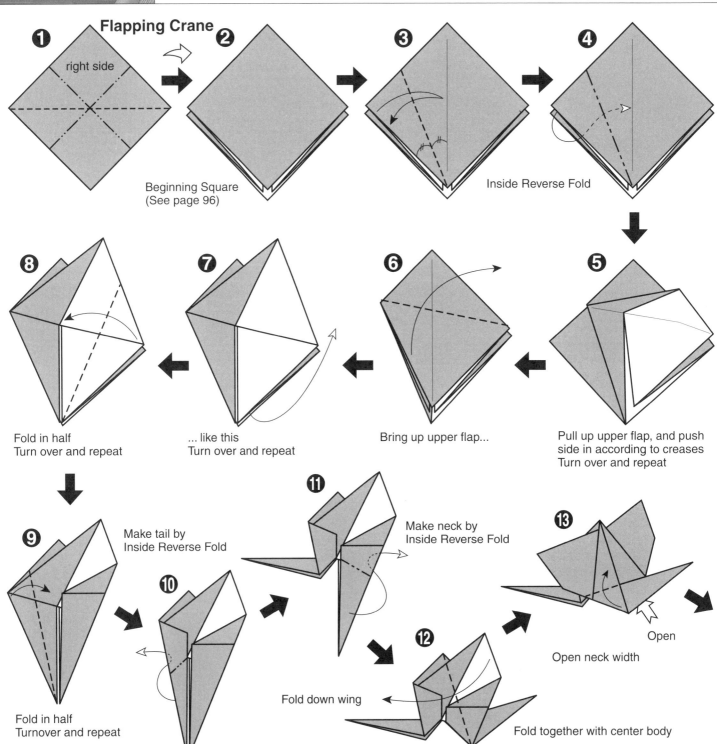

Flapping Crane

1. right side

2. Beginning Square (See page 96)

3.

4. Inside Reverse Fold

5. Pull up upper flap, and push side in according to creases
Turn over and repeat

6. Bring up upper flap...

7. ... like this
Turn over and repeat

8. Fold in half
Turn over and repeat

9. Make tail by Inside Reverse Fold
Fold in half
Turnover and repeat

10.

11. Make neck by Inside Reverse Fold

12. Fold down wing
Fold together with center body

13. Open
Open neck width

#17 Chopstick Cover
Page 27

Materials

2" square patterned *washi* paper for good-luck crane
5"×10" block printed *washi* paper for cover
1½"×2" patterned *washi* paper

See page 52 for folding cover.
Refer to pages 2-3 for crane folding.

Good-luck Crane

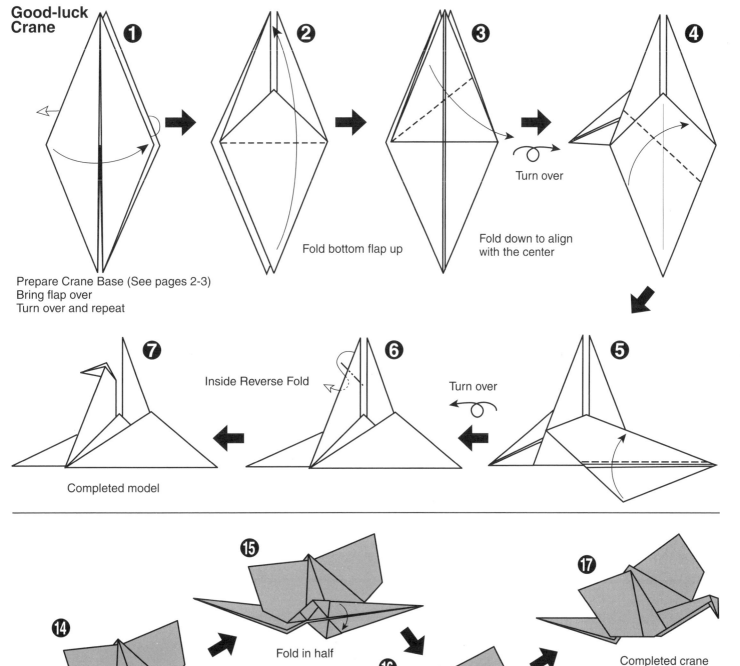

❶ Prepare Crane Base (See pages 2-3)
Bring flap over
Turn over and repeat

❷ Fold bottom flap up

❸ Fold down to align with the center

Turn over

❹

❺ Turn over

❻ Inside Reverse Fold

❼ Completed model

⓮ Fold in to shape neck

⓯ Fold in half

⓰ Make head by Inside Reverse Fold

⓱ Completed crane

#13 #16 Chopstick Rests

Page 26

Materials for both cranes (Makes 2)

7" square metallic origami paper
½"× 1¼" metallic origami paper for #13
6" #28 craft wire for #16

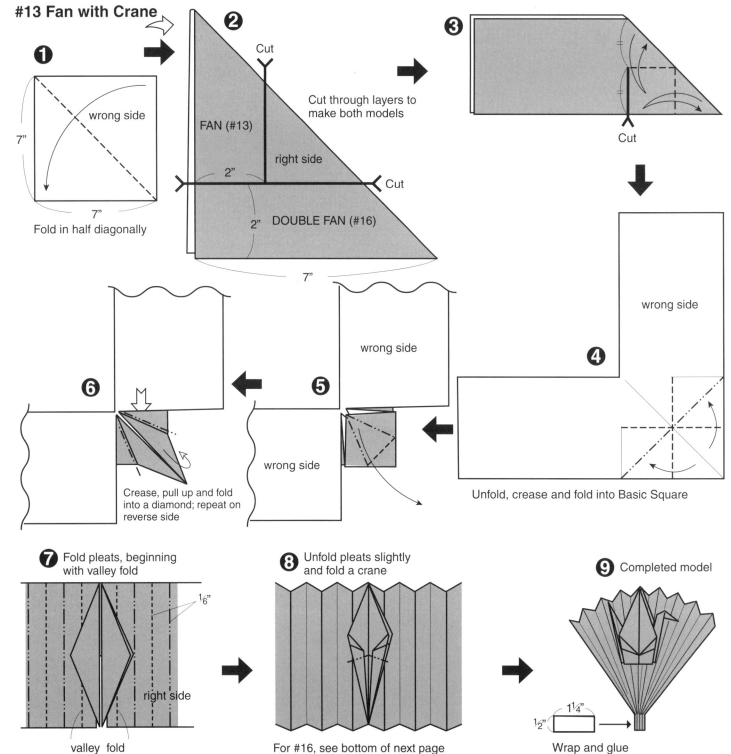

#13 Fan with Crane

❶ Fold in half diagonally

7"
7"
wrong side

❷ Cut through layers to make both models

Cut
Cut
FAN (#13)
right side
DOUBLE FAN (#16)
2"
2"
7"

❸ Cut

❹ Unfold, crease and fold into Basic Square

wrong side

❺ wrong side

wrong side

❻ Crease, pull up and fold into a diamond; repeat on reverse side

❼ Fold pleats, beginning with valley fold

1/6"
right side
valley fold

❽ Unfold pleats slightly and fold a crane

For #16, see bottom of next page

❾ Completed model

1¼"
½"
Wrap and glue

SENBAZURU (THOUSAND CRANES) Page 1

Materials

1000 squares origami paper, as small as 2" or 3"
Cotton thread
Cardboard or bead

See pages 2-3 for crane folding.

DISPLAY

Method A
Single Direction

Method B
Alternate Direction

Method C
Straight neck/head

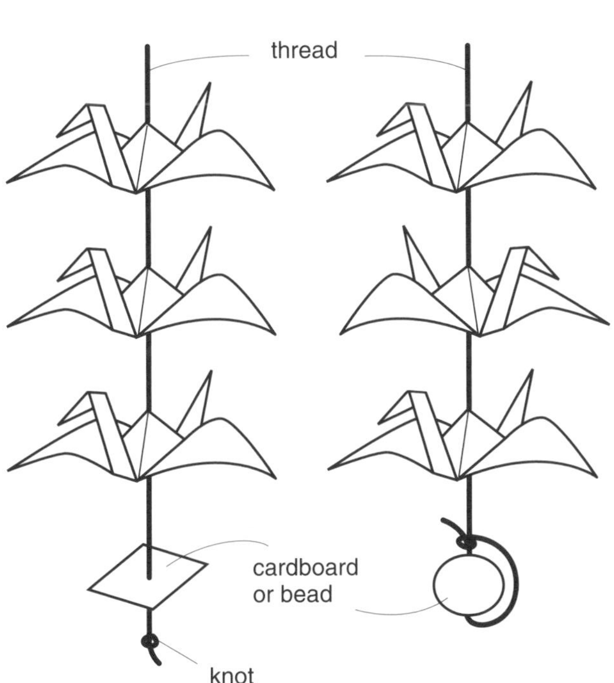

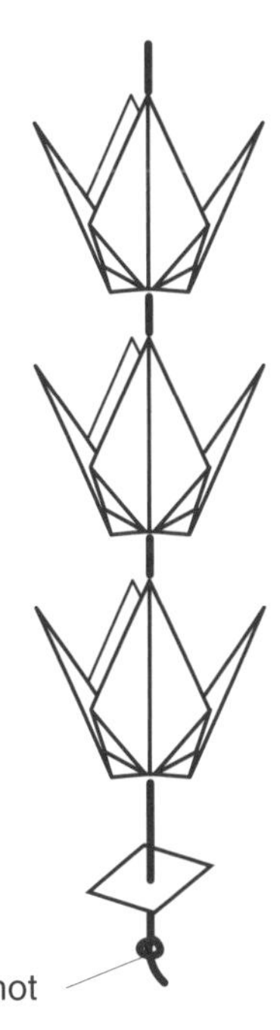

String cranes of a certain number. Repeat until all 1000 cranes are threaded, and tie ends of threads into a knot. Divide the threads into three tufts, and make a braid. Make a hoop by tying a knot again.

#16 Double Fan with Crane

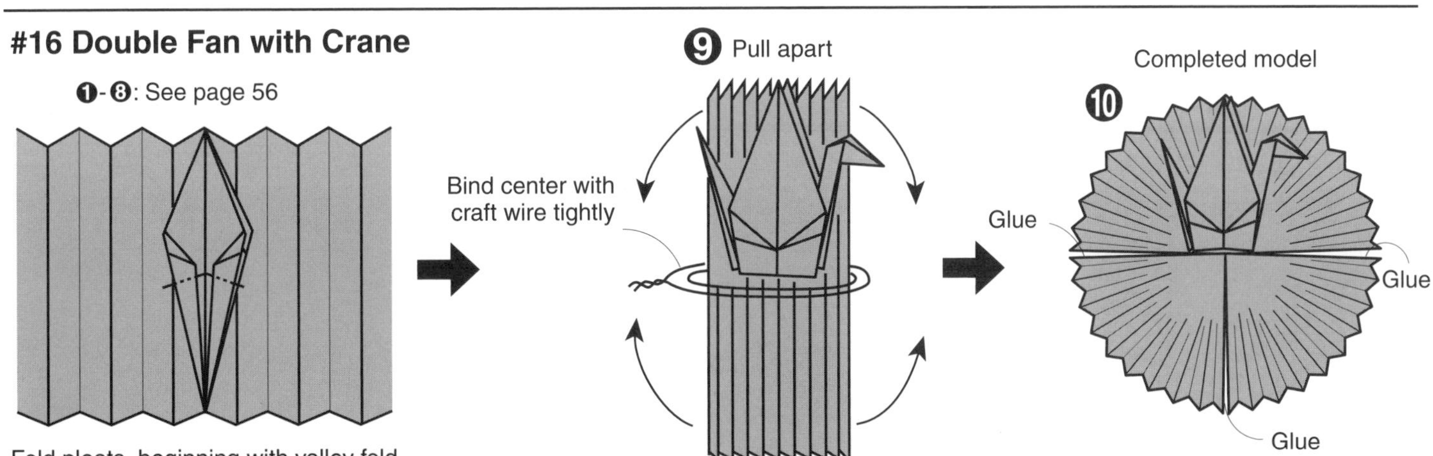

#14 Chopstick Rest

Page 26

Materials

Approximately 3"×9" paper
or commercial chopstick cover (folded type)

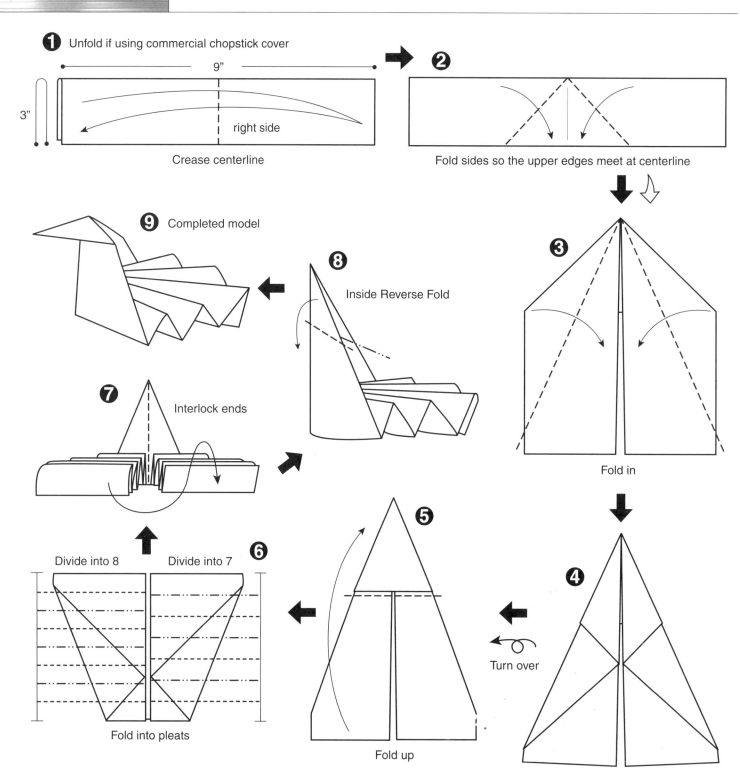

#12 Chopstick Rest Page 26

Materials

6" square double-sided metallic origami paper (use half)
See page 96 for crane folding.

If using a thick type paper, omit Steps ❷-❹, and cut a slit. Fold a crane with one side, then repeat with the other side up.

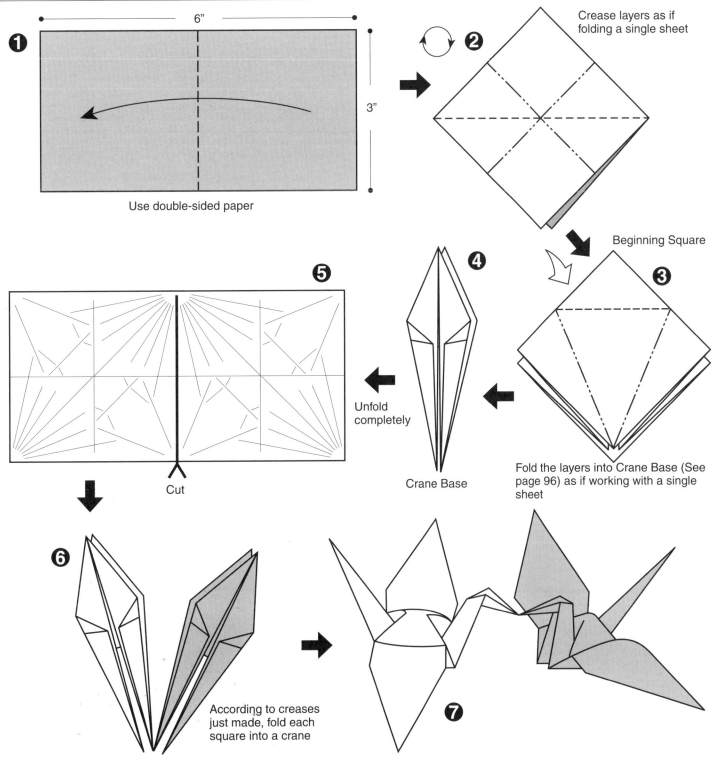

❶

6"

3"

Use double-sided paper

❷

Crease layers as if folding a single sheet

❸

Beginning Square

Fold the layers into Crane Base (See page 96) as if working with a single sheet

❹

Crane Base

Unfold completely

❺

Cut

❻

According to creases just made, fold each square into a crane

❼

#21 #22 #23 Plate Doilies   Page 28

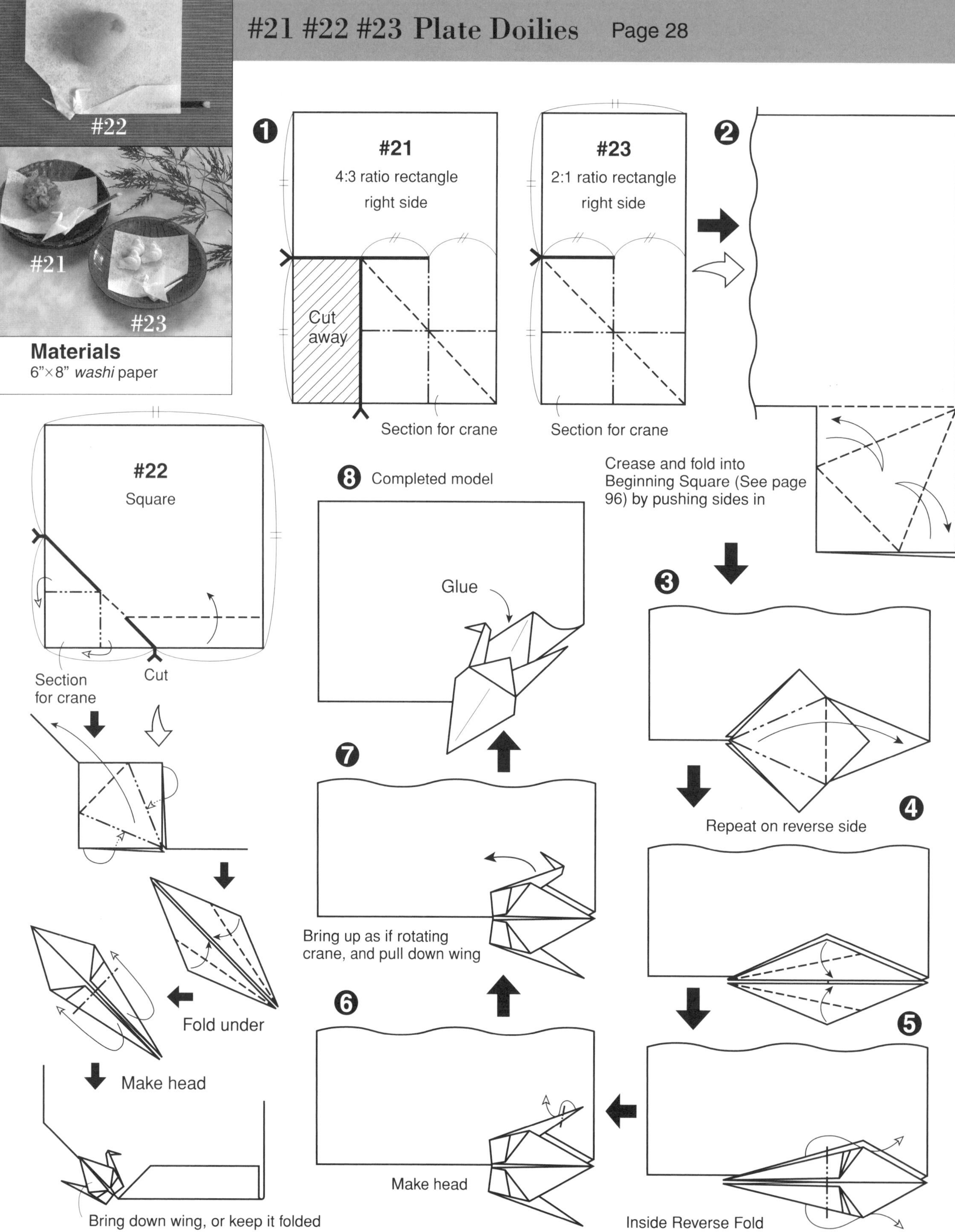

Materials
6"×8" *washi* paper

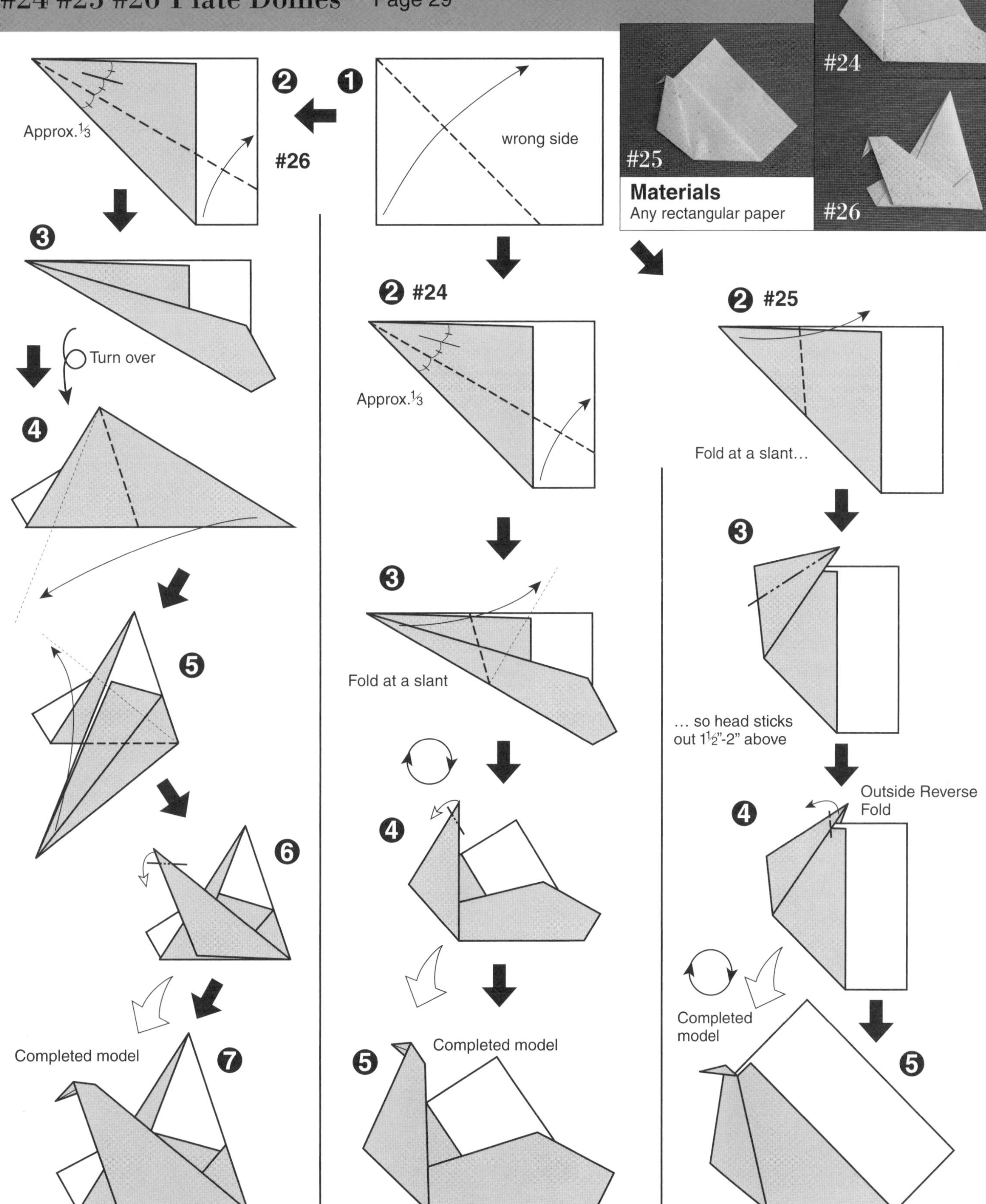
#24
#25
#26
Materials
Any rectangular paper
1
wrong side
2
#26
Approx.⅓
3
Turn over
4
5
6
Completed model
7
2 #24
Approx.⅓
3
Fold at a slant
4
Completed model
5
2 #25
Fold at a slant…
3
… so head sticks
out 1½"-2" above
Outside Reverse
Fold
4
Completed
model
5

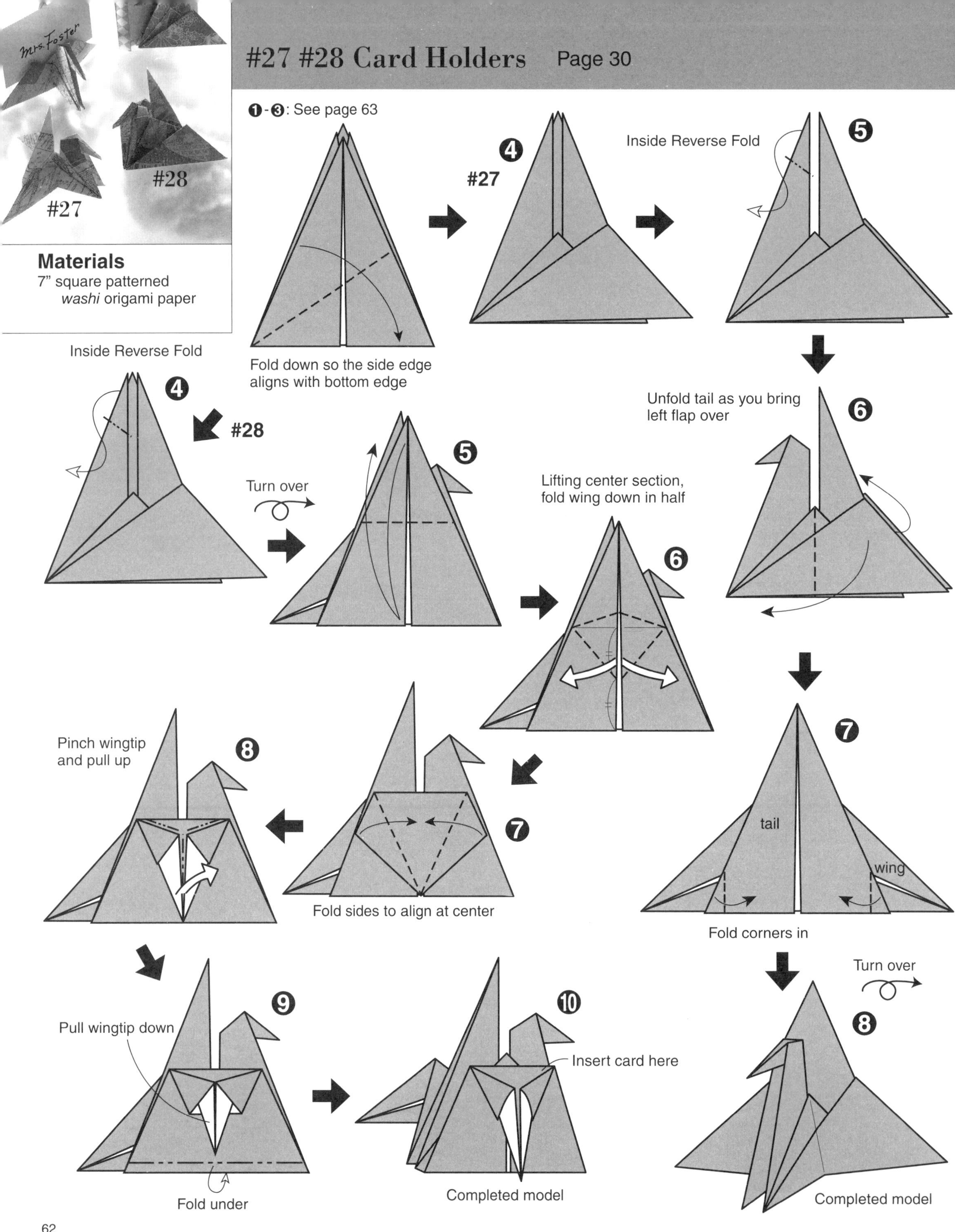

#27 #28 Card Holders
Page 30
Mrs. Foster
#28
#27
Materials
7" square patterned washi origami paper
❶-❸: See page 63
Fold down so the side edge aligns with bottom edge
❹
#27
Inside Reverse Fold
❺
Unfold tail as you bring left flap over
❻
Inside Reverse Fold
❹
#28
Turn over
❺
Lifting center section, fold wing down in half
❻
❼
tail
wing
Fold corners in
Pinch wingtip and pull up
❽
❼
Fold sides to align at center
Turn over
❽
Completed model
❾
Pull wingtip down
Fold under
❿
Insert card here
Completed model

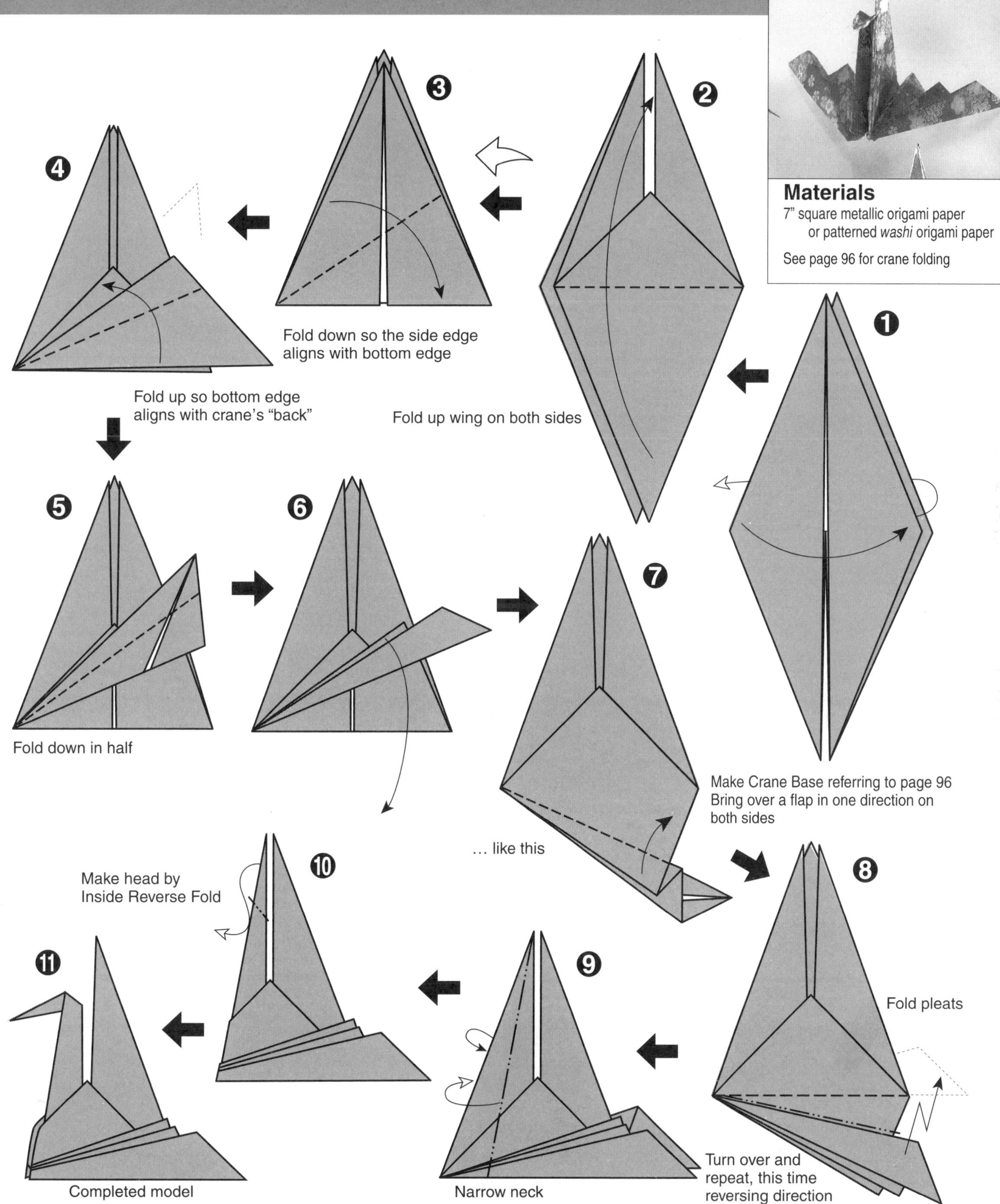
Materials
7" square metallic origami paper
or patterned *washi* origami paper
See page 96 for crane folding
1
Make Crane Base referring to page 96
Bring over a flap in one direction on both sides
2
Fold up wing on both sides
3
Fold down so the side edge aligns with bottom edge
4
Fold up so bottom edge aligns with crane's "back"
5
Fold down in half
6
7
… like this
8
Fold pleats
Turn over and repeat, this time reversing direction
9
Narrow neck
10
Make head by Inside Reverse Fold
11
Completed model

#31 Gift Envelope Page 32

Materials

16"×22" woodblock printed *washi* paper
16"×6" patterned *washi* paper
4" square patterned *washi* origami paper

For crane folding, see page 96.

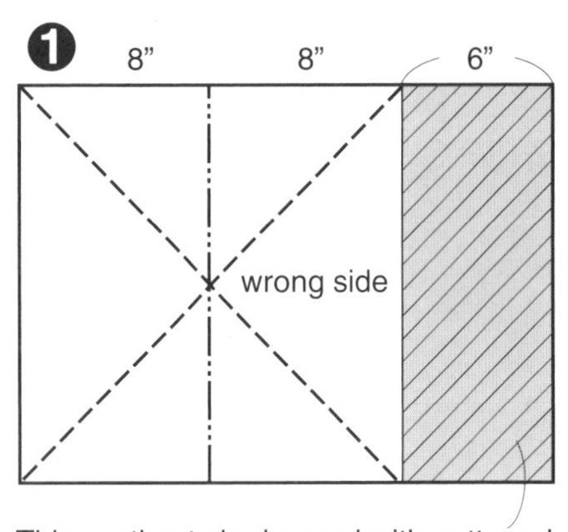

This section to be layered with pattened *washi* paper (Step ⓬)

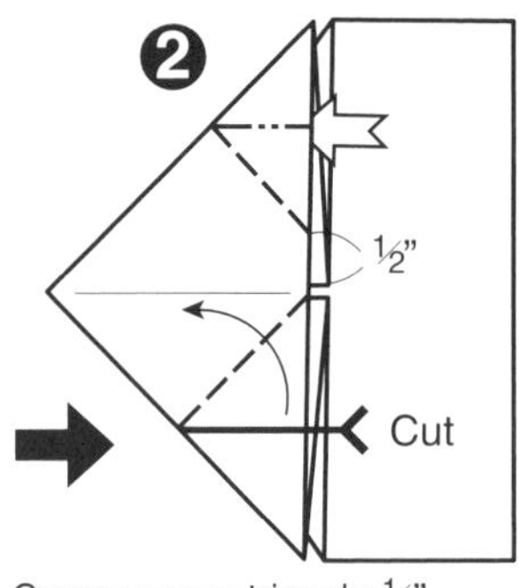

Crease upper triangle, ½" above center
Insert your finger and bring down, flattening into a square
Cut away bottom triangle
Fold up bottom to align with horizontal centerline

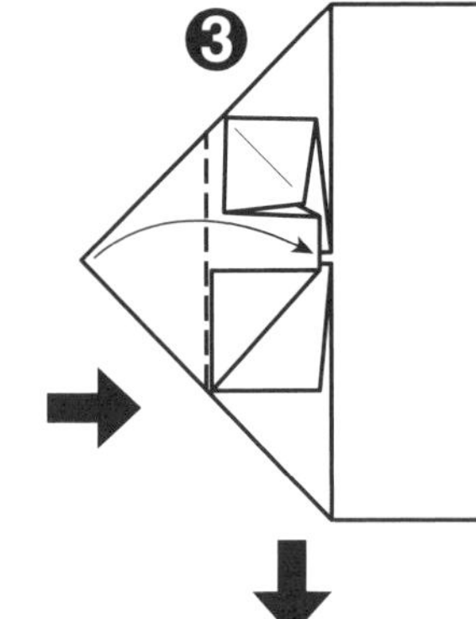

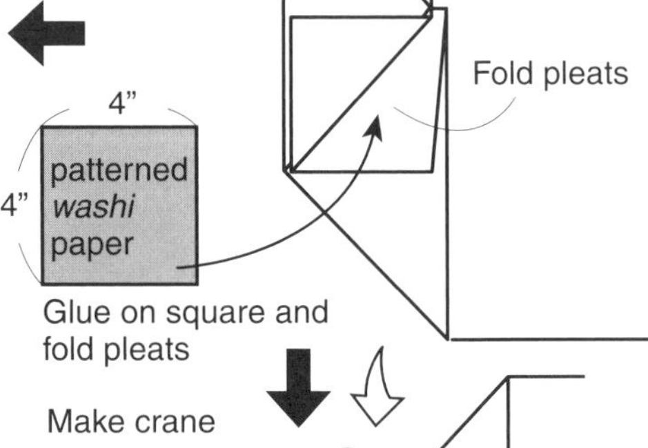

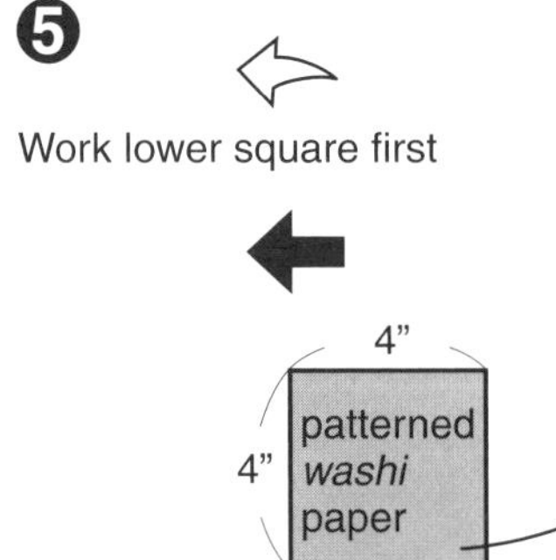

Glue on square and fold pleats

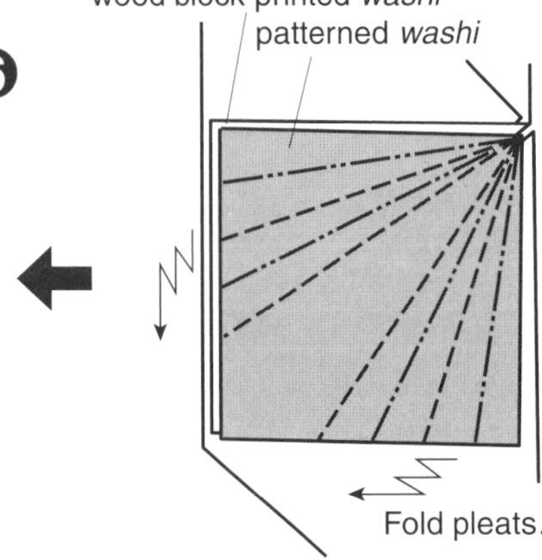

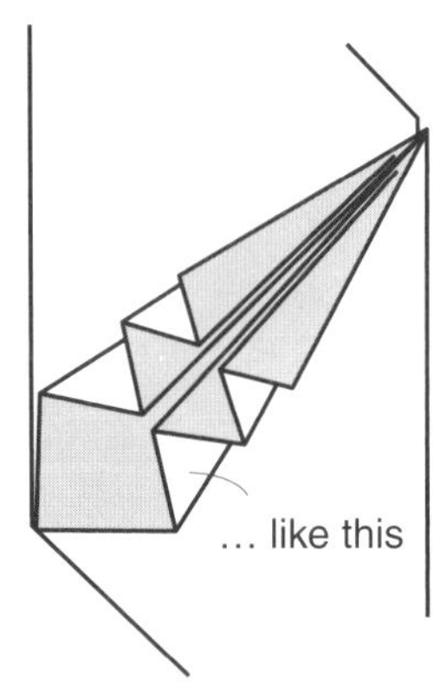

Make crane

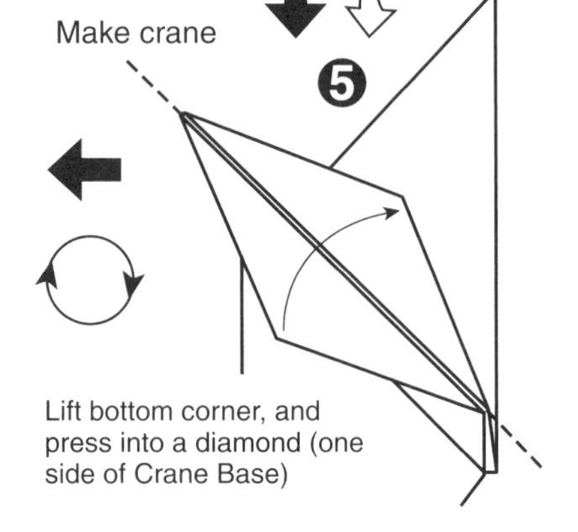

Lift bottom corner, and press into a diamond (one side of Crane Base)

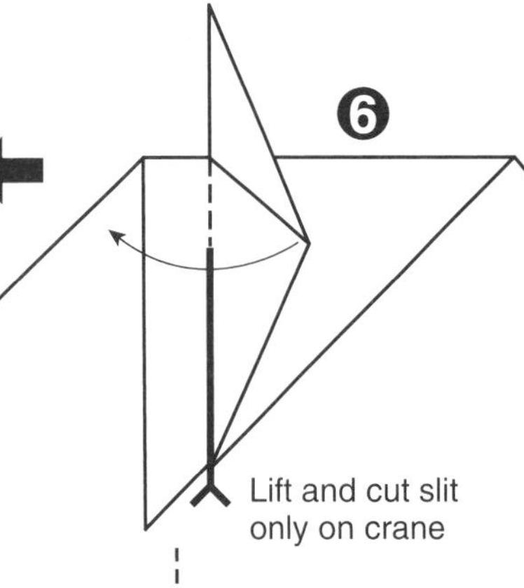

Lift and cut slit only on crane

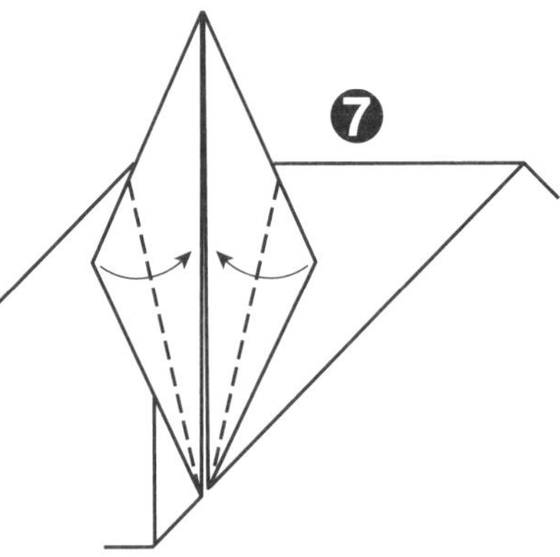

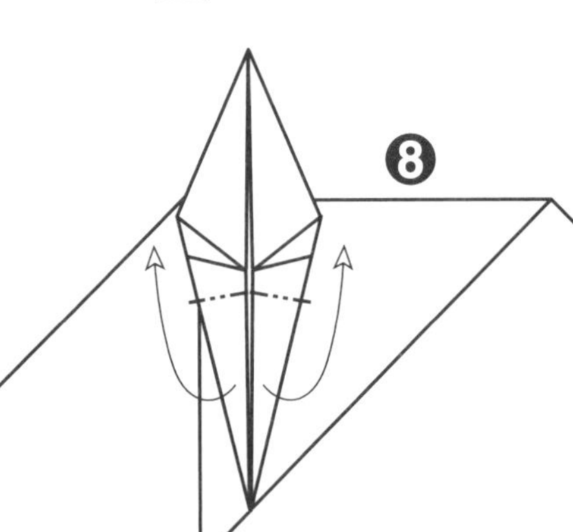

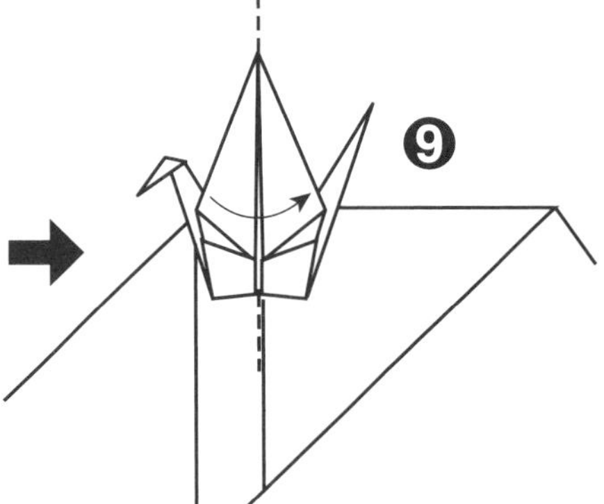

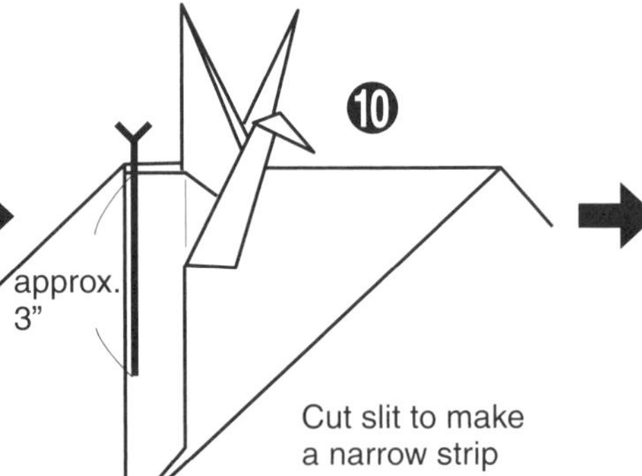

Cut slit to make a narrow strip

#30 Gift Envelope Page 32

Materials
1 10" square white *washi* paper
2 2" squares patterned *washi* origami paper

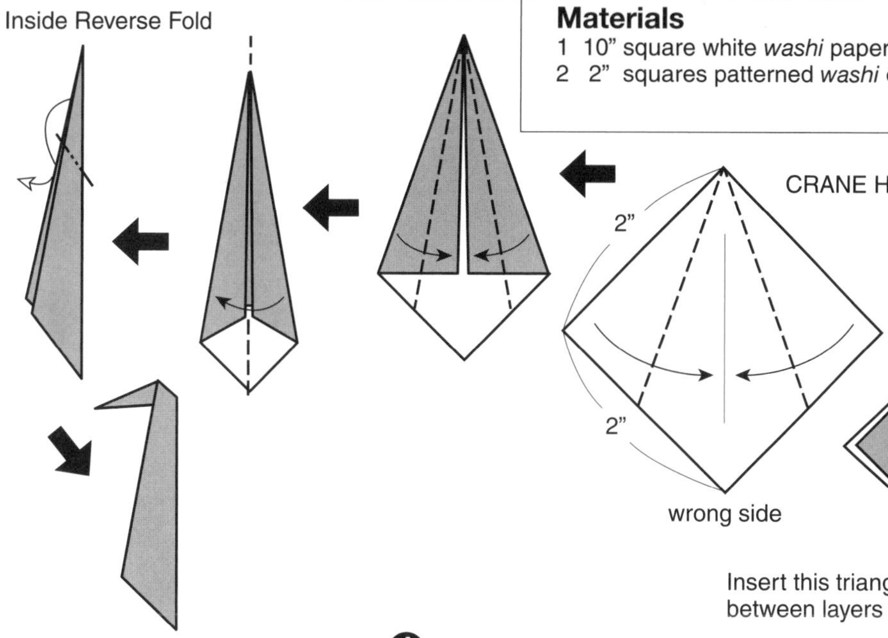

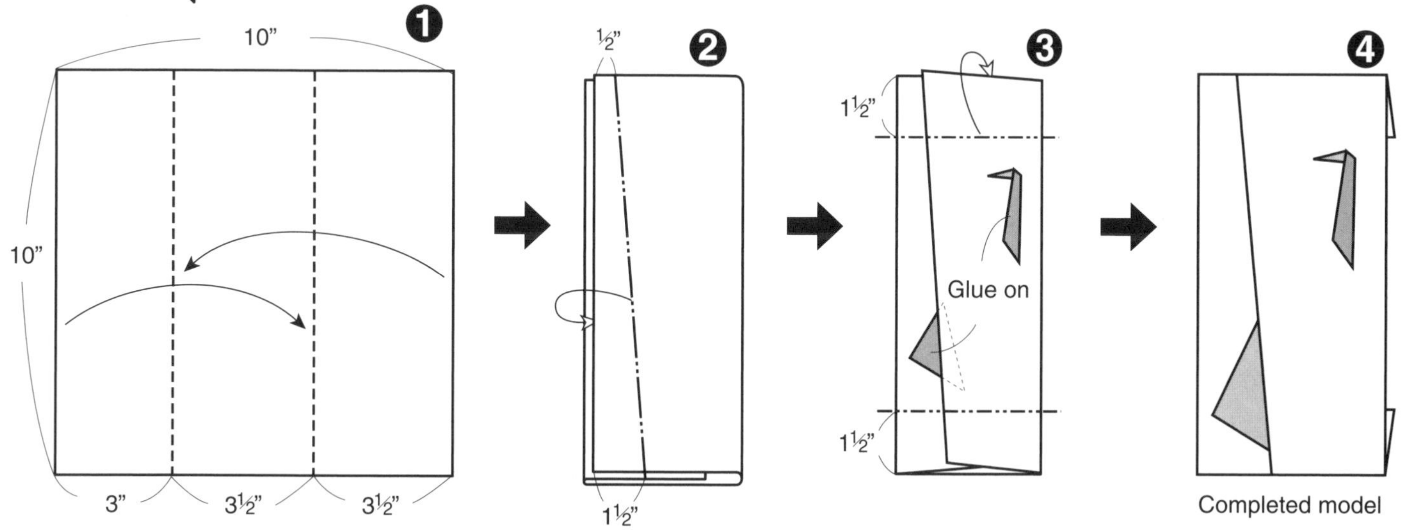

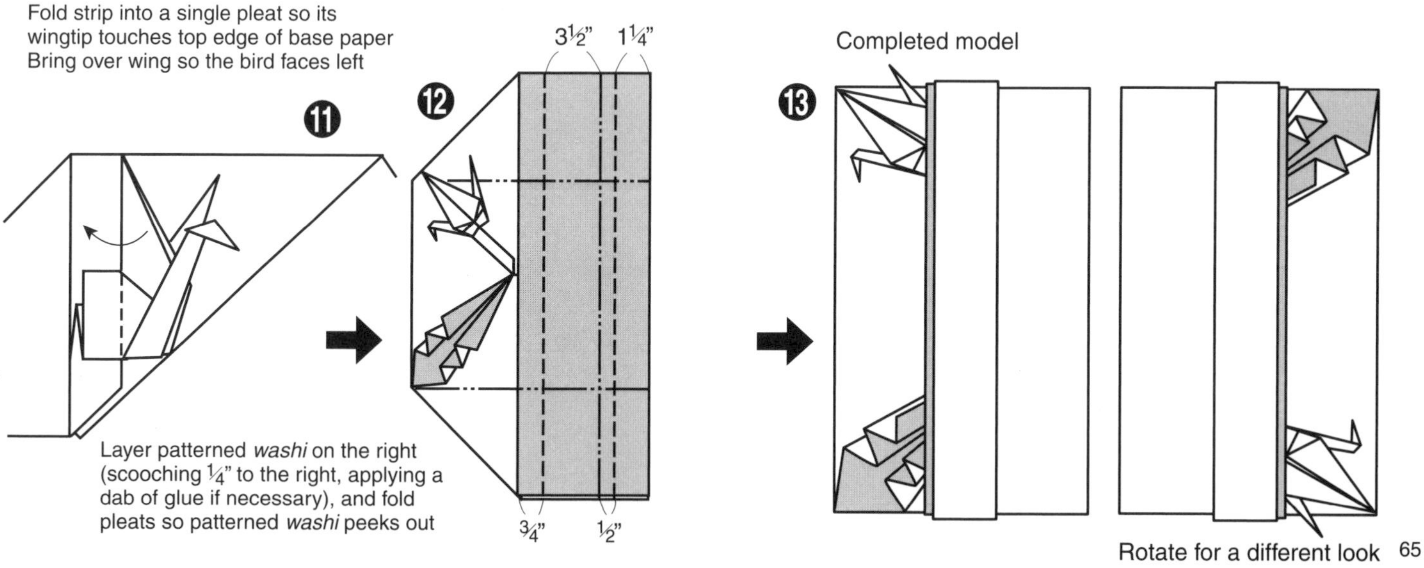

Inside Reverse Fold

CRANE HEAD

2"

2"

wrong side

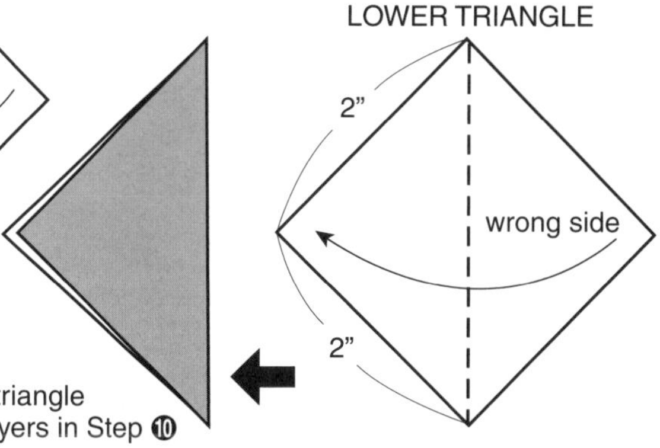

LOWER TRIANGLE

2"

wrong side

2"

Insert this triangle between layers in Step ⑩

❶

10"

10"

3" 3½" 3½"

❷

½"

1½"

❸

1½"

Glue on

1½"

❹

Completed model

Fold strip into a single pleat so its wingtip touches top edge of base paper Bring over wing so the bird faces left

⑪

⑫

3½" 1¼"

¾" ½"

Layer patterned *washi* on the right (scooching ¼" to the right, applying a dab of glue if necessary), and fold pleats so patterned *washi* peeks out

⑬

Completed model

Rotate for a different look

#32 Gift Envelope Page 32

Materials
9"×13" thin to medium *washi* paper or printing paper

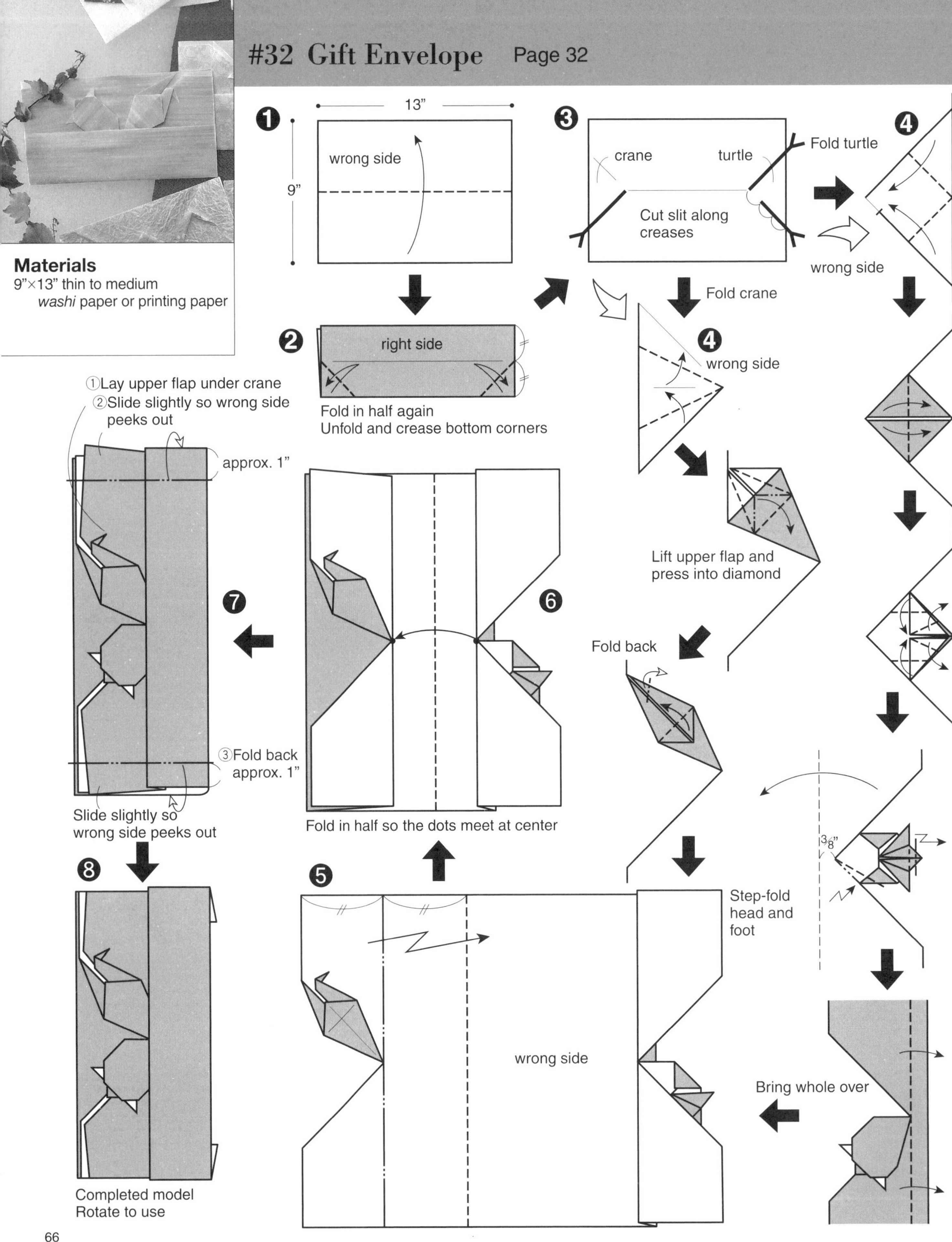

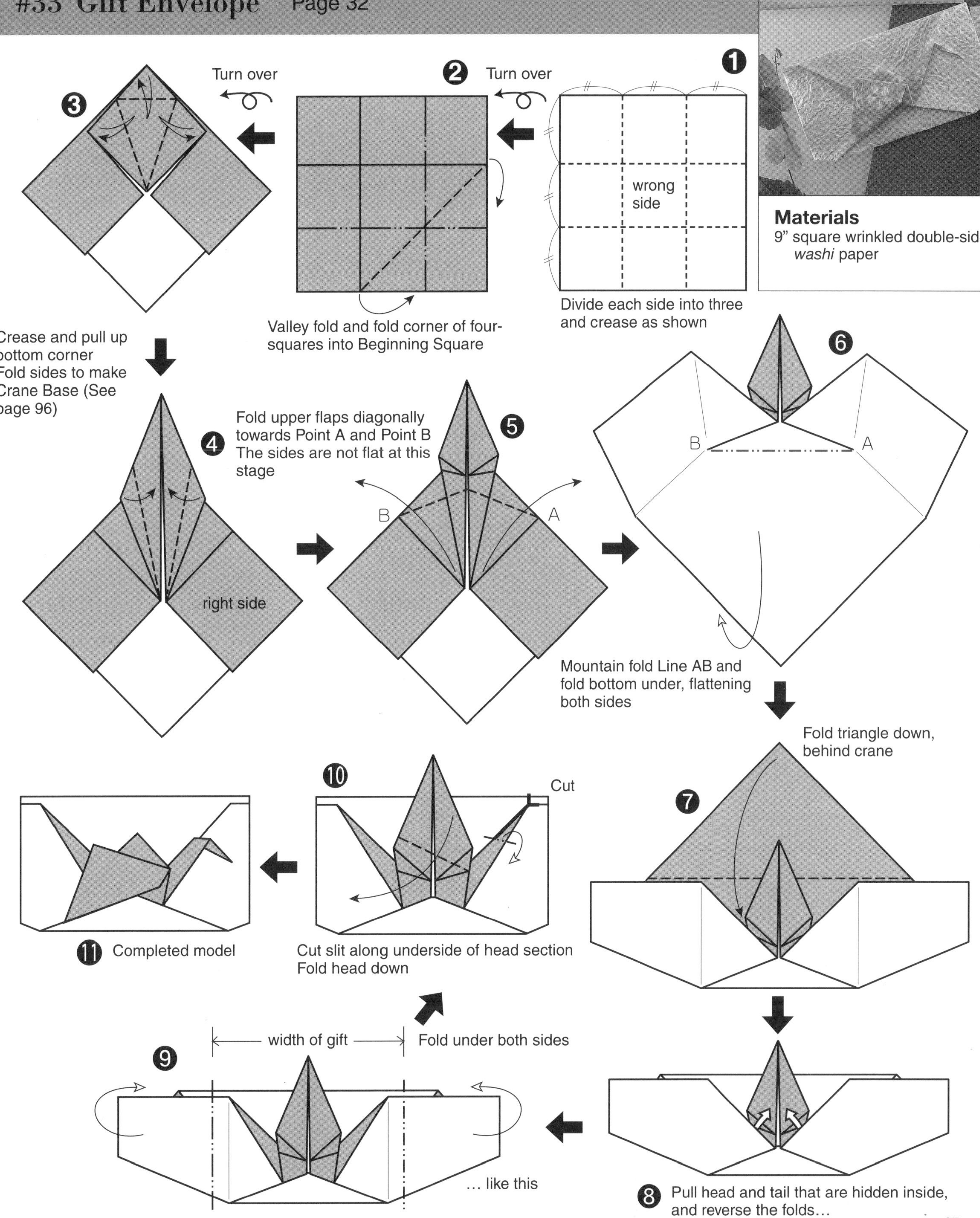
Materials
9” square wrinkled double-sided washi paper
1
Divide each side into three and crease as shown
wrong side
2
Turn over
Valley fold and fold corner of four-squares into Beginning Square
3
Turn over
Crease and pull up bottom corner
Fold sides to make Crane Base (See page 96)
4
right side
Fold upper flaps diagonally towards Point A and Point B
The sides are not flat at this stage
5
B
A
6
B
A
Mountain fold Line AB and fold bottom under, flattening both sides
7
Fold triangle down, behind crane
8
Pull head and tail that are hidden inside, and reverse the folds…
9
width of gift
Fold under both sides
… like this
10
Cut
Cut slit along underside of head section
Fold head down
11
Completed model

#36 #37 #38 Gift Envelopes

Page 34

Materials for #36
5"×10" white *washi* paper
5"×2½" block printed *washi* paper for crane
¼"×5" block printed *washi* paper for band

Materials for #37
6"×7½" white *washi* paper or block printed *washi* paper
¼"×2" *hosho washi* paper (red) for band

Materials for #38
7" square patterned *washi* origami paper

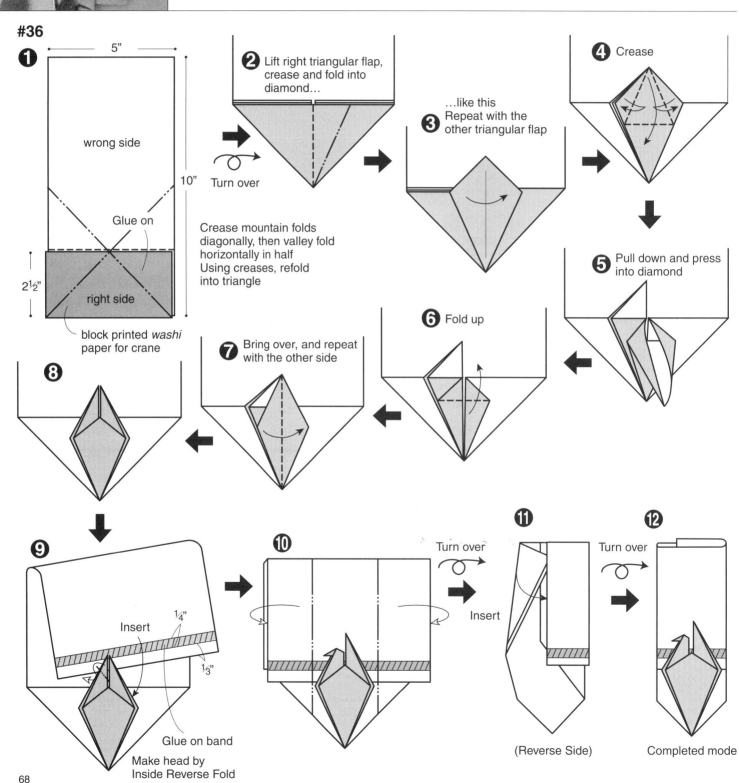

#36

#38 For crane folding, see page 96.

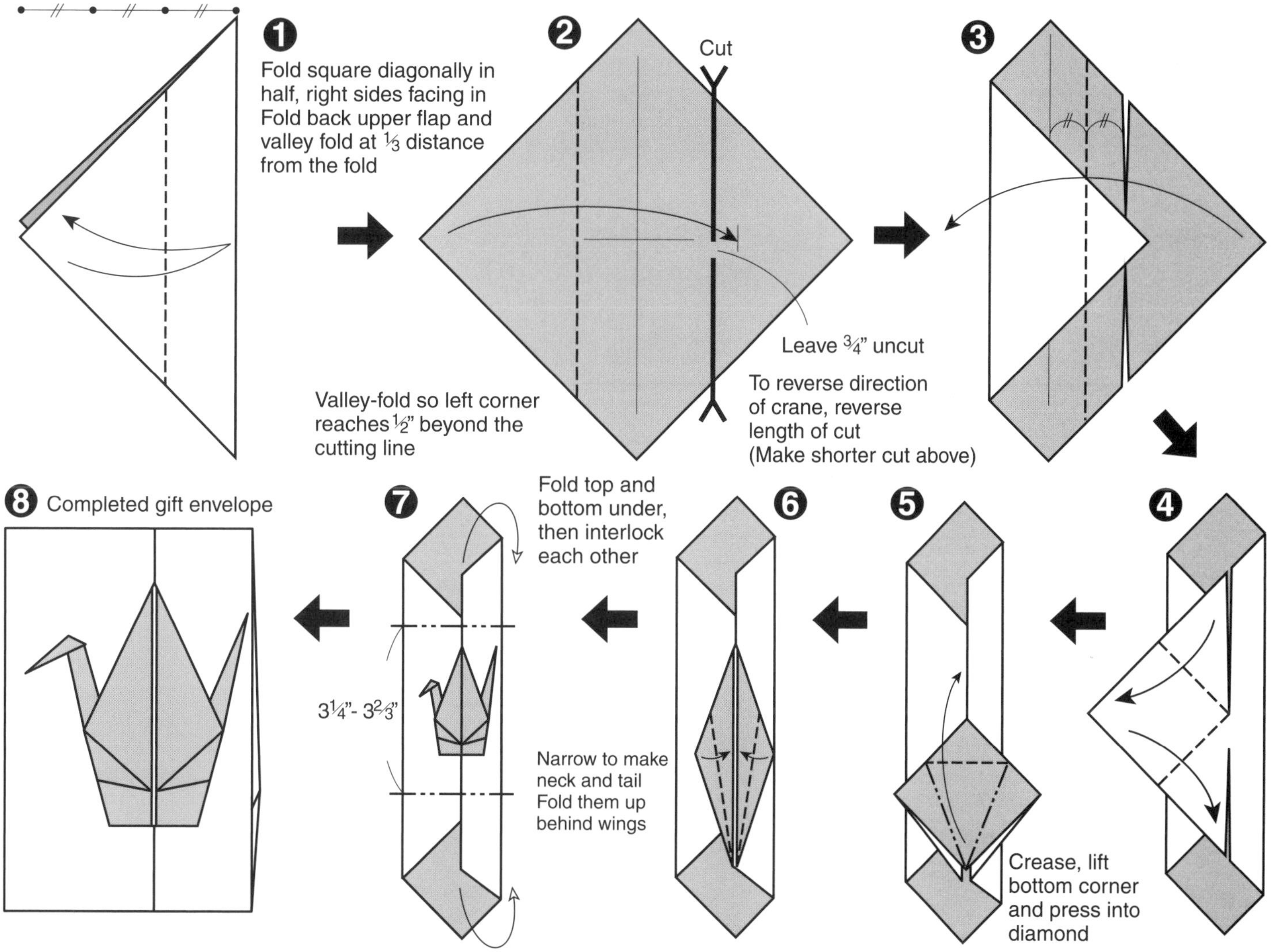

❶ Fold square diagonally in half, right sides facing in Fold back upper flap and valley fold at ⅓ distance from the fold

❷ Cut

Valley-fold so left corner reaches ½" beyond the cutting line

Leave ¾" uncut

To reverse direction of crane, reverse length of cut (Make shorter cut above)

❸

❹

❺ Crease, lift bottom corner and press into diamond

❻ Narrow to make neck and tail Fold them up behind wings

❼ Fold top and bottom under, then interlock each other

3¼"- 3⅔"

❽ Completed gift envelope

#37 ❶-❼: See page 68

❽ Fold according to numbers, ① and then ②

Turn over

❾

⅓"

❿

Turn over

⓫ ¼"

⅛"

Make band by folding up and attach by tucking ends under pleats

⓬ Completed model

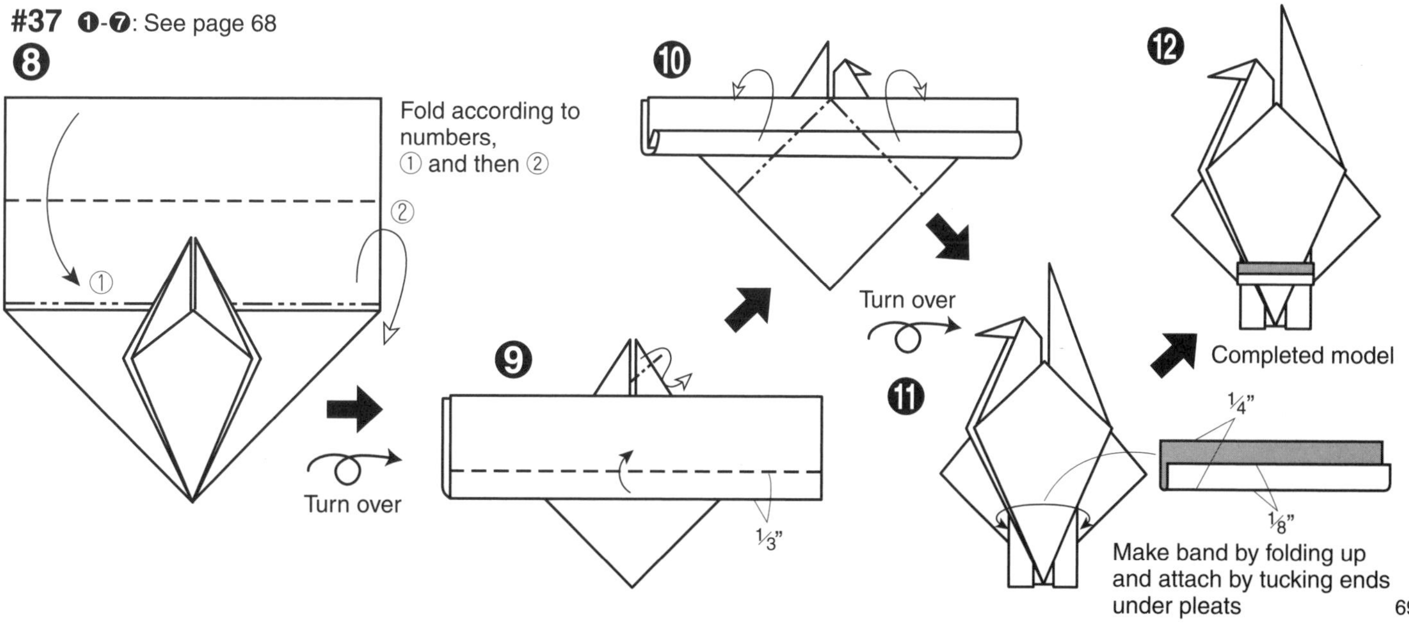

#39 #40 Gift Card Envelopes Page 35

Materials for #39
5"×10" double-sided wrapping paper
(Use any rectangular sheet of 1:2 ratio)

Piece strips if necessary.

Materials for #40
5"×15" double-sided wrapping paper
(Use any rectangular sheet of 1:3 ratio)

#39

1. Crease and fold accordingly

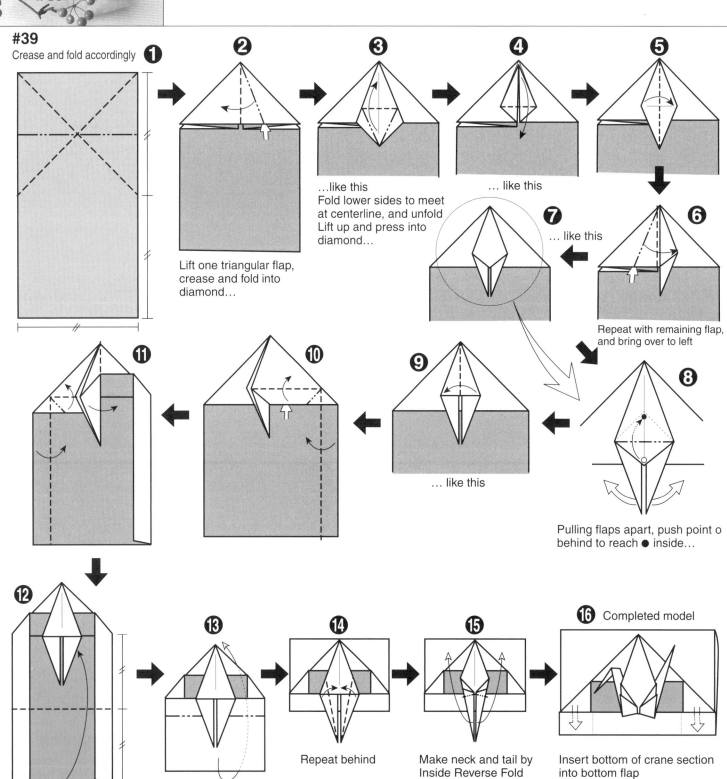

2. Lift one triangular flap, crease and fold into diamond…

3. …like this
Fold lower sides to meet at centerline, and unfold
Lift up and press into diamond…

4. … like this

5.

6. Repeat with remaining flap, and bring over to left

7. … like this

8. Pulling flaps apart, push point o behind to reach ● inside…

9. … like this

10.

11.

12.

13.

14. Repeat behind

15. Make neck and tail by Inside Reverse Fold

16. Completed model
Insert bottom of crane section into bottom flap

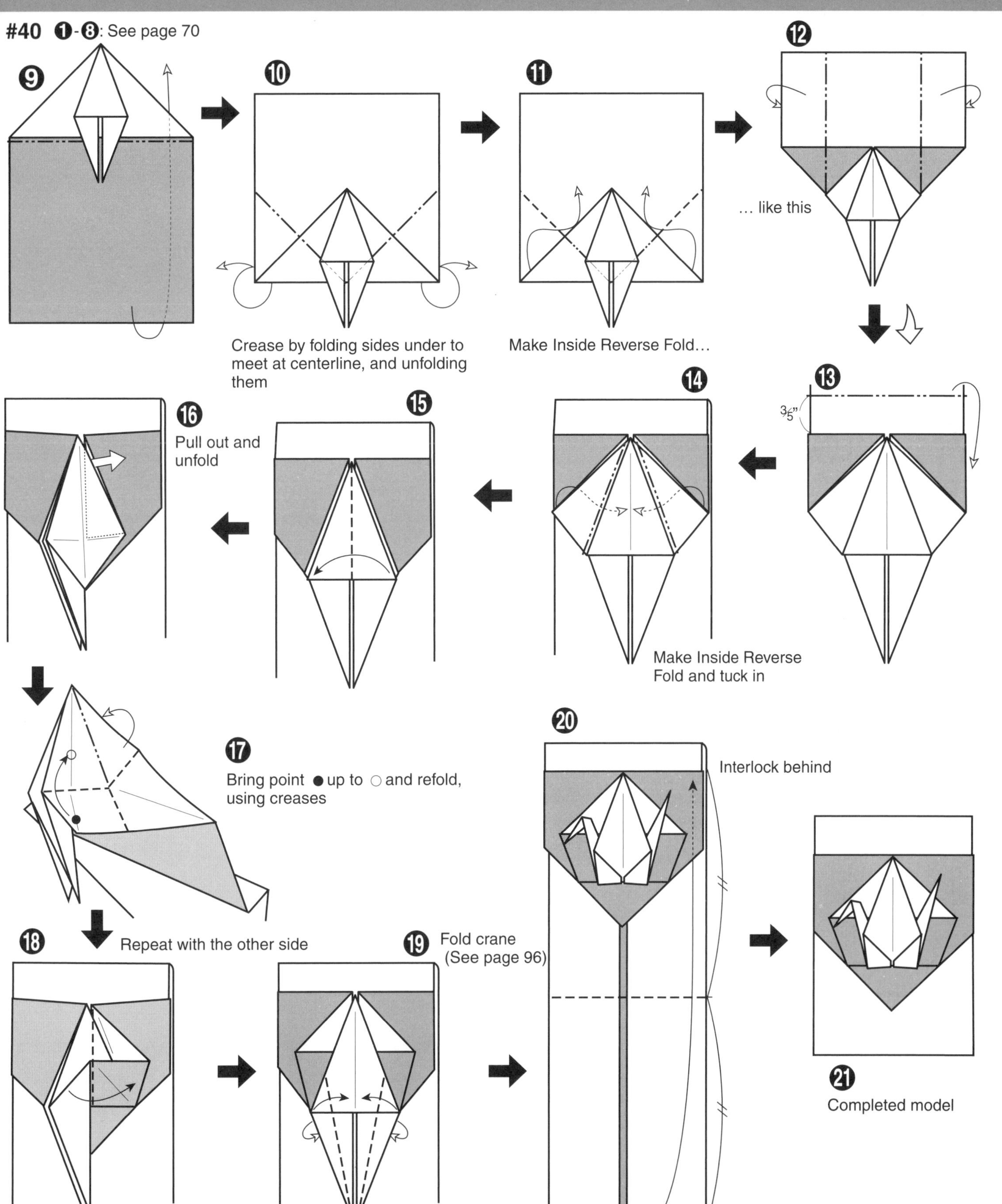
#40 ❶-❽: See page 70
❾
❿
Crease by folding sides under to meet at centerline, and unfolding them
⓫
Make Inside Reverse Fold…
⓬
… like this
⓭
3/5"
⓮
Make Inside Reverse Fold and tuck in
⓯
⓰
Pull out and unfold
⓱
Bring point ● up to ○ and refold, using creases
⓲
Repeat with the other side
⓳
Fold crane (See page 96)
⓴
Interlock behind
㉑
Completed model

#41 #42 #43 Color Block Cranes Page 36

Materials per each
1 square origami paper

Three patterns are created by initial folding directions.

#41 Mark the center by folding in half twice

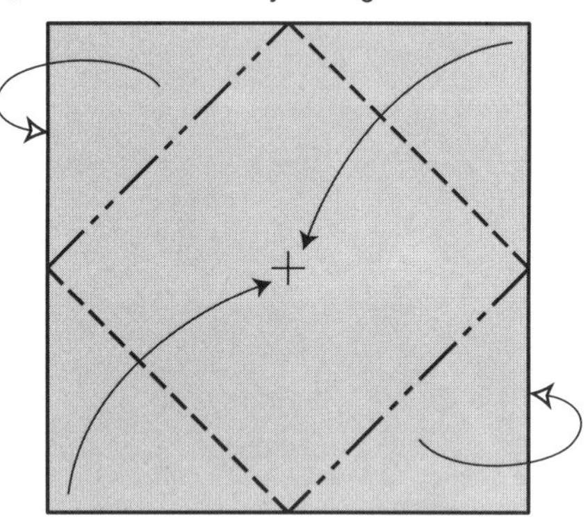

Bring all corners to center, valley-folding and mountain-folding as indicated

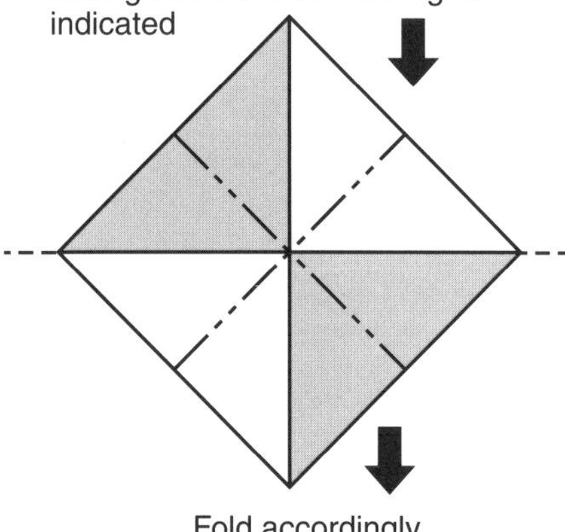

Fold accordingly

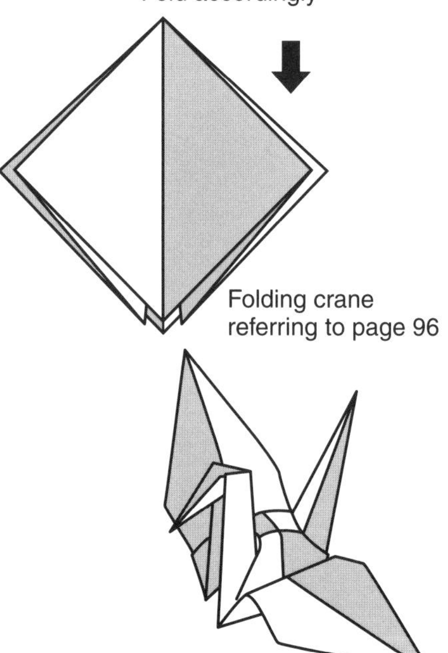

Folding crane referring to page 96

#42 Mark the center by folding in half twice

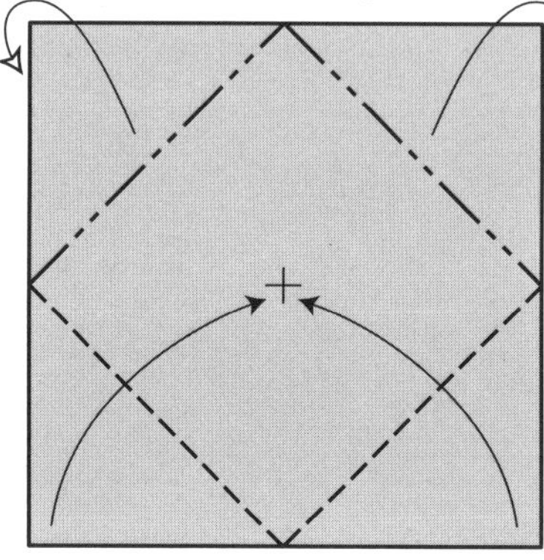

Bring all corners to center, valley-folding and mountain-folding as indicated

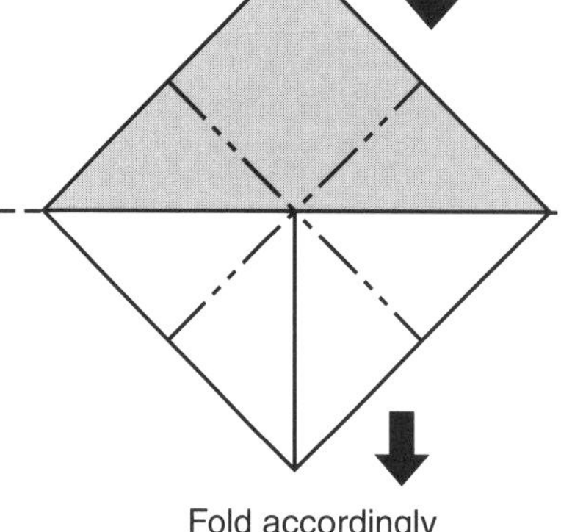

Fold accordingly

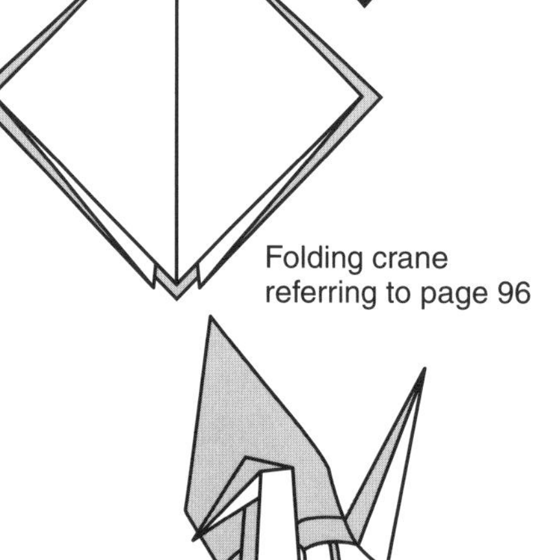

Folding crane referring to page 96

#43 Mark the center by folding in half twice

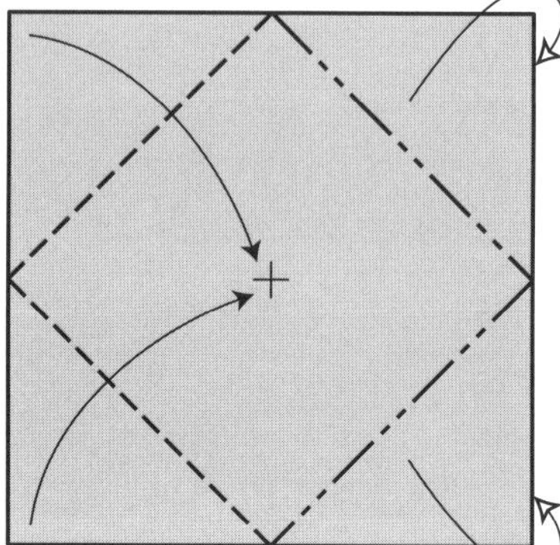

Bring all corners to center, valley-folding and mountain-folding as indicated

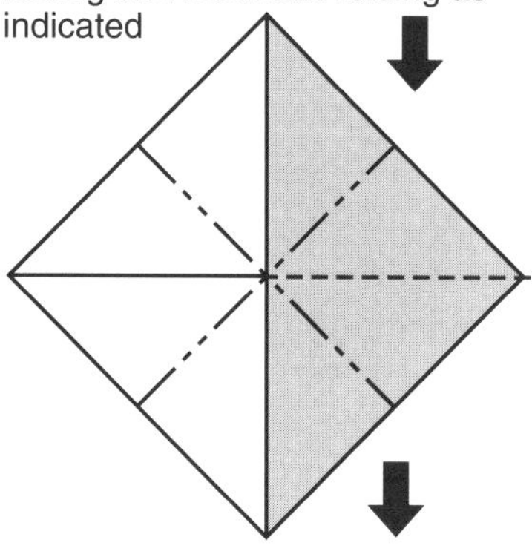

Fold accordingly

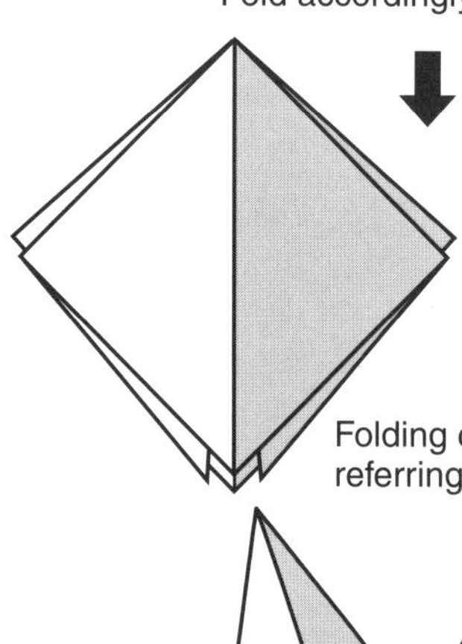

Folding crane referring to page 96

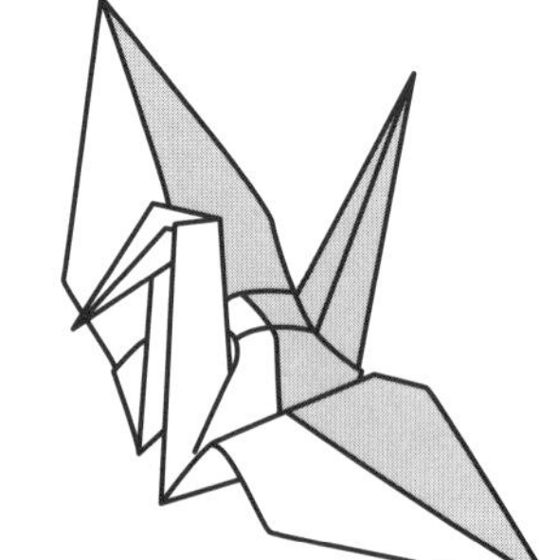

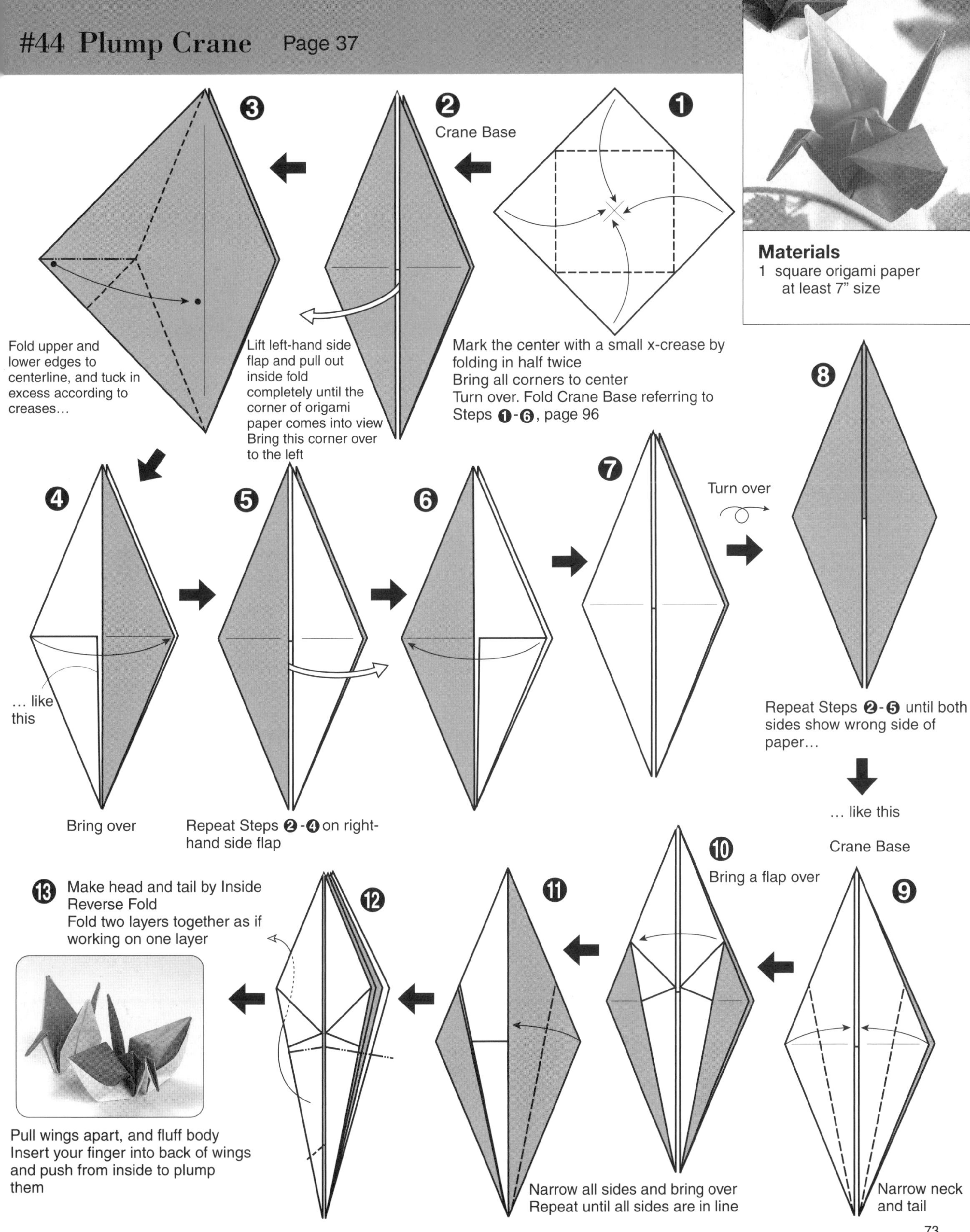
#44 Plump Crane Page 37
Materials
1 square origami paper at least 7" size
1
Mark the center with a small x-crease by folding in half twice
Bring all corners to center
Turn over. Fold Crane Base referring to Steps 1-6, page 96
2
Crane Base
Lift left-hand side flap and pull out inside fold completely until the corner of origami paper comes into view
Bring this corner over to the left
3
Fold upper and lower edges to centerline, and tuck in excess according to creases…
4
… like this
Bring over
5
Repeat Steps 2-4 on right-hand side flap
6
7
Turn over
8
Repeat Steps 2-5 until both sides show wrong side of paper…
… like this
Crane Base
9
Narrow neck and tail
10
Bring a flap over
11
Narrow all sides and bring over
Repeat until all sides are in line
12
13
Make head and tail by Inside Reverse Fold
Fold two layers together as if working on one layer
Pull wings apart, and fluff body
Insert your finger into back of wings and push from inside to plump them

#45 Crane Containers

Page 38

Materials per each
Large : 16" square *washi* paper
Medium : 9" square patterned *washi* paper
Small : 7" square shaded *washi* paper

1 wrong side

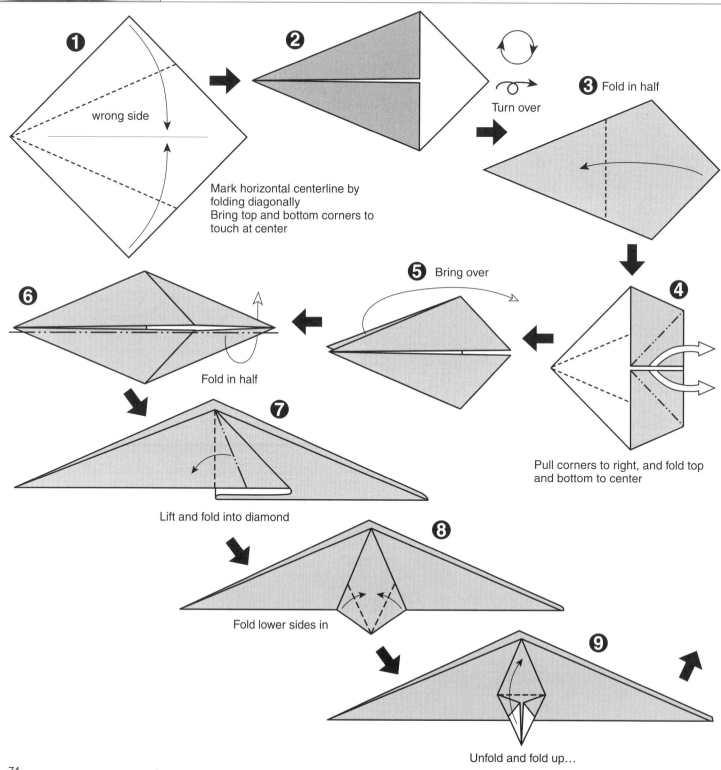

Mark horizontal centerline by folding diagonally
Bring top and bottom corners to touch at center

2

Turn over

3 Fold in half

4

Pull corners to right, and fold top and bottom to center

5 Bring over

6

Fold in half

7

Lift and fold into diamond

8

Fold lower sides in

9

Unfold and fold up…

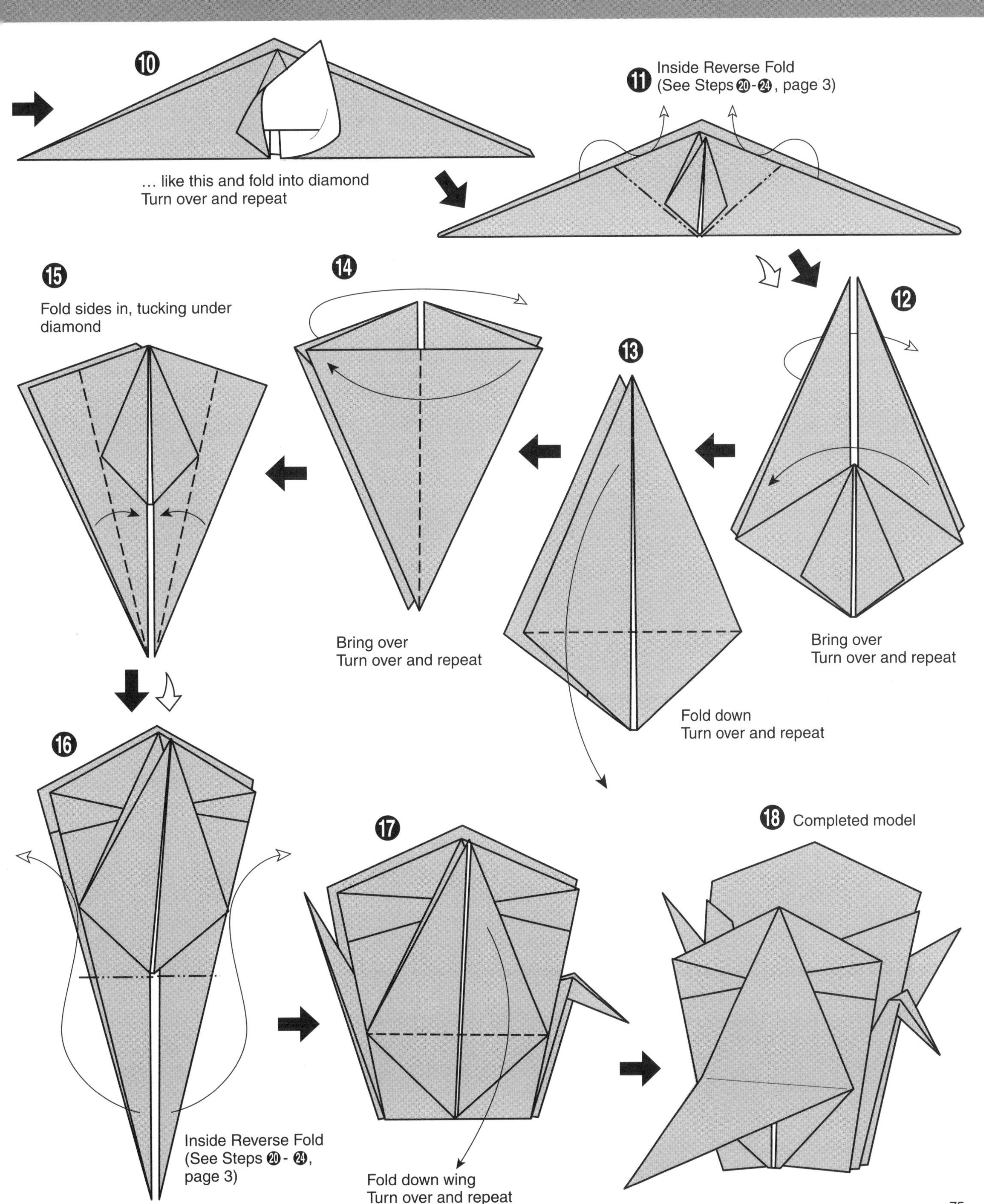

10
… like this and fold into diamond
Turn over and repeat
11 Inside Reverse Fold
(See Steps 20-24, page 3)
12
Bring over
Turn over and repeat
13
Fold down
Turn over and repeat
14
Bring over
Turn over and repeat
15
Fold sides in, tucking under diamond
16
Inside Reverse Fold
(See Steps 20 - 24,
page 3)
17
Fold down wing
Turn over and repeat
18 Completed model

#46 #47 #48 Crane Boxes

Page 39

Materials per each
9" square patterned *washi* paper or metallic origami paper

#46
Box Base

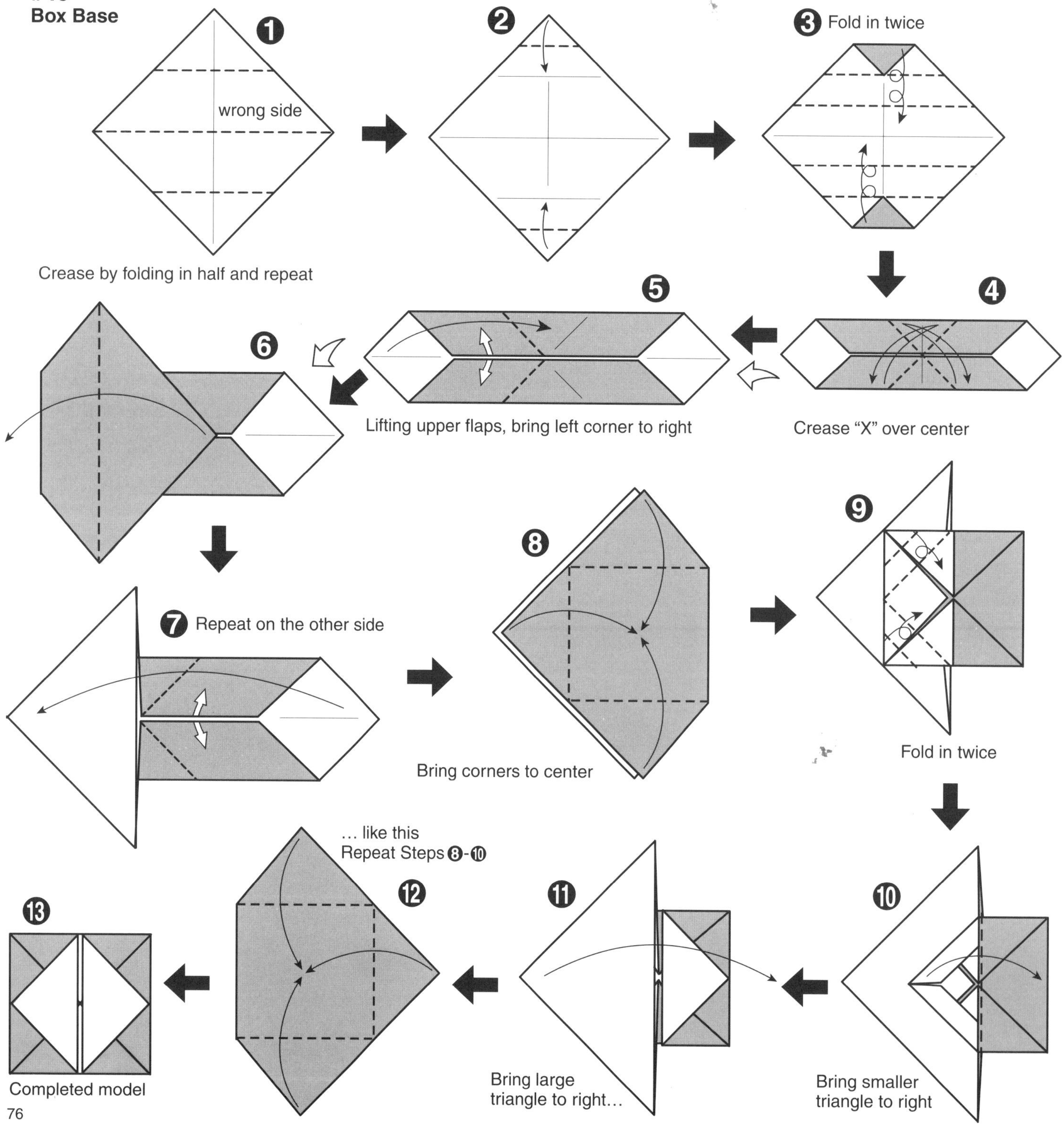

1 wrong side

Crease by folding in half and repeat

2

3 Fold in twice

4 Crease "X" over center

5 Lifting upper flaps, bring left corner to right

6

7 Repeat on the other side

8 Bring corners to center

9 Fold in twice

10 Bring smaller triangle to right

11 Bring large triangle to right...

12 ... like this
Repeat Steps 8-10

13 Completed model

#47 Make Box Base referring to previous page, Steps ❶-❼

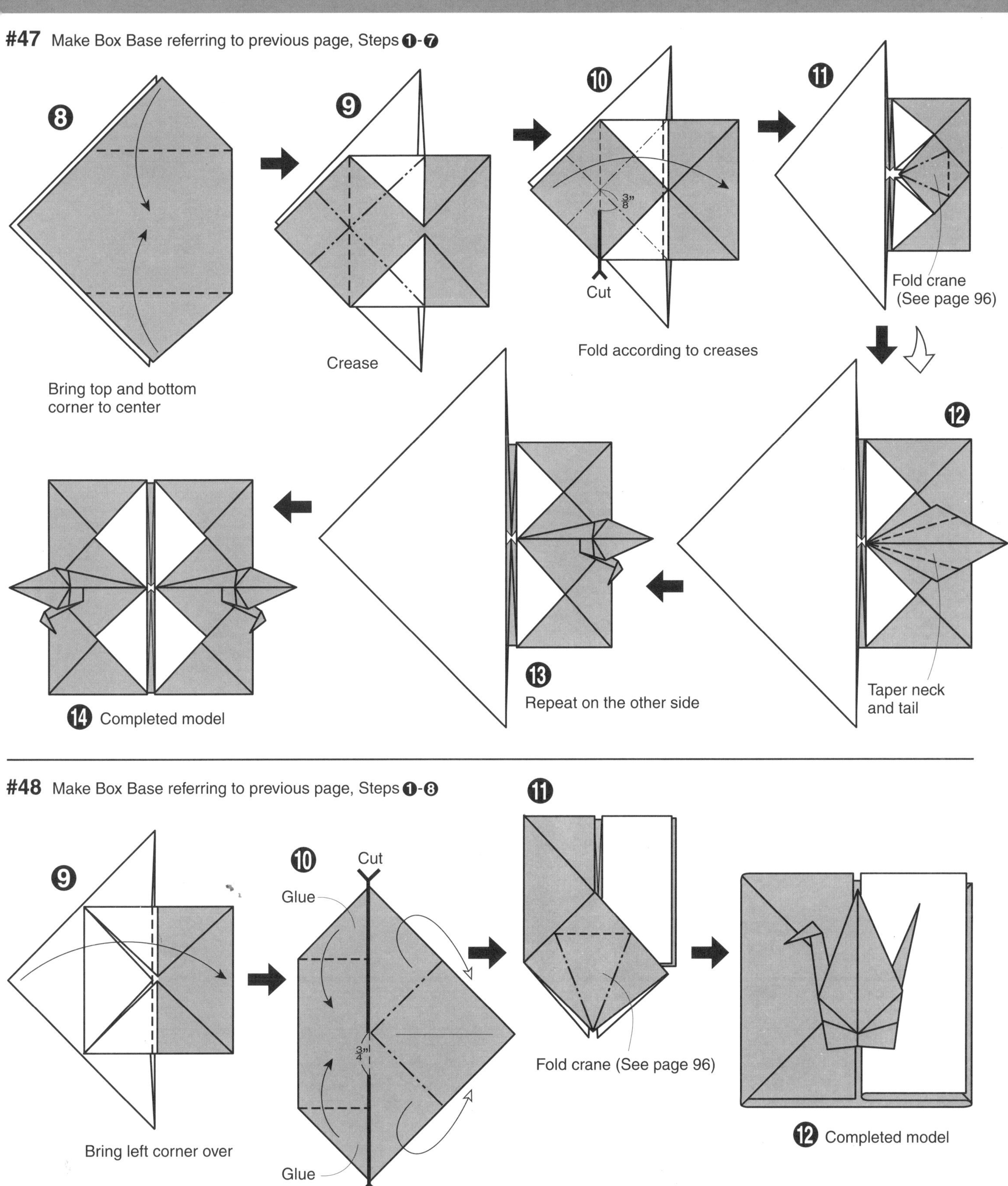

#49 Sitting Cranes Page 40

Materials
Large: 9" square mesh origami paper
Small: 7" square metallic origami paper

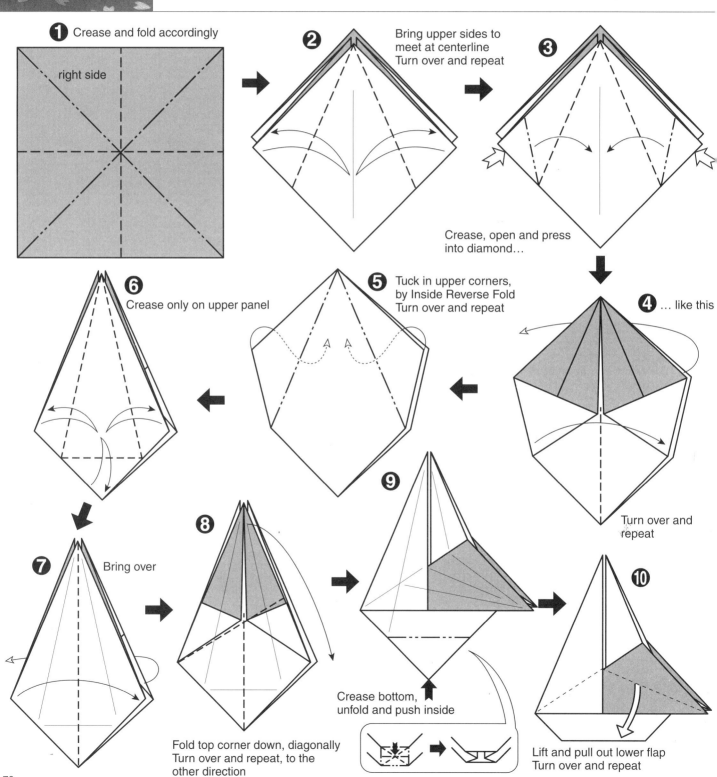

1. Crease and fold accordingly
right side

2. Bring upper sides to meet at centerline
Turn over and repeat

3. Crease, open and press into diamond…

4. … like this
Turn over and repeat

5. Tuck in upper corners, by Inside Reverse Fold
Turn over and repeat

6. Crease only on upper panel

7. Bring over

8. Fold top corner down, diagonally
Turn over and repeat, to the other direction

9. Crease bottom, unfold and push inside

10. Lift and pull out lower flap
Turn over and repeat

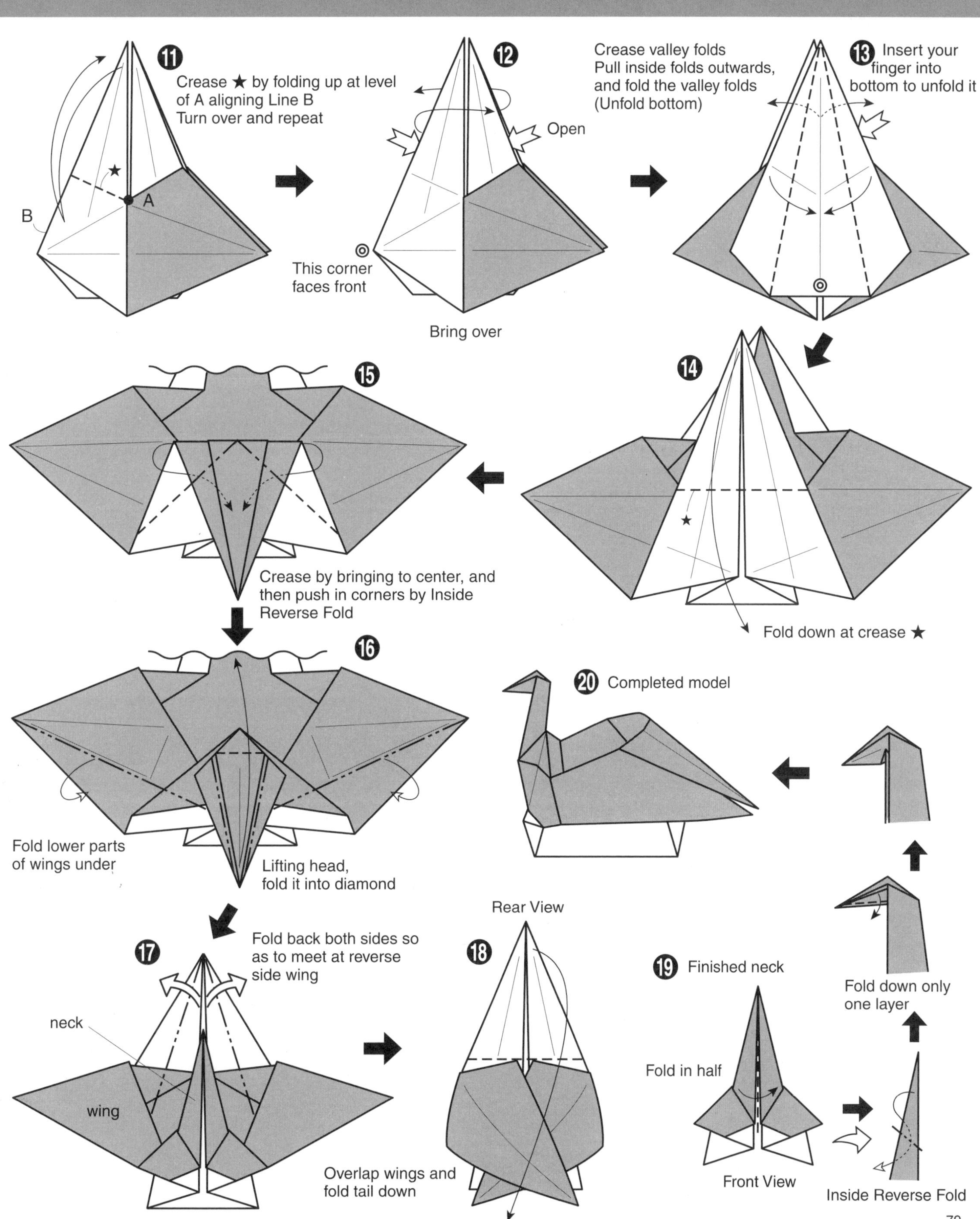
11
Crease ★ by folding up at level of A aligning Line B
Turn over and repeat
★
A
B
12
Open
This corner faces front
Bring over
Crease valley folds
Pull inside folds outwards, and fold the valley folds
(Unfold bottom)
13 Insert your finger into bottom to unfold it
14
★
Fold down at crease ★
15
Crease by bringing to center, and then push in corners by Inside Reverse Fold
16
Fold lower parts of wings under
Lifting head, fold it into diamond
20 Completed model
Fold down only one layer
17
Fold back both sides so as to meet at reverse side wing
neck
wing
Rear View
18
Overlap wings and fold tail down
19 Finished neck
Fold in half
Front View
Inside Reverse Fold

#34 #35 Flying Crane Quartets Page 33

Materials
6" square shaded *washi* paper

For crane folding, see page 96.

1 Make creases carefully (this is important)

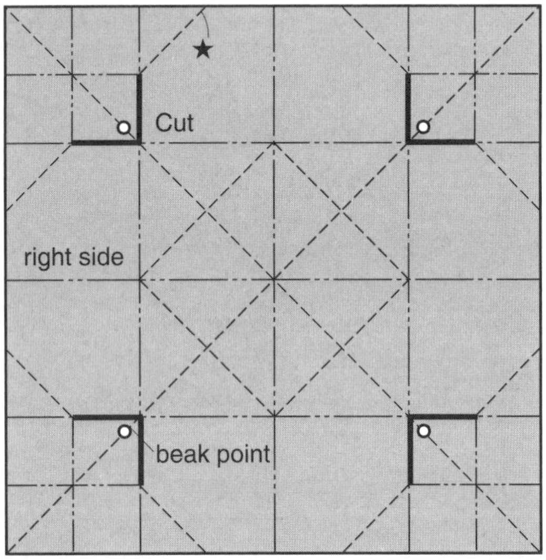

Cut

right side

beak point

Cut before creasing ★

2 Fold each small corner into crane

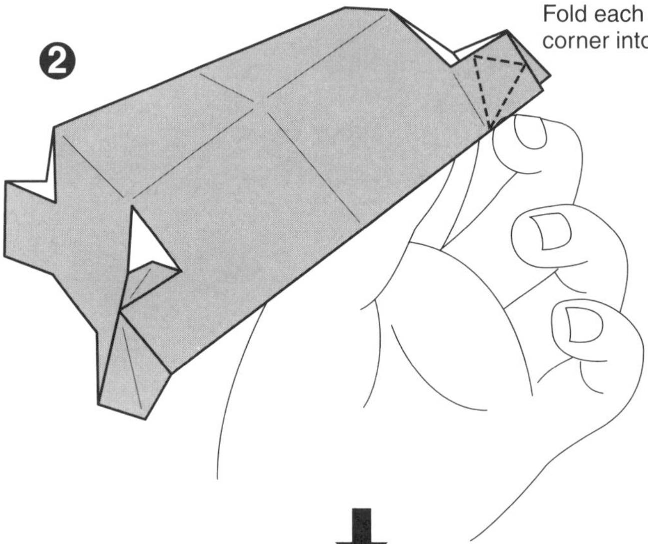

3 Hold to form a box, and make neck of crane

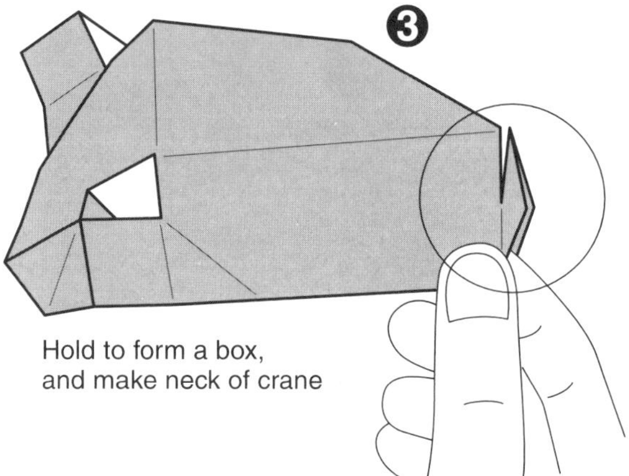

4

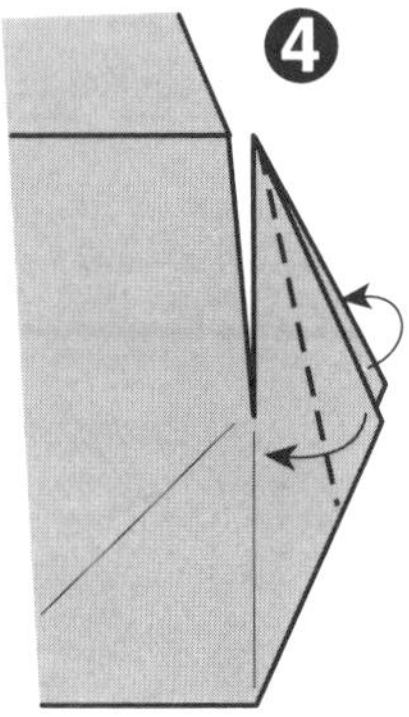

5 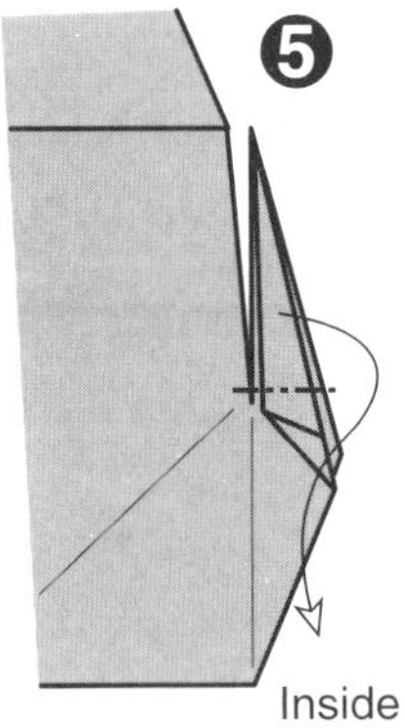 Inside Reverse Fold

6 Make head by Inside Reverse Fold
Repeat on remaining corners

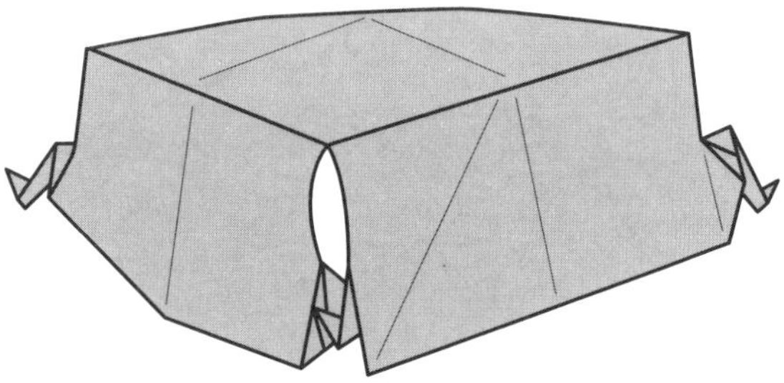

7 Carefully reverse the folds to bring inside out
Make tail for each crane

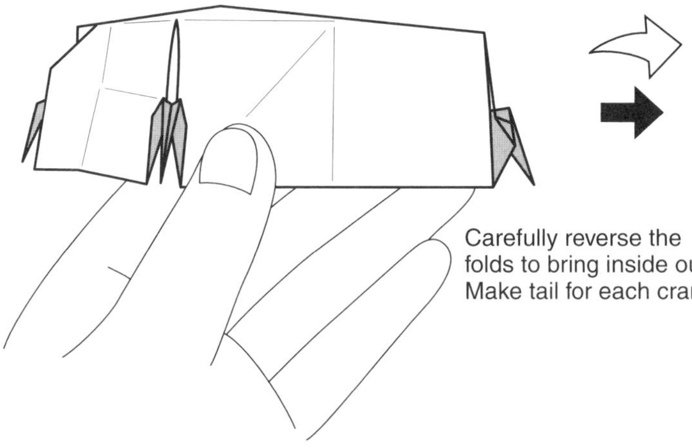

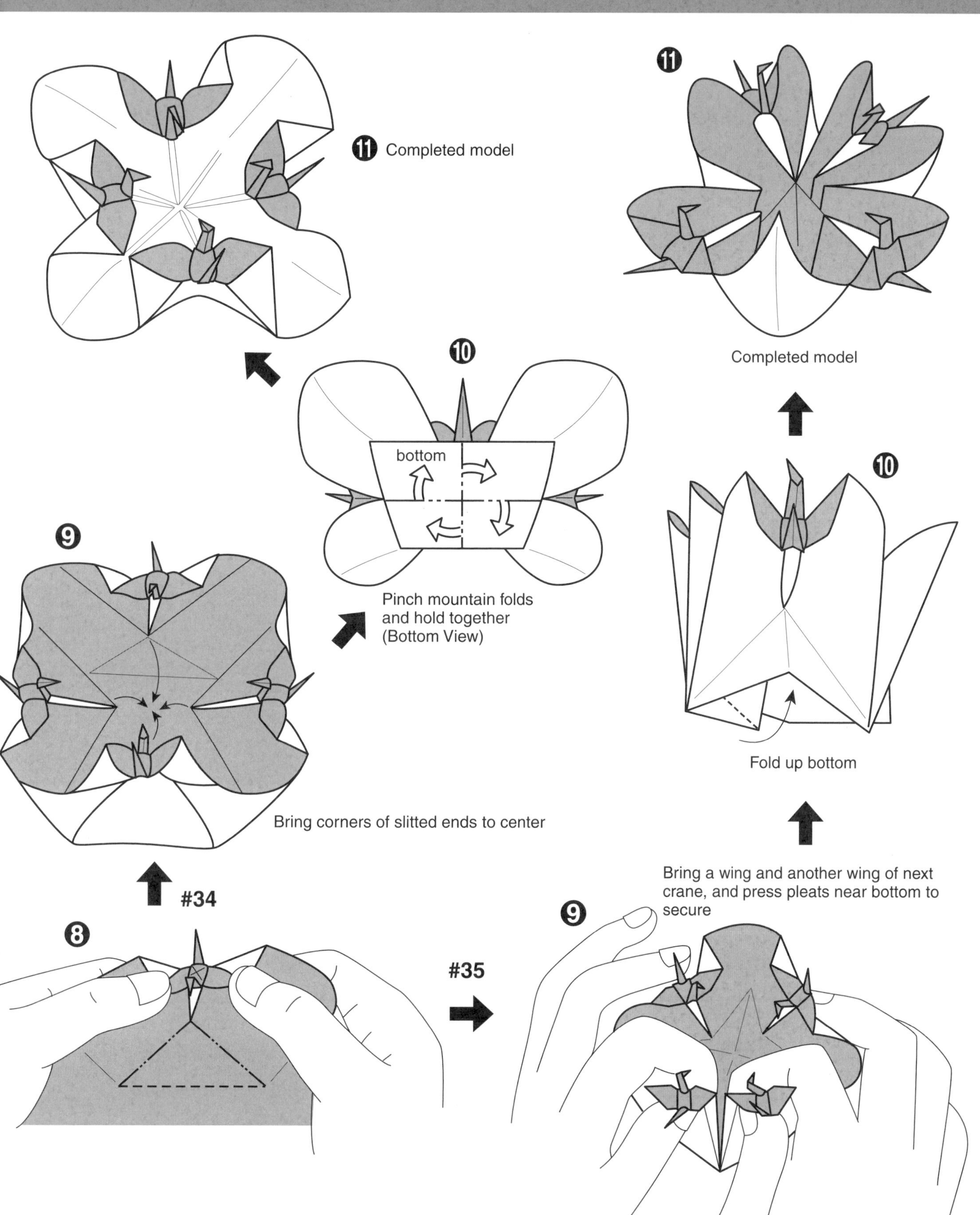

11 Completed model
11
Completed model
10
bottom
10
9
Pinch mountain folds
and hold together
(Bottom View)
Fold up bottom
Bring corners of slitted ends to center
#34
Bring a wing and another wing of next
crane, and press pleats near bottom to
secure
8
#35
9

#15 #50 Good Luck Cranes

Page 26 and 41

Materials for #15
3" square metallic origami paper

Materials for #50
9" square metallic origami paper

1. Crease and fold accordingly

Crease to make Basic Square (See page 2)

2.

3.

4.

5.

Turn over

6.

Lift and press to fold

7.

8. Lift and press to fold

9. Crease by folding sides to meet at centerline

10. Lift and press to fold

11. Repeat with all flap

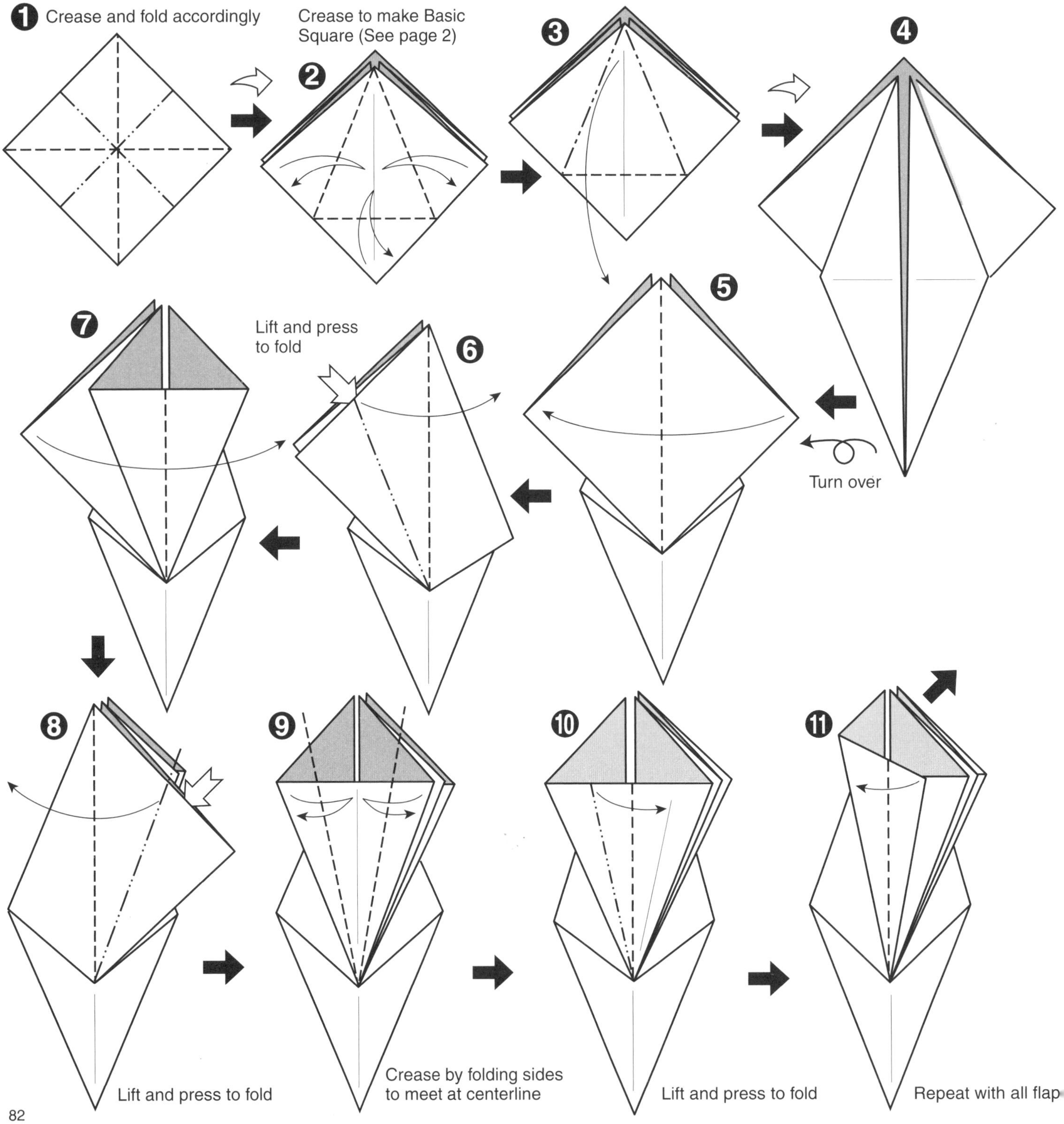

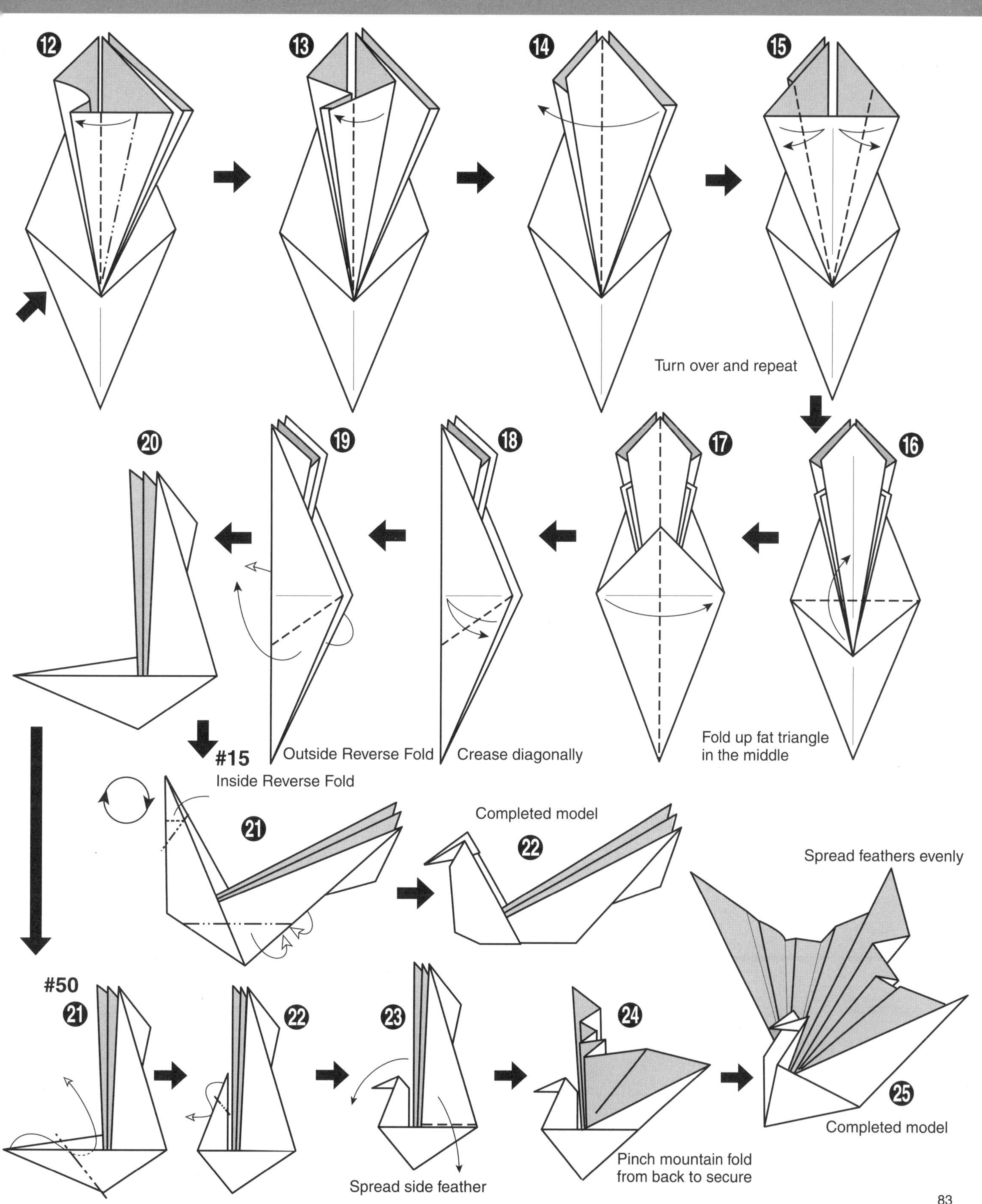
12
13
14
15
Turn over and repeat
20
19
18
17
16
Outside Reverse Fold
Crease diagonally
Fold up fat triangle
in the middle
#15
Inside Reverse Fold
21
Completed model
22
Spread feathers evenly
#50
21
22
23
24
25
Spread side feather
Pinch mountain fold
from back to secure
Completed model

#51 Happy Crane

Page 41

Materials
4½"×9" metallic origami paper

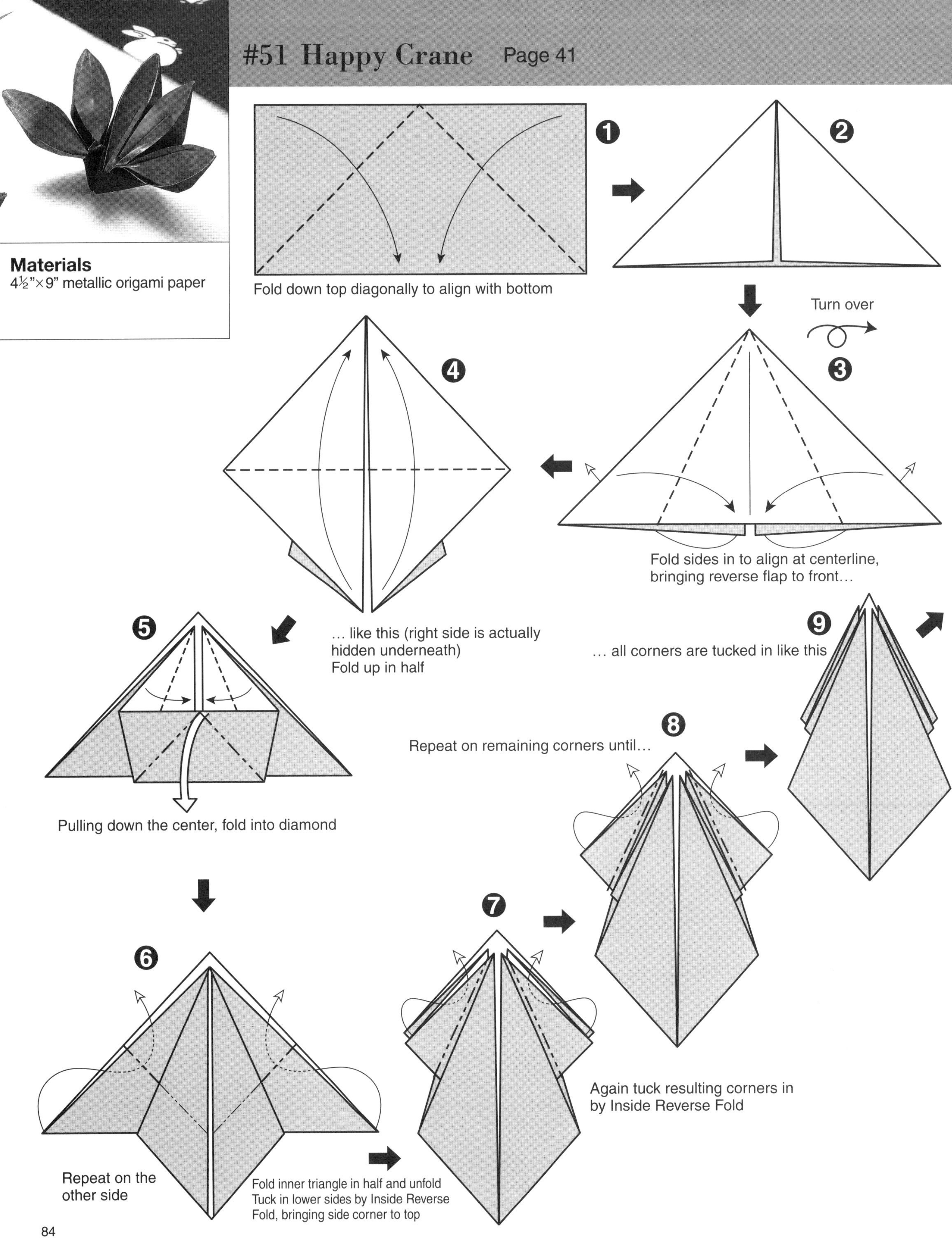

1
Fold down top diagonally to align with bottom
2
Turn over
3
Fold sides in to align at centerline, bringing reverse flap to front…
4
… like this (right side is actually hidden underneath)
Fold up in half
5
Pulling down the center, fold into diamond
6
Repeat on the other side
Fold inner triangle in half and unfold
Tuck in lower sides by Inside Reverse Fold, bringing side corner to top
7
Again tuck resulting corners in by Inside Reverse Fold
8
Repeat on remaining corners until…
9
… all corners are tucked in like this

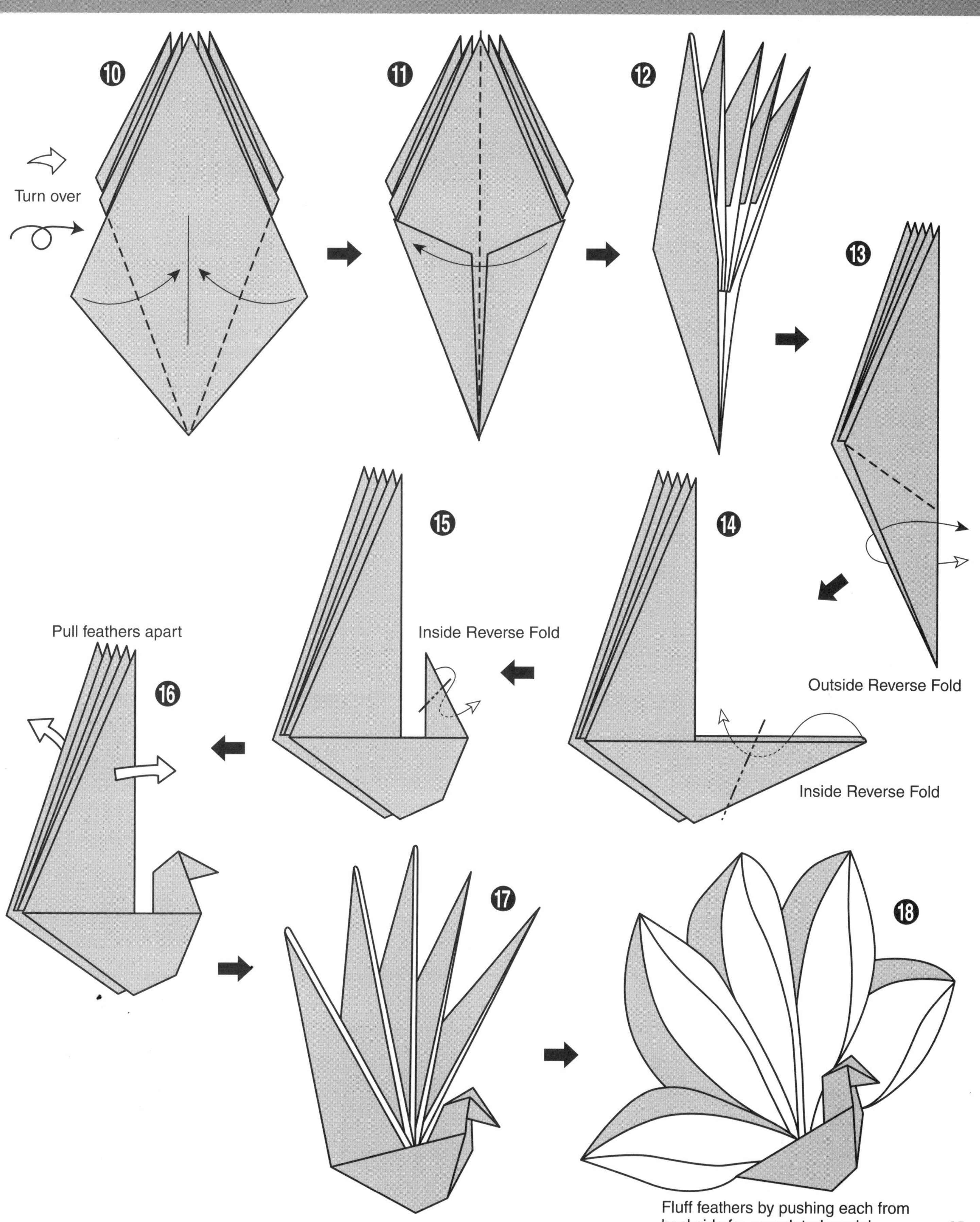
10
Turn over
11
12
13
Outside Reverse Fold
14
Inside Reverse Fold
15
Inside Reverse Fold
16
Pull feathers apart
17
18
Fluff feathers by pushing each from
backside for completed model

#52 New Year Wreath

Page 42

Materials

2 3"×24" strips wrinkled thick *washi* paper (dark green)
2 6" squares metallic origami paper (gold/red) for cranes
2 2" squares wrinkled *washi* paper (light green) for bamboo
4 2"×3" strips wrinkled *washi* paper (green) for pine
3 1½" squares gold-freckled *washi* paper (red) for blossom
2 1½" squares gold-freckled *washi* paper (white) for blossom
9" styrofoam wreath base
Floral wire

MAKE WREATH

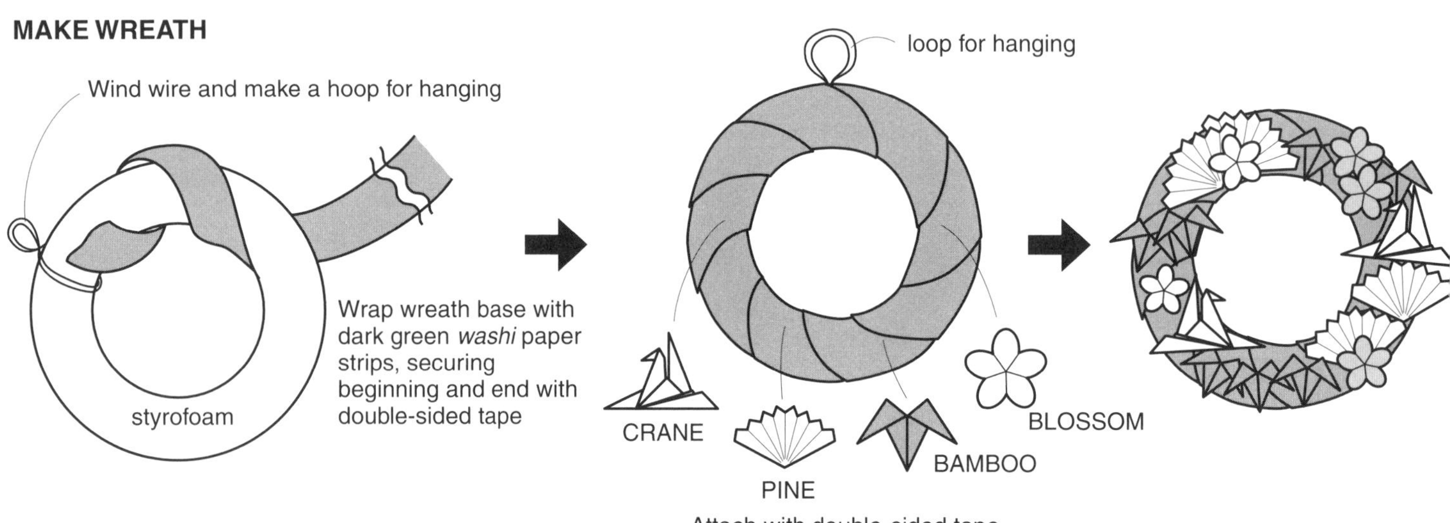

PINE

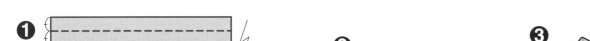

1. Fold lengthwise in half, and unfold
Turn over and fold each section in half
Repeat to make 8-section pleats

2. Fold in half and secure ends with glue

3. Completed pine
Make 4

BAMBOO

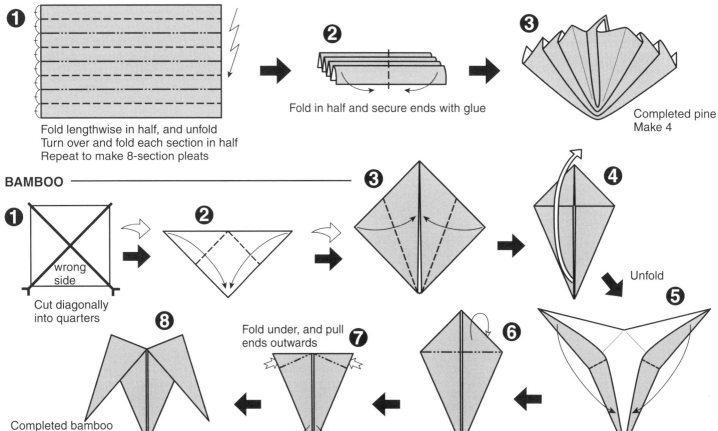

1. wrong side
Cut diagonally into quarters

2.

3.

4.

Unfold

5.

6.

7. Fold under, and pull ends outwards

8. Completed bamboo
Make 7

BLOSSOM

1 right side

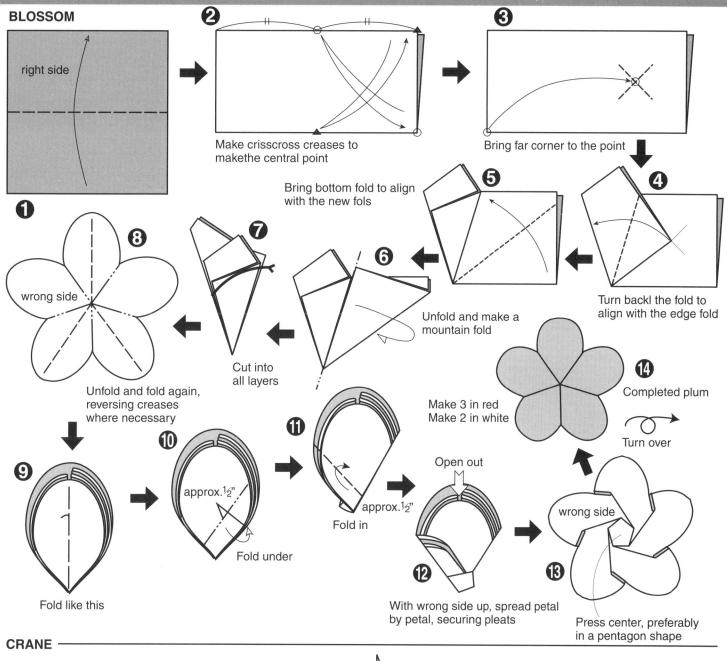

2 Make crisscross creases to makethe central point

3 Bring far corner to the point

4 Turn backl the fold to align with the edge fold

5 Bring bottom fold to align with the new fols

6 Unfold and make a mountain fold

7 Cut into all layers

8 wrong side

Unfold and fold again, reversing creases where necessary

9 Fold like this

10 approx.½" Fold under

11 Fold in approx.½"

12 Open out

With wrong side up, spread petal by petal, securing pleats

13 wrong side

Press center, preferably in a pentagon shape

14 Completed plum

Make 3 in red
Make 2 in white

Turn over

CRANE

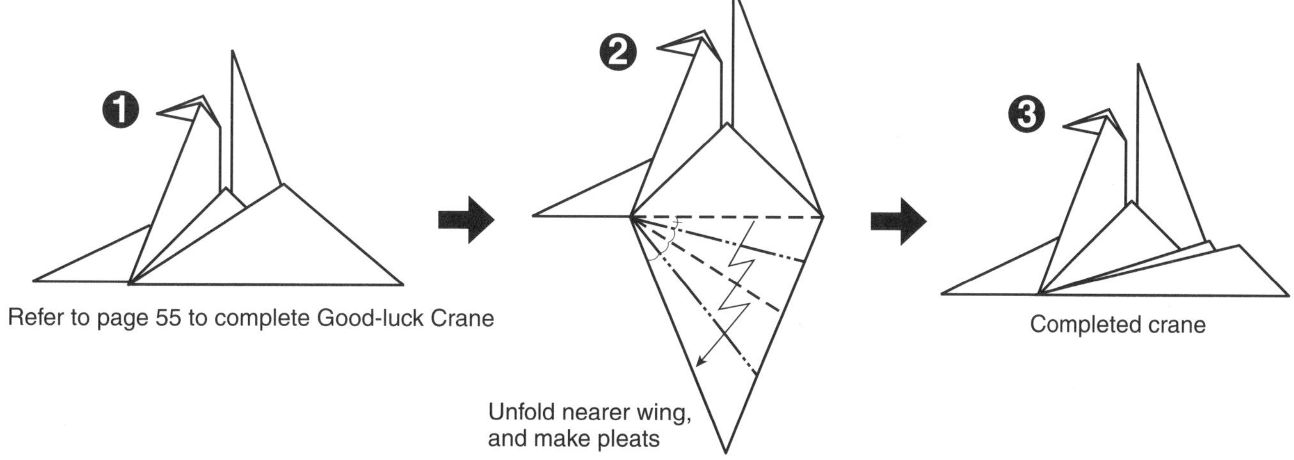

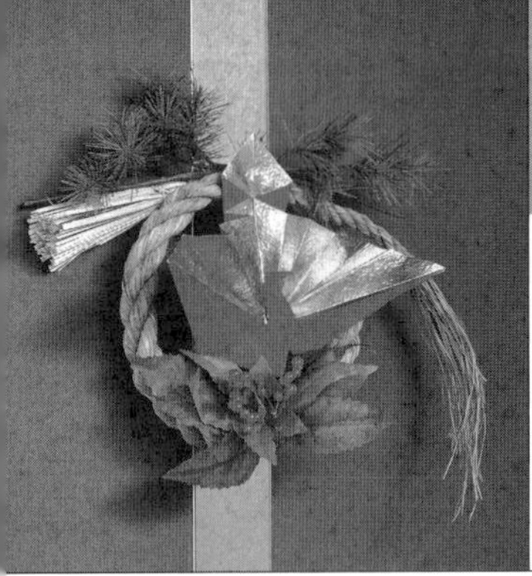

#54 New Year Wreath Page 42

Materials

9½" square metallic origami paper (red / gold)
approx. 40" long commercial straw rope
Pine twigs
Berry twigs
Floral wire

CRANE Refer to page 83 and work until Step ⑳ is done

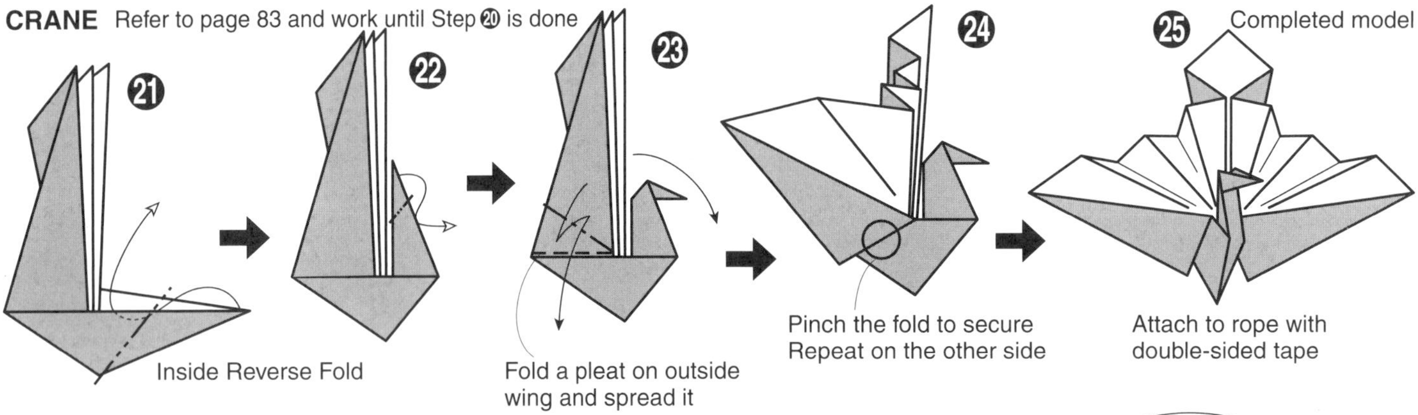

21
Inside Reverse Fold
22
23
Fold a pleat on outside wing and spread it
24
Pinch the fold to secure
Repeat on the other side
25
Completed model
Attach to rope with double-sided tape

WREATH

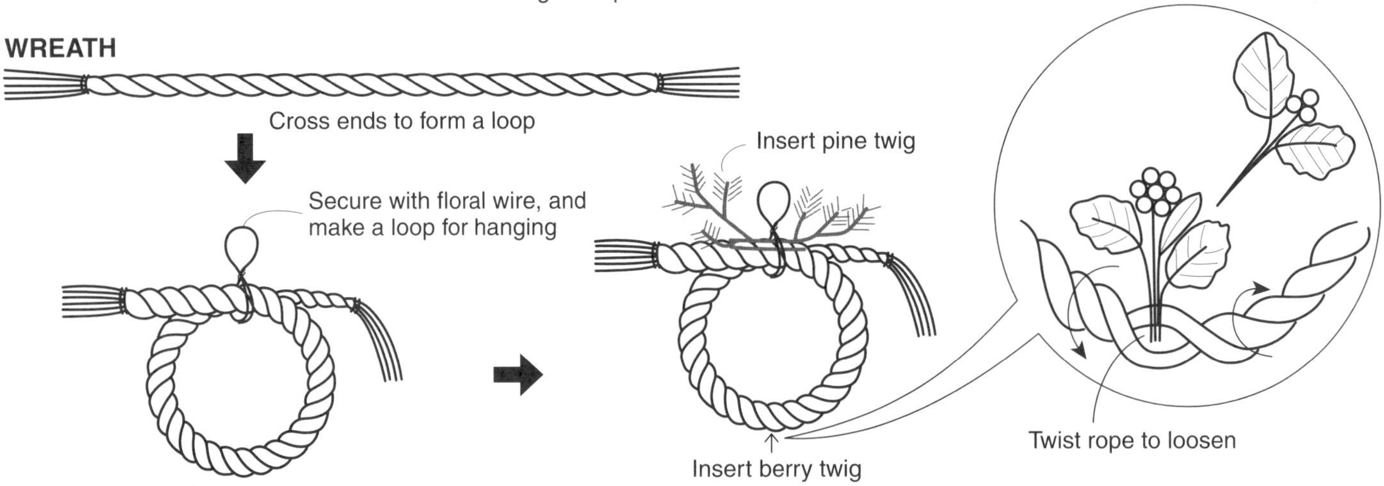

Cross ends to form a loop
Secure with floral wire, and make a loop for hanging
Insert pine twig
Insert berry twig
Twist rope to loosen

Materials

1 6" square metallic origami paper (red / gold)
1 6" diameter commercial looped straw rope
15 20" long *mizuhiki* cords (gold / white)
3 pine twigs
1 plum twig
1 ear of rice

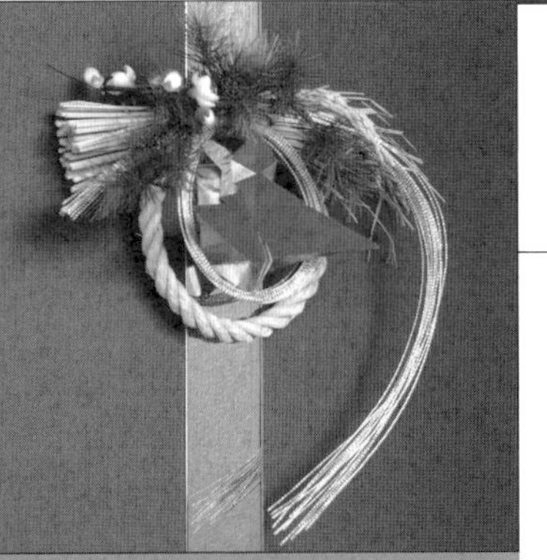

#53 New Year Wreath
Page 42

Measure internal diameter as length "a"
a
Secure with wire
wire
a
Using all *mizuhiki* cords, make a loop of length "a" as external diameter
Secure with wire

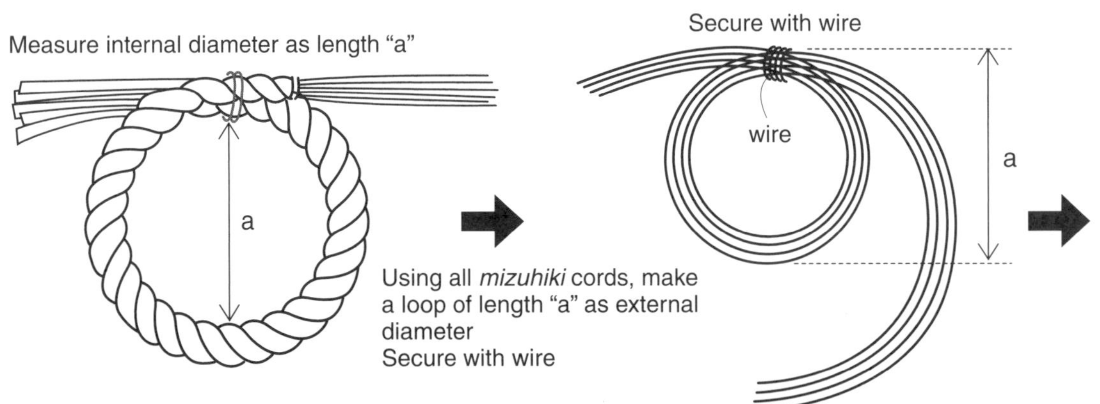

#55 Bobbing Cranes and Balloons Page 43

Materials

Approx. 20 4" square patterned *washi* origami paper (assorted)
Approx. 20 3" square shaded *washi* origami paper
8 $\frac{1}{12}$" wide 28" long stripwood or bamboo sticks
Thick cotton thread for sewing

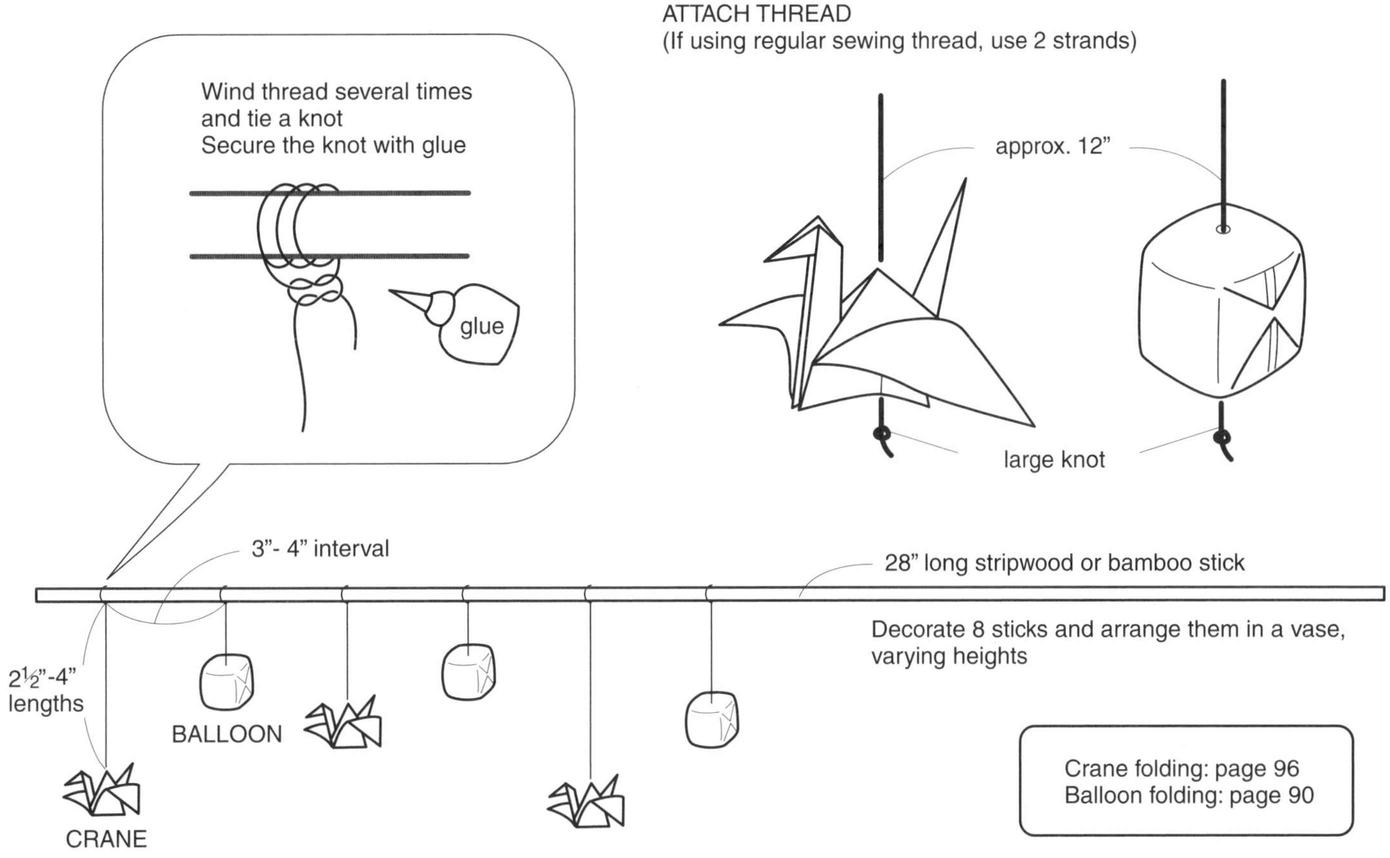

Wind thread several times and tie a knot
Secure the knot with glue

glue

ATTACH THREAD
(If using regular sewing thread, use 2 strands)

approx. 12"

large knot

3"- 4" interval

28" long stripwood or bamboo stick

Decorate 8 sticks and arrange them in a vase, varying heights

2½"-4" lengths

BALLOON

CRANE

Crane folding: page 96
Balloon folding: page 90

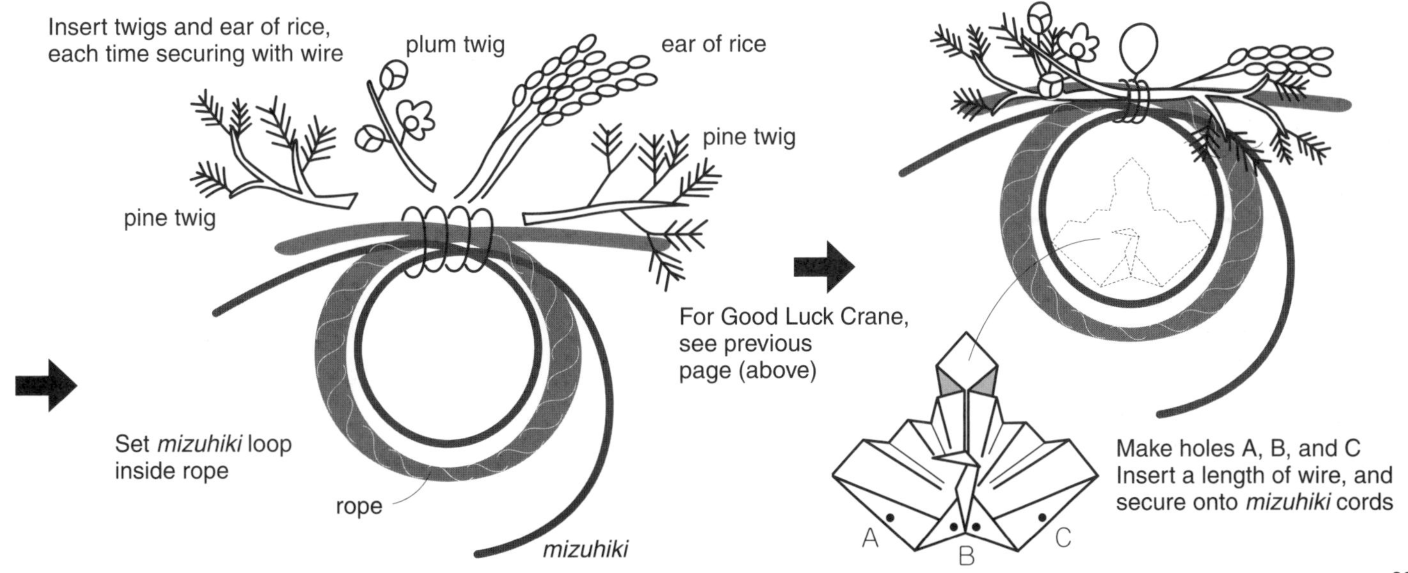

Insert twigs and ear of rice, each time securing with wire
plum twig
ear of rice
pine twig
pine twig
For Good Luck Crane, see previous page (above)
Set *mizuhiki* loop inside rope
rope
mizuhiki
Make holes A, B, and C
Insert a length of wire, and secure onto *mizuhiki* cords
A
B
C

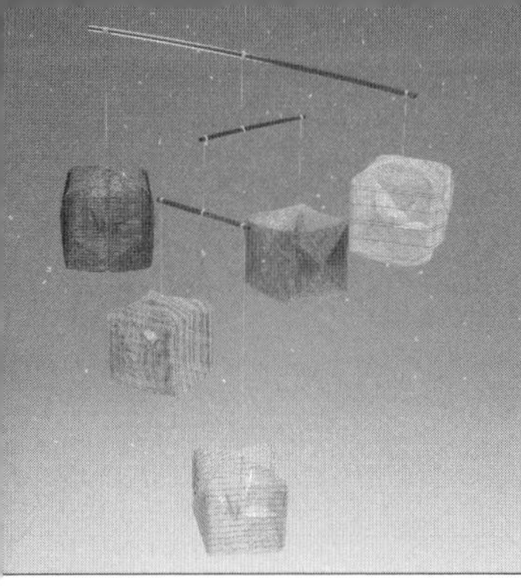

#58 Caged Crane Mobile Page 45

Materials

5 9½" squares mesh origami paper for balloons
5 3" squares Aurora origami paper for cranes
Approx. 30 1" long bugle beads
⅛" wide 20" long acrylic rod
#30 cotton thread

For crane folding, see pages 2-3.

BALLOON

1 Crease as shown
right side
2
Turn over
3
4
5
6
7

Completed balloon

Inflate to fluff

Fold down and tuck into pockets

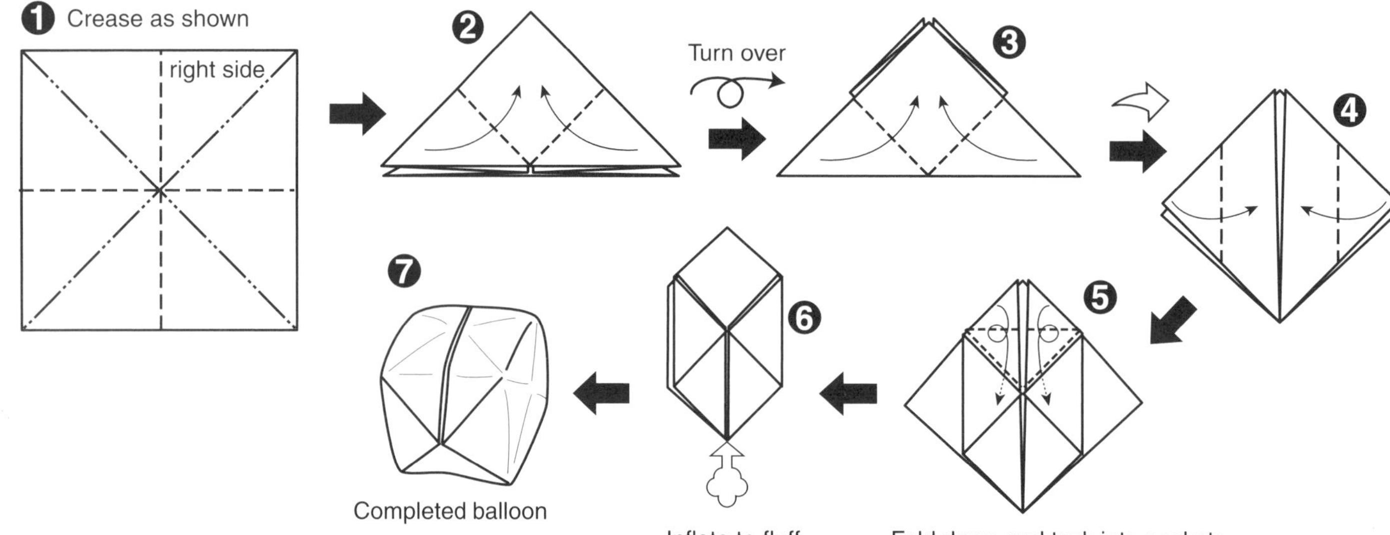

CRANE IN BALLOON

12" long cotton thread
needle
5-6 bugle beads
Tie a large knot
bugle beads

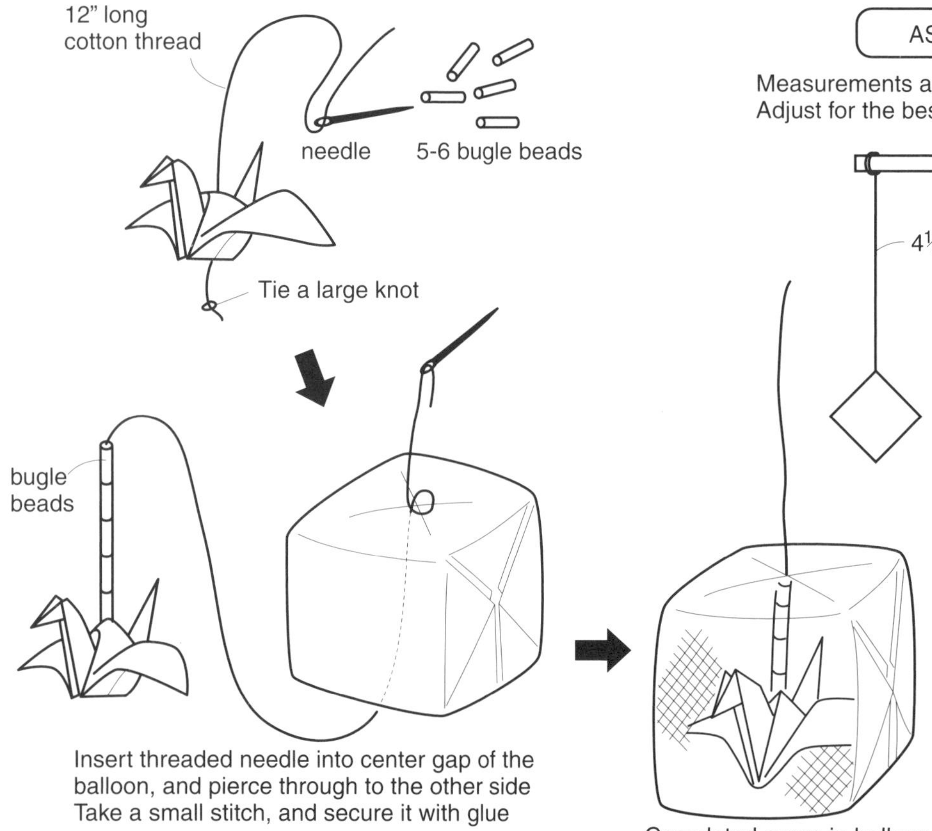

Insert threaded needle into center gap of the balloon, and pierce through to the other side
Take a small stitch, and secure it with glue

Completed crane in balloon

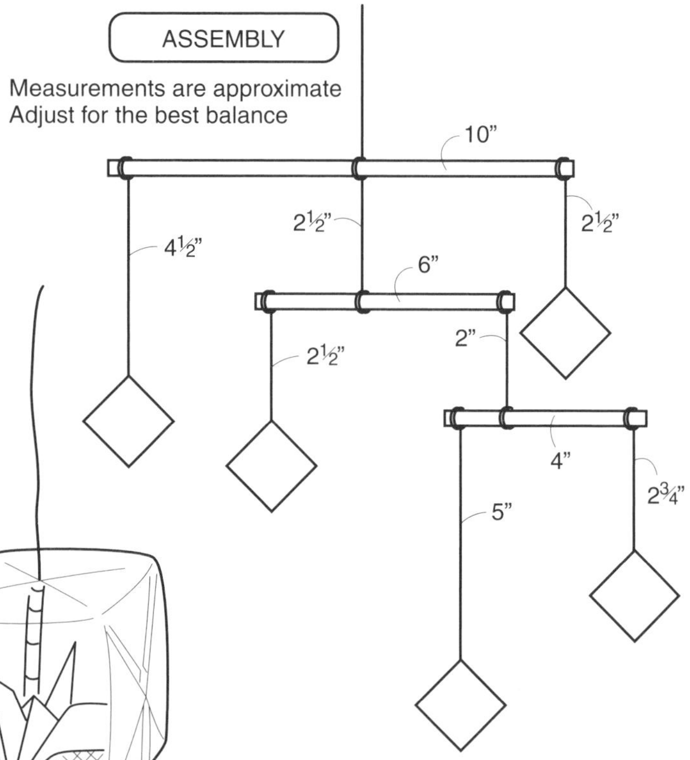

ASSEMBLY
Measurements are approximate
Adjust for the best balance
10"
2½"
2½"
4½"
6"
2"
2½"
4"
2¾"
5"

#59 *Washi* Screen Page 45

pressure rod
Hang with pegs
Attach cranes using double-sided tape

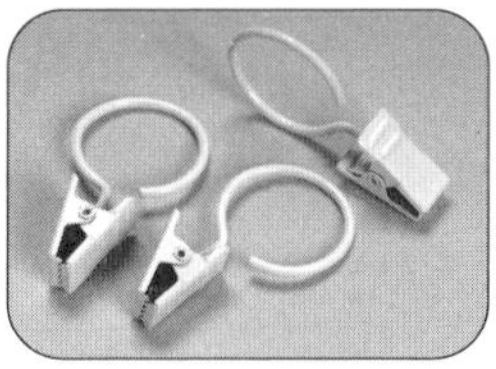

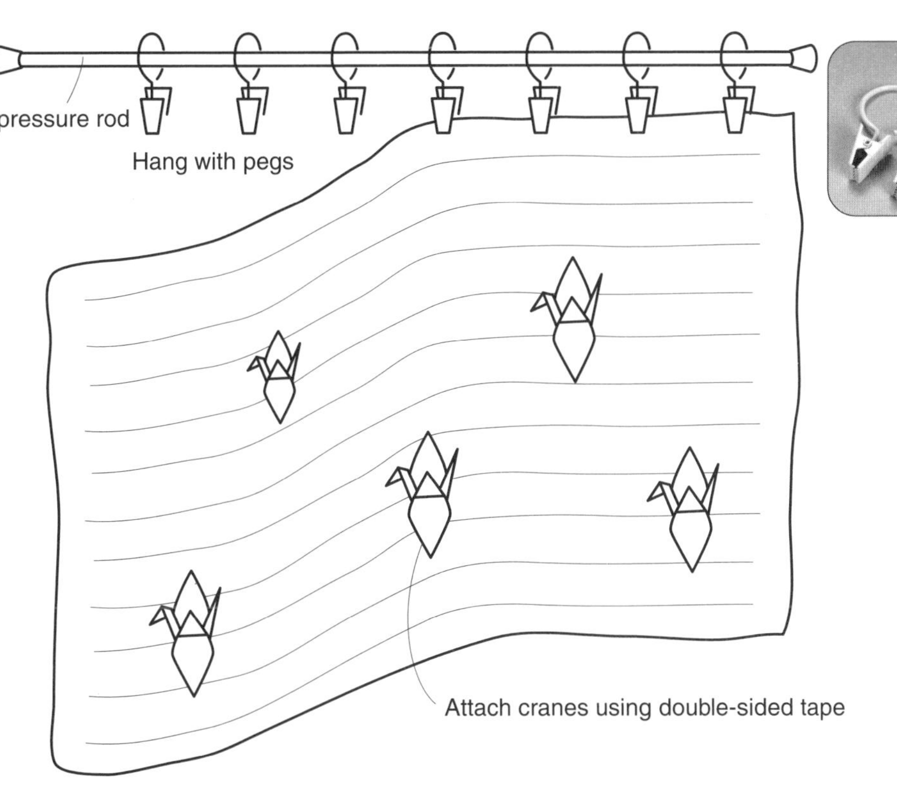

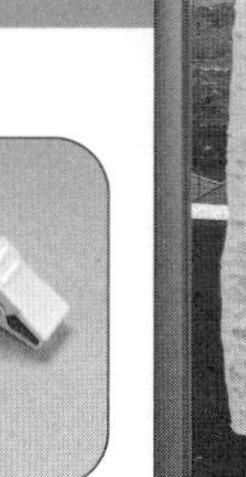

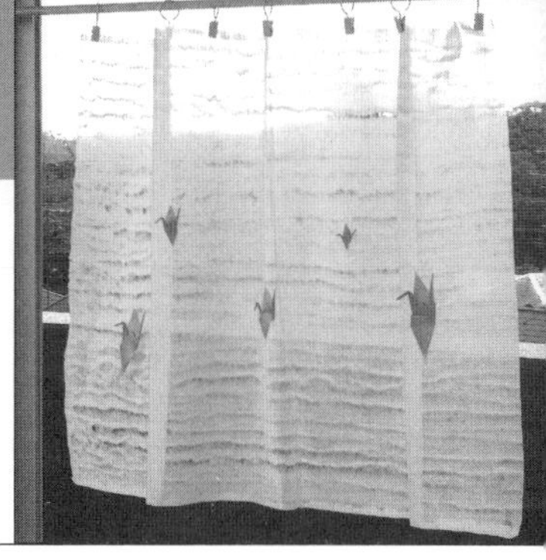

Materials
Approx. 22”×30” *Tosa Sazanami* (ripples) *washi* paper
Cranes: 1 square each 1½”, 2¼”, 3”, 4”, and 4¾” shaded *washi* paper

For crane folding, see pages 2-3.

#57 Clustered Flowers Page 44

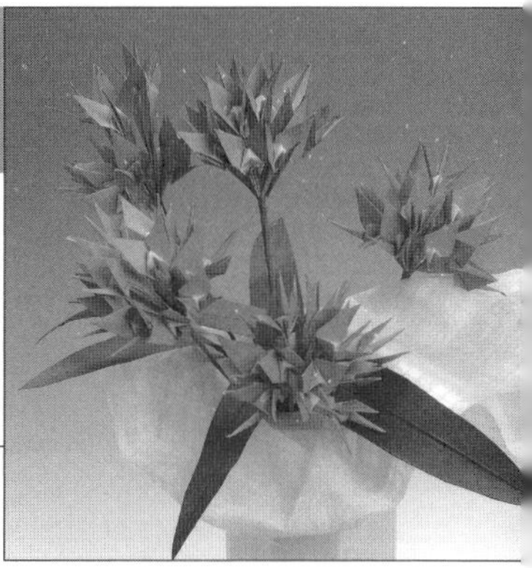

Materials per stem
15 3” squares origami paper
15 pieces #24 floral wire
Floral tape

For crane folding, see page 96.

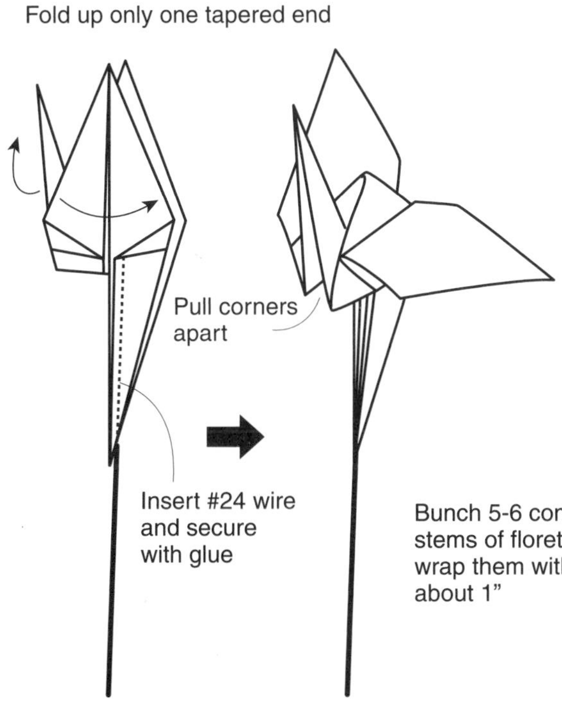

Fold up only one tapered end
Pull corners apart
Insert #24 wire and secure with glue

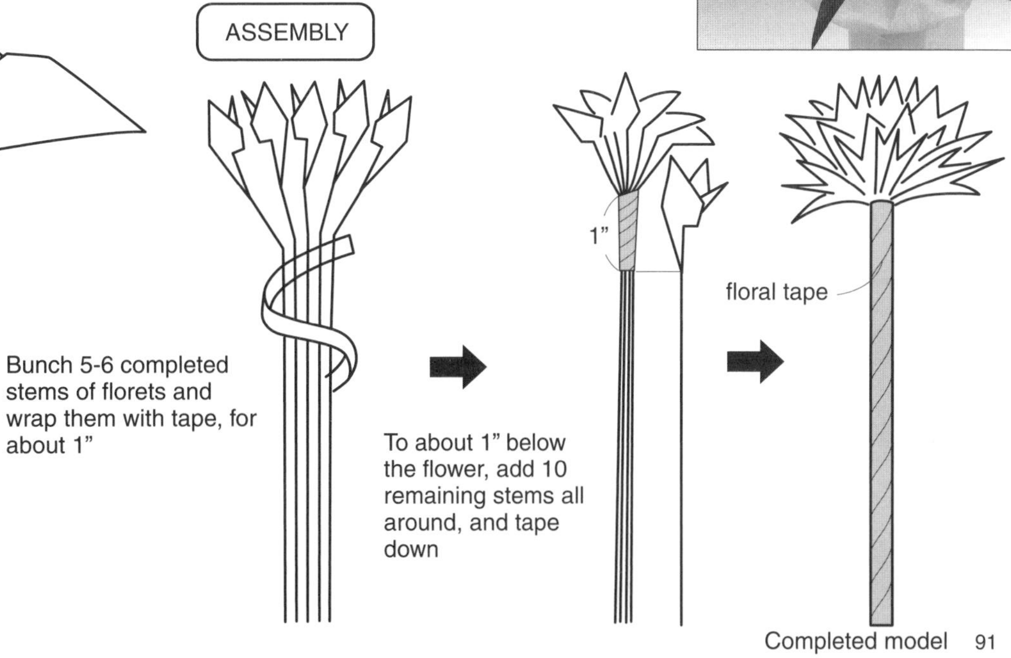

ASSEMBLY
Bunch 5-6 completed stems of florets and wrap them with tape, for about 1”
1”
To about 1” below the flower, add 10 remaining stems all around, and tape down
floral tape
Completed model

#56 Wall Hanging Page 44
#60 Light Diffuser Page 46

Materials for #56 Wall Hanging

Approx. 28" square handmade *washi* paper
Approx. 25"×36" hand made *Inshu washi* paper
4 6" squares *washi* origami paper with fiber glass
3 5" squares *washi* origami paper with fiber glass
1 4" square *washi* origami paper with fiber glass
4 1" wide 32" long balsa wood
String for hanging

#56 Wall Hanging

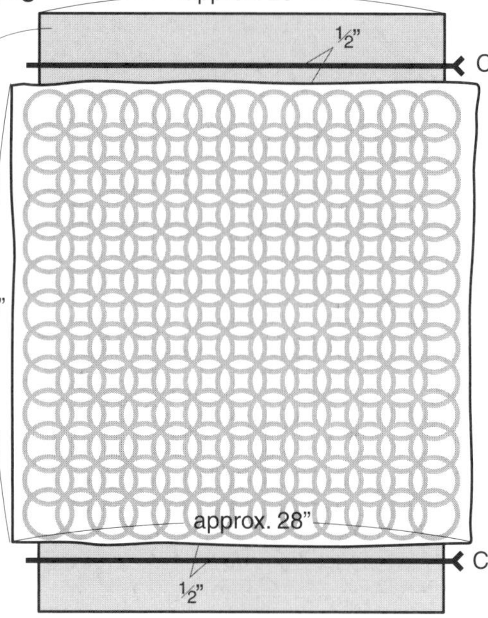

approx. 25"

½"

Cut

Inshu Aurora-*zome washi* paper

approx. 28"

approx. 28"

Cut

½"

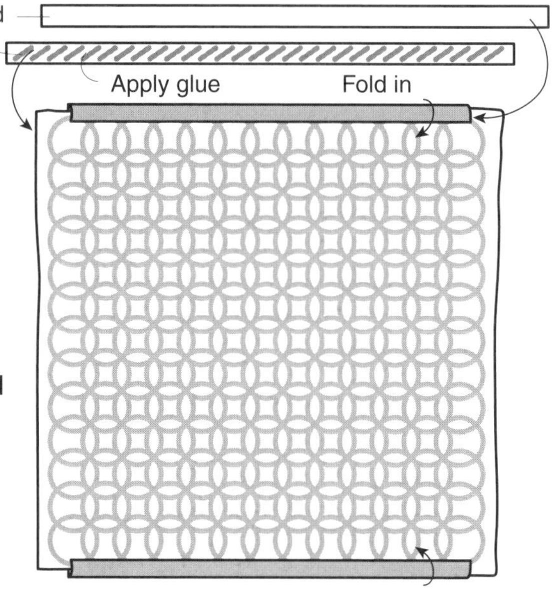

1" wide balsa stripwood

Apply glue

Fold in

Sandwich top and bottom edges with 2 balsa wood pieces, each with glued inside

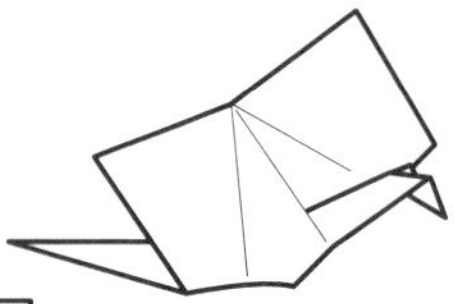

Fold in

For Flapping Crane folding, see page 54

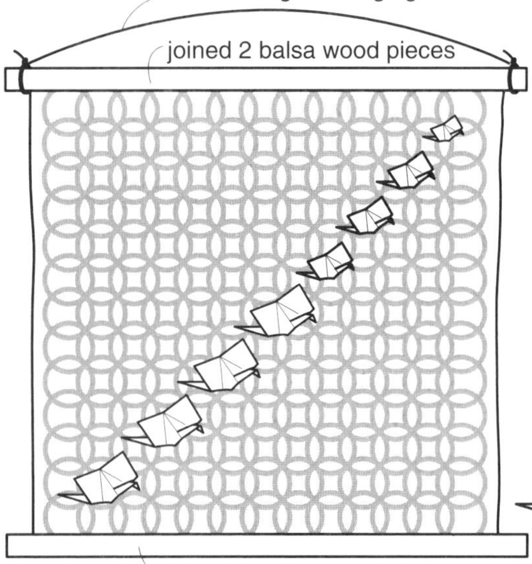

Tie string for hanging

joined 2 balsa wood pieces

joined 2 balsa wood pieces

Glue on Flapping Cranes

#60 Light Diffuser

Check the size of pendant, and cut enough size of paper to wrap around with no overlapping

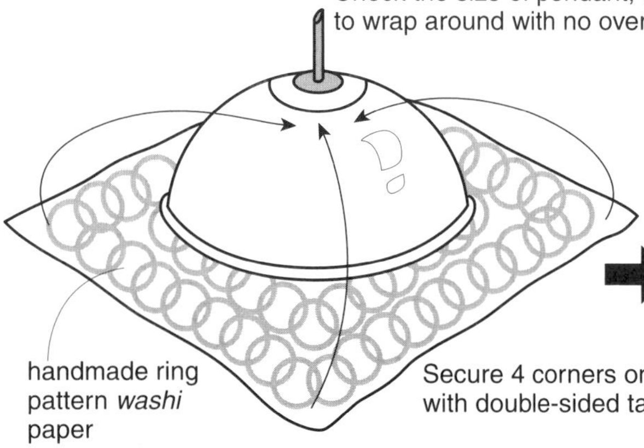

handmade ring pattern *washi* paper

Secure 4 corners onto shade with double-sided tape

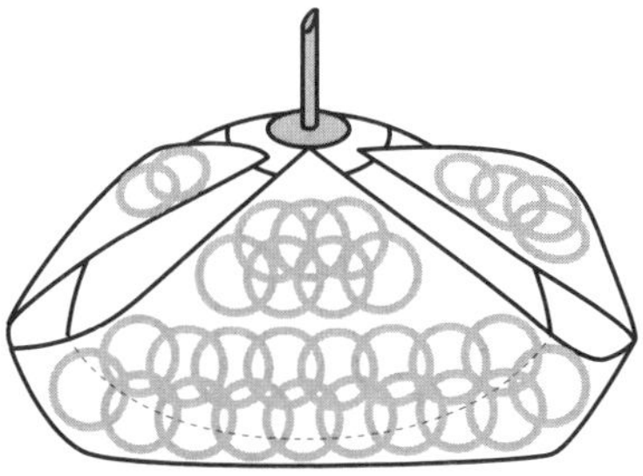

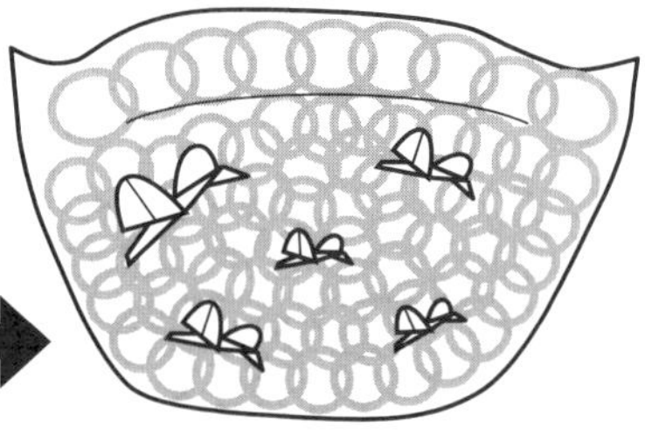

Arrange positions of Flapping Cranes in a balanced manner when looked from below

#62 Lamp Shade Page 47

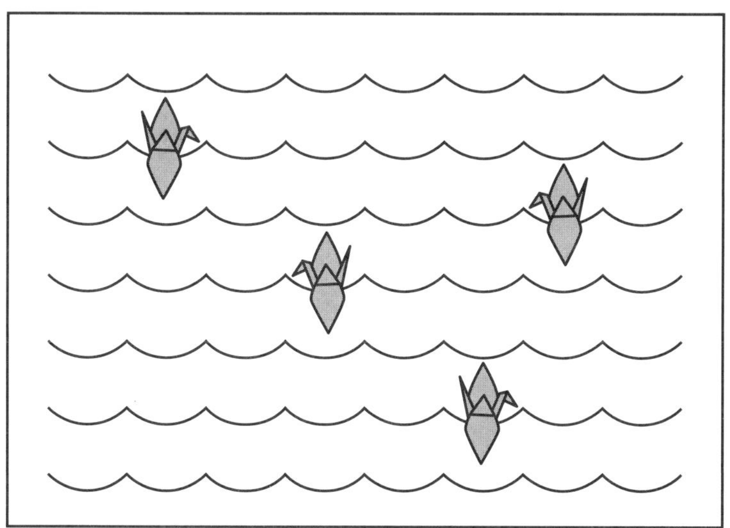

Position folded cranes in a balanced manner
Make tiny rings with extra *washi* paper, apply glue, and use as sticky tape

Materials
Approx. 22"×30" handmade *washi* paper
4-6 4" squares shaded *washi* origami paper

For crane folding, see pages 2-3.

floor setting lamp base

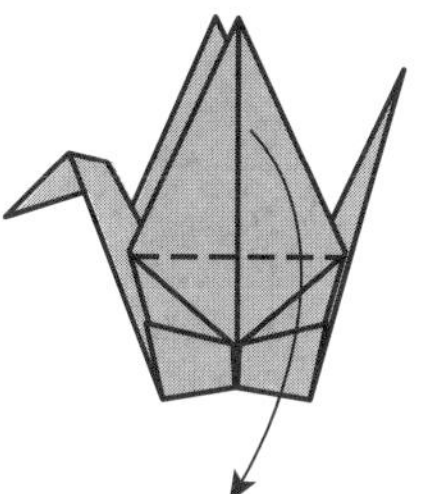

Fold down front wing

#61 Nightlight Page 46

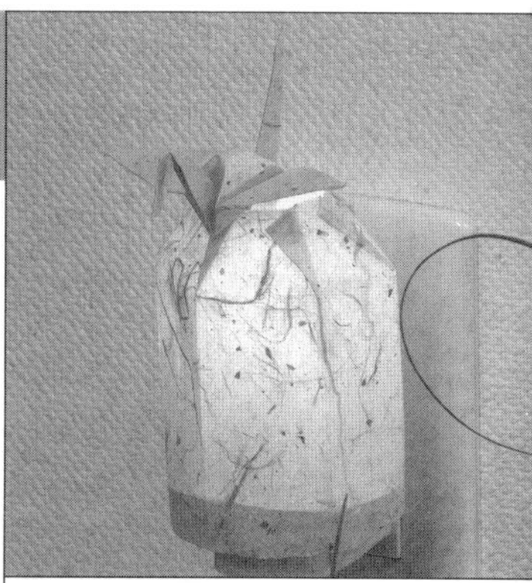

Materials
3½"×8" *washi* paper with fiber for cover
4" square *washi* paper with fiber for crane
Card for reinforcement

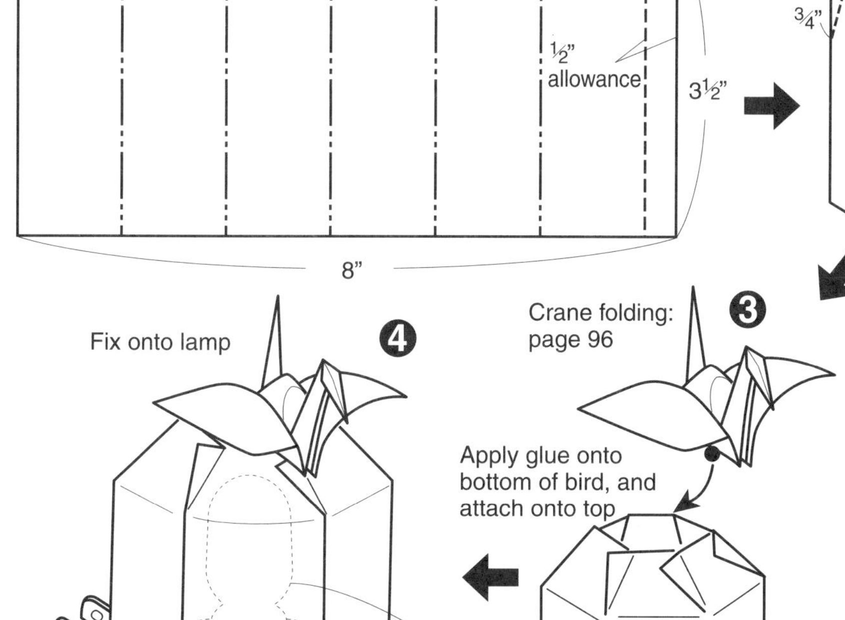

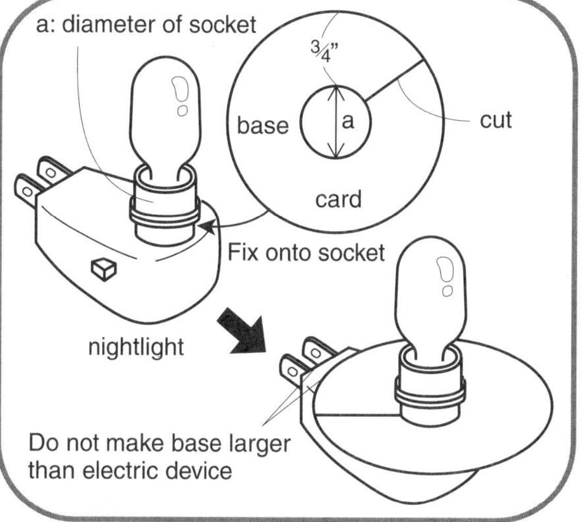

#63 Lamp Shade

Page 47

Materials

Approx 13"×38" handmade *washi* paper with fiber
6 3½" squares wax paper

For crane folding, see pages 2-3.

lamp base with frame

1

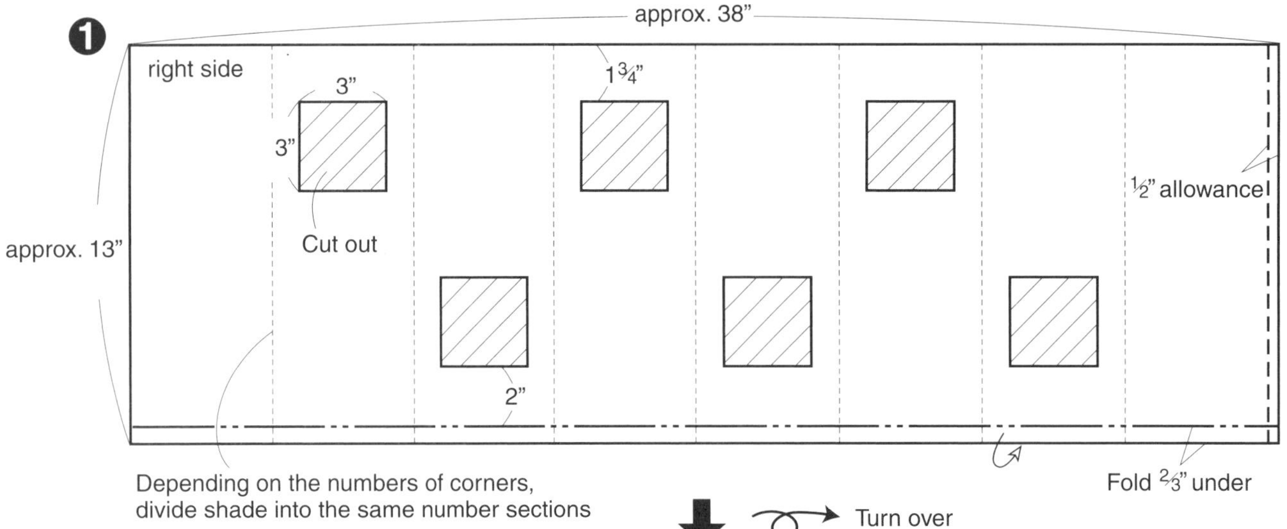

approx. 38"

right side

3"

3"

1¾"

Cut out

½" allowance

approx. 13"

2"

Depending on the numbers of corners, divide shade into the same number sections

Fold ⅔" under

Turn over

2

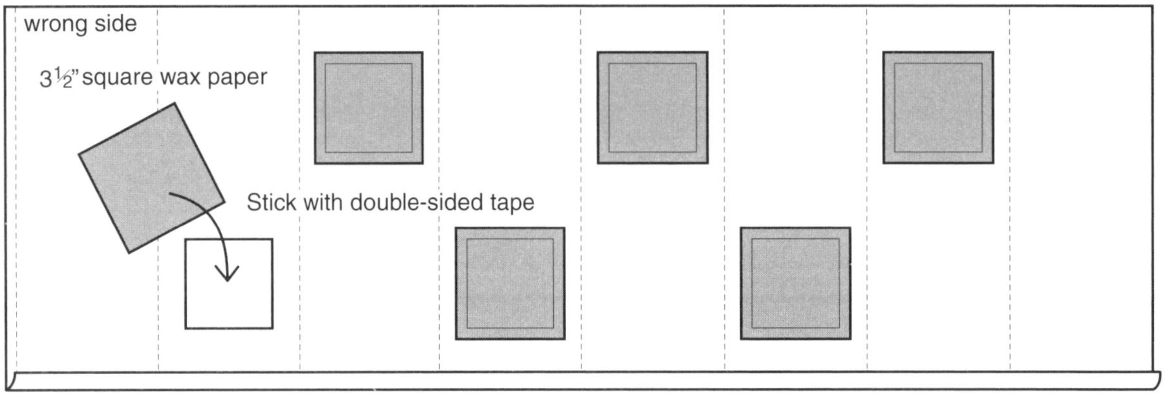

wrong side

3½" square wax paper

Stick with double-sided tape

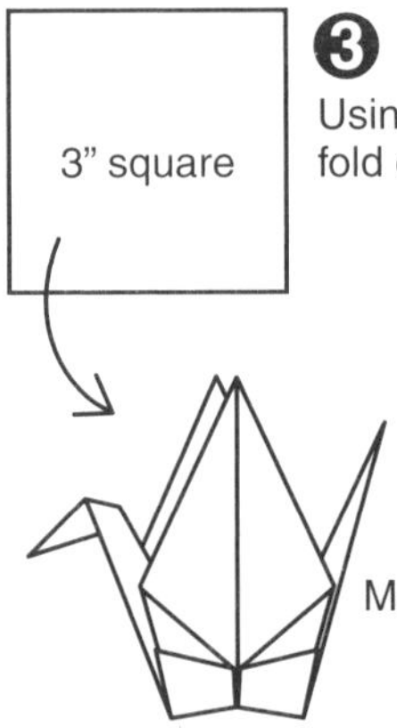

3 Using cut-out, fold crane

3" square

Make 6

4 Wrap frame with *washi* paper

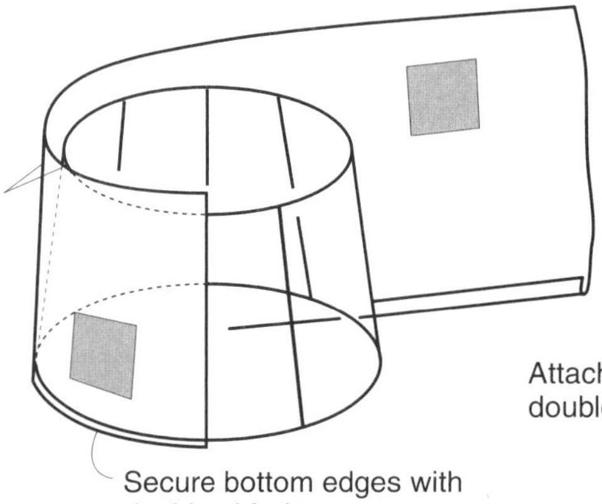

Do not attach top edges

Keep frame and paper apart

Secure bottom edges with double-sided tape

5 Stick double-sided tape onto allowance and secure

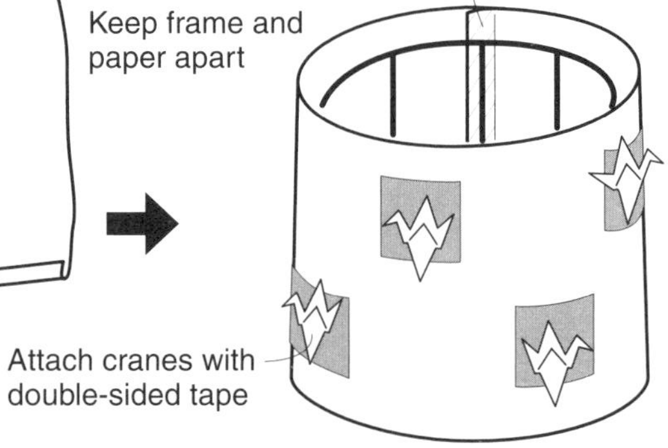

Attach cranes with double-sided tape

Completed lamp shade

#64 Artistic Room Divider Page 48

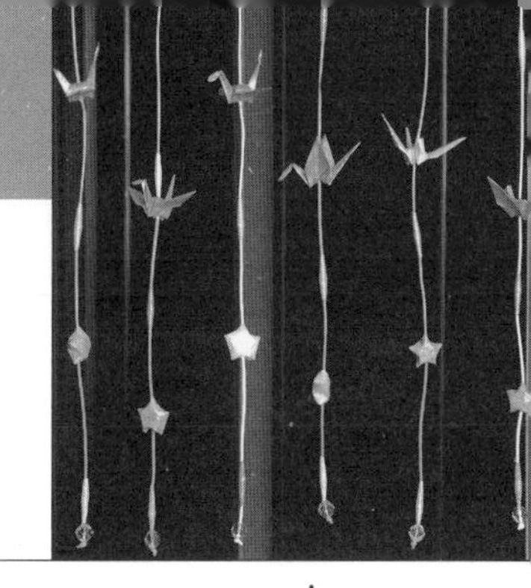

Materials

20 4" squares origami paper for cranes
30 ¾"× approx. 8" strips origami paper for stars
50 1⅕" wide 6" long triangular strips for paper beads
(Aurora origami paper is used for this project)

10 36" long pieces colored plastic tube
10 12mm acrylic beads
Wooden toothpick
1¼" wide 40" long plastic paper-holder

For crane folding, see pages 2-3 or page 96

ORIGAMI STAR

Tie strip into a single knot

Press down to crease tightly
Tuck in short end to form a pentagon

Fold long end over, and roll until there is no strip

Trim end and tuck in

Pull edges to make 3D star

Completed star

PAPER BEAD

1⅕" 6" origami paper

3/5" 1⅕" 3/5"

Cut into isosceles triangles

Roll around a wooden toothpick

When glue is completly dry, remove pick
Make 50

Glue end

ASSEMBLY

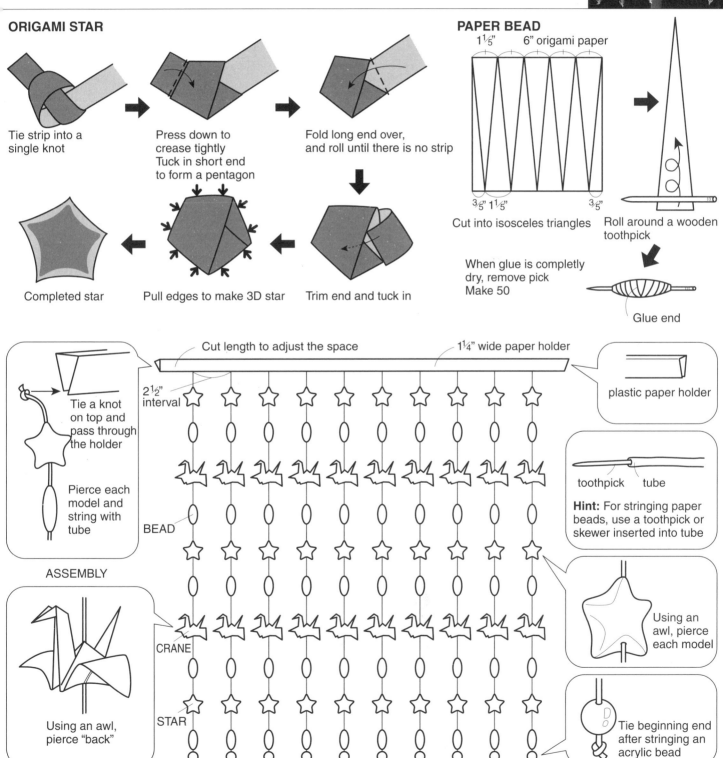

Cut length to adjust the space

1¼" wide paper holder

plastic paper holder

2½" interval

Tie a knot on top and pass through the holder

Pierce each model and string with tube

BEAD

CRANE

STAR

toothpick tube

Hint: For stringing paper beads, use a toothpick or skewer inserted into tube

Using an awl, pierce each model

Using an awl, pierce "back"

Tie beginning end after stringing an acrylic bead

FOLDING CRANE WITH SMOOTH WINGS

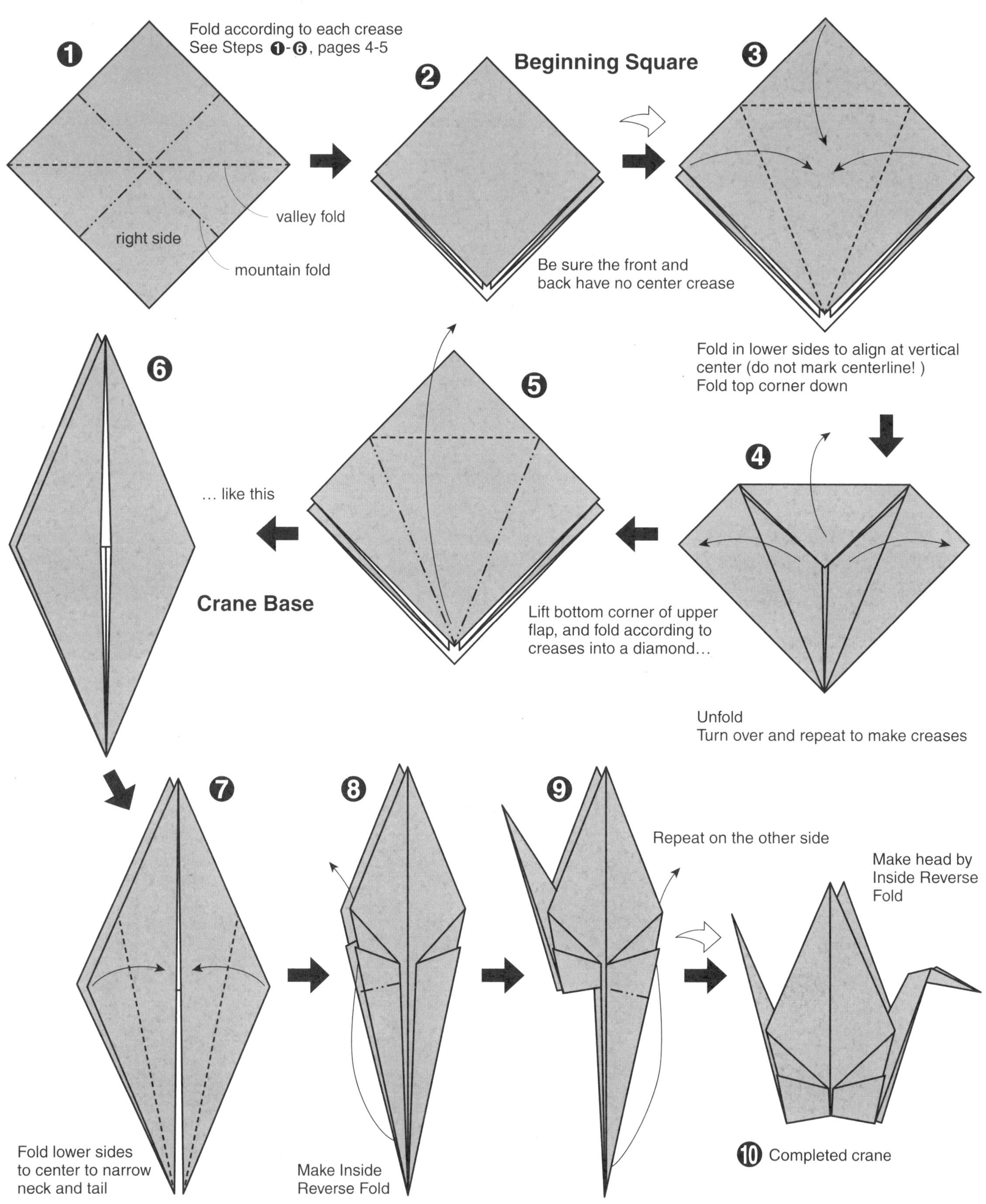

1
Fold according to each crease
See Steps 1-6, pages 4-5
valley fold
right side
mountain fold
2
Beginning Square
Be sure the front and
back have no center crease
3
Fold in lower sides to align at vertical
center (do not mark centerline!)
Fold top corner down
4
Unfold
Turn over and repeat to make creases
5
Lift bottom corner of upper
flap, and fold according to
creases into a diamond...
... like this
6
Crane Base
7
Fold lower sides
to center to narrow
neck and tail
8
Make Inside
Reverse Fold
9
Repeat on the other side
Make head by
Inside Reverse
Fold
10 Completed crane